W9-AWA-383

A Programmer's Introduction to Visual Basic .NET

Craig Utley

SAMS

201 West 103rd St., Indianapolis, Indiana, 46290 USA

MARLBOROUGH PUBLIC LIBRARY
MARLBOROUGH, MA

A Programmer's Introduction to Visual Basic .NET

Copyright © 2002 by Sams Publishing

All rights reserved. No part of this book shall be reproduced, stored in a retrieval system, or transmitted by any means, electronic, mechanical, photocopying, recording, or otherwise, without written permission from the publisher. No patent liability is assumed with respect to the use of the information contained herein. Although every precaution has been taken in the preparation of this book, the publisher and author assume no responsibility for errors or omissions. Nor is any liability assumed for damages resulting from the use of the information contained herein.

International Standard Book Number: 0-672-32264-1

Library of Congress Catalog Card Number: 2001093565

Printed in the United States of America

First Printing: December 2001

04	03	02	01		4	3	2	1

Trademarks

All terms mentioned in this book that are known to be trademarks or service marks have been appropriately capitalized. Sams Publishing cannot attest to the accuracy of this information. Use of a term in this book should not be regarded as affecting the validity of any trademark or service mark.

Warning and Disclaimer

Every effort has been made to make this book as complete and as accurate as possible, but no warranty or fitness is implied. The information provided is on an "as is" basis. The author and the publisher shall have neither liability nor responsibility to any person or entity with respect to any loss or damages arising from the information contained in this book.

EXECUTIVE EDITOR
Shelley Kronzek

DEVELOPMENT EDITOR
Kevin Howard

MANAGING EDITOR
Charlotte Clapp

PROJECT EDITOR
Carol Bowers

COPY EDITOR
Michael Henry

INDEXER
Eric Schroeder

PROOFREADERS
Charlotte Clapp
Bob LaRoche

TECHNICAL EDITOR
Boyd Nolan

TEAM COORDINATOR
Pamalee Nelson

MULTIMEDIA DEVELOPER
Dan Scherf

INTERIOR DESIGNER
Gary Adair

COVER DESIGNER
Gary Adair

PAGE LAYOUT
Octal Publishing, Inc.

Contents at a Glance

Table of Contents

About the Author

Craig Utley is President of CIOBriefings LLC, a consulting and training firm focused on helping customers develop enterprise-wide solutions with Microsoft technologies. Craig has been using Visual Basic since version 1.0, and he has guided customers through the creation of highly scalable Web applications using Active Server Pages, Visual Basic, MTS/Component Services, and SQL Server. Craig's skills in analyzing and designing enterprise-wide solutions have been used by large corporations and start-up companies alike. A frequent conference speaker as well as a book, courseware, and article author, Craig has recently spent much time writing about VB.NET and ASP.NET for both Sams and Volant Training.

Dedication

Dedicated to the rescue workers who, in response to the September 11 attacks, worked tirelessly under unspeakable conditions. You are proof that heroes still exist.

Acknowledgments

Sams Publishing deserves much of the credit for this book. After buying into my idea for a book targeted at helping VB6 developers move to VB .NET, Shelley Kronzek, the executive editor, asked me to write a 200-page version of the book in three weeks, which Sams would distribute for free. That book has been handed out to and downloaded by more than 70,000 people, and the number continues to climb every day.

This is the full realization of the book. Shelley Kronzek provided the prodding, and final kick, needed to see the book through to fruition. Kevin Howard, the development editor, has been great at keeping the process moving and helping make the book better, by catching many of my mistakes. Mike Henry made sure my English teachers felt that I had learned what they taught me. Carol Bowers, the Project Editor, made sure I always had a chapter or two to review and kept us all on schedule. I know there are many others at Sams without whom this book would not have been possible.

Boyd Nolan acted as the technical editor again, and I appreciate his efforts and respect his abilities. Every suggestion resulted in improvements to the book. Special thanks to Chris Payne, who jumped in and provided critical support at crunch time.

Just as I couldn't have done this without help from the team at Sams, Microsoft provided invaluable support. Ari Bixhorn and Ed Robinson answered many questions and put me in touch with a host of people on the VB .NET team. Susan Warren was absolutely fantastic at answering my questions within minutes. To all those who helped, thanks for taking the time while also working hard to get Visual Studio .NET out the door.

Having this book as the second version means that I got great feedback from the first, smaller edition. Thanks to Walter Scrivens, William Corry, John Beresford, Cindy Kee, and Stephanie DiMaggio, five readers of the first book who took the time to offer feedback, comments, and encouragement. I enjoy teaching people how to use technology, and feedback on any ways to improve that teaching are always appreciated.

Despite all the reviews done by various people, any mistakes in this book are strictly mine.

Tell Us What You Think!

As the reader of this book, *you* are our most important critic and commentator. We value your opinion and want to know what we're doing right, what we could do better, what areas you'd like to see us publish in, and any other words of wisdom you're willing to pass our way.

As an Executive Editor for Sams, I welcome your comments. You can fax, e-mail, or write me directly to let me know what you did or didn't like about this book—as well as what we can do to make our books stronger.

Please note that I cannot help you with technical problems related to the topic of this book, and that due to the high volume of mail I receive, I might not be able to reply to every message.

When you write, please be sure to include this book's title and author as well as your name and phone or fax number. I will carefully review your comments and share them with the author and editors who worked on the book.

Fax: 317-581-4770

E-mail: feedback@samspublishing.com

Mail: Shelley Kronzek
         Executive Editor
         Sams Publishing
         201 West 103rd Street
         Indianapolis, IN 46290 USA

Introduction

Why Does This Book Exist?

This book is meant to give you a head start on the changes from Visual Basic to Visual Basic .NET (VB .NET). Most of the book assumes that you are comfortable with Visual Basic 6.0 (VB6), so the book endeavors to be a quick introduction to the major differences between VB6 and the new VB .NET.

I've been using Visual Basic since version 1.0. The most dramatic shift had been in the move from VB3 to VB4, when class modules were introduced, and VB started on its long, slow path to becoming object oriented. For the first time, you could build COM components in VB, leading to an explosion in n-tier application development. VB4 brought COM development to the average programmer, so it was no longer a technology known only to a few C++ developers.

When I first started looking at the differences between VB6 and VB .NET, I realized that the change would be even more significant than it had been from VB3 to VB4. I thought it would be good to put together a book that helped VB6 developers transition to VB.NET. To that end, I pitched the idea for a book named something like *Migrating from VB to VB .NET* to a couple of different companies. Sams Publishing liked the idea, and one day they called me and asked me about doing a miniature version of the book. . .in three weeks.

The story of the miniature version is detailed in the miniature version. The plan was always to produce a larger book, and that is what you are holding. This book goes into much more detail and covers numerous topics not in the smaller book. It has also been updated to later, more stable builds of Visual Studio .NET.

There is no doubt: VB .NET will be an exciting change for us all. There is so much new material to learn that it can be somewhat daunting at first. However, the benefits of the .NET Framework are significant, and in the end can greatly reduce the effort required today to build enterprise-ready distributed applications.

Why VB .NET Instead of C#?

A lot of press has been given to the new language Microsoft has created: C# (pronounced "C-Sharp"). This is a new language, based on C/C++. C#, like VB .NET, is built specifically for the .NET Framework, and much has been written about it. Given all the hype, some people might wonder why they should choose VB .NET over C#.

Although both VB .NET and C# projects are created in the Visual Studio .NET environment, VB .NET was created specifically for VB developers and has a number of unique features that make it a great choice for building .NET applications. VB .NET is still the only language in

VS .NET that includes background compilation, which means that it can flag errors immediately, while you type. VB .NET is the only .NET language that supports late binding. In the VS .NET IDE, VB .NET provides a drop-down list at the top of the code window with all the objects and events; the IDE does not provide this functionality for any other language. VB .NET is also unique for providing default values for optional parameters, and for having a collection of the controls available to the developer. Don't forget, too, that C#, like its C and C++ brethren, is case-sensitive, something that drives most experienced VB developers crazy. In addition, C# uses different symbols for equality (=) and comparison (==). Finally, let's face it: If you know VB, you are further down the road with VB .NET than you are with C#. Even though much has changed, the basic syntax of VB .NET is similar to VB, so you already know how to declare variables, set up loops, and so on.

As you can see, VB .NET has some advantages over the other .NET languages. If you're curious about the advantages of VB .NET over traditional VB, you'll have to read this book.

Who Should Read This Book?

This book is targeted at current VB developers. If you don't know VB, parts of the book might not make sense to you. The goal here is to cover what has changed. So, if something hasn't changed, I have to assume that you already know it. If you know VB, and want to learn VB .NET or at least see what it can do for you, this book is for you.

If you are currently using Visual InterDev to create Web applications, this book is also for you, because Visual InterDev has been integrated throughout Visual Studio .NET. This means you can create Visual InterDev-like Web Applications using VB .NET (and C#). You get several advantages with this new approach, including the ability to write in full VB .NET instead of VBScript, and the advantages of .NET's Web application architecture (ASP.NET) over the current ASP model are significant.

No matter what you will be doing with VB .NET, the place to start is with the .NET Framework. Without understanding the .NET Framework, you won't be able to write good VB .NET applications, regardless of whether they are Windows or Web applications. Therefore, prepare to get started by examining the .NET Framework.

Why Should You Move to Visual Basic .NET?

IN THIS CHAPTER

A number of people have been grumbling about Visual Basic .NET (VB .NET). The main concern is the fact that they have to learn a new language, when they are comfortable with the current Visual Basic language. It's true that there are some dramatic changes, and that current VB developers have had three years to become comfortable with version 6.0. However, there are some compelling reasons to move to VB .NET, and the learning curve, although steep at first, can be tackled with an understanding of some of the new concepts, chiefly the .NET Framework.

Visual Basic .NET: A New Framework

One of the most common questions today is, "Why should I move to .NET?" .NET is new, and there are many questions about what it can do for you. From a Visual Basic standpoint, it's important to understand some of the dramatic benefits that can be achieved by moving to Visual Basic .NET.

Many people have looked at VB .NET and grumbled about the changes. In fact, one industry trade publication contained an article in which several long-time Visual Basic developers complained that the changes were too much and that they felt blindsided. After all, there are significant changes to the language: a new error handling structure (which is optional), namespaces, true inheritance, true multithreading, and many others. Some see these changes as merely a way that Microsoft can place a check mark next to a certain feature and be able to say, "Yeah, we do that."

Most developers, however, feel there are good reasons for the changes in VB .NET. The world of applications is changing, continuing the evolution that has been occurring over the past several years. If you went back to 1991 and showed a Visual Basic 1.0 developer an n-tier application with an Active Server Pages (ASP) front end, a VB COM component middle tier complete with Microsoft Transaction Server, and a SQL Server back end full of stored procedures, it would look quite alien to him. Yet, over the past few years, the vast majority of developers have been using Visual Basic to create COM components, and they have become quite versed in ADO for their database access. The needs for reusability and centralization (a way to avoid distributing components to the desktop) have driven this move to the n-tier model.

The next logical step in the evolution of n-tier systems was to have a Web-enabled application. Unfortunately, the move to the Web revealed some problems. Scalability was an issue, but more complex applications had other requirements, such as transactions that spanned multiple components, multiple databases, or both. To address these issues, Microsoft created Microsoft Transaction Server (MTS) and COM+ Component Services. MTS (in Windows NT 4) and Component Services (an updated MTS in Windows 2000) acted as an object-hosting environment, allowing you to gain scalability and distributed transactions with relative ease. However,

VB components could not take full advantage of all that Component Services had to offer, such as object pooling, because VB did not support true multithreading.

Opening Up on the Web

In the ASP/VB6 model, Microsoft had developers building a component and then calling it via an ASP. Microsoft realized that it would be a good idea to make the component directly callable over HTTP, so that an application anywhere in the world could use that component. Microsoft threw its support behind the Simple Object Access Protocol, or SOAP, which allows developers to call a component over HTTP using an XML string. The data is then returned via HTTP in an XML string. Components exposed via SOAP sport URLs, making them as easy to access as any other Web item. SOAP has the advantage of having been a cross-industry standard, and not just a Microsoft creation. This has given rise to a number of vendors, including Microsoft's archrivals, lauding the benefits of Web services.

At this point, you might be tempted to think that SOAP is all you need, and that you can just stick with VB6. Therefore, it is important to understand what VB .NET gives you, and why it probably makes sense for you, and many other developers, to upgrade to .NET. For example, you create components and want them to be callable via SOAP, but how do you let people know that those components exist? .NET includes a discovery mechanism that allows you to find components that are available to you. You'll find out more about this mechanism, including the "disco" file, in Chapter 9, "Building Web Services with VB .NET." .NET also provides many other features, such as garbage collection for freeing up resources, true inheritance for the first time, debugging that works across languages and against running applications, and the ability to create Windows services and console applications.

What Does the ".NET" Mean?

Before proceeding, it's important to understand a little bit more about what is meant by *.NET*. There are many .NETs here. There is VB .NET, which is the new version of Visual Basic. There is Visual Studio .NET (an integrated development environment that hosts VB .NET), C# (pronounced "C sharp"), and C++.NET. Microsoft is even calling most of its server product ".NET Servers" now. Underlying all this is the . NET Framework and its core execution engine, the Common Language Runtime.

In the .NET model, you write applications that target the .NET Framework. This gives them automatic access to such benefits as garbage collection (which destroys objects and reclaims memory for you), debugging, security services, inheritance, and more. When you compile the code from any language that supports the .NET Framework, it compiles into something called MSIL, or Microsoft Intermediate Language. This MSIL file is binary, but it is not machine code; instead, it is a format that is platform independent and can be placed on any machine running the .NET Framework. Within the .NET Framework is a compiler called the Just-In-Time, or JIT, compiler. It compiles the MSIL down to machine code specific to that hardware and operating system.

In looking at the fundamental changes, it's important to understand that the number-one feature request from Visual Basic developers, for years, has been inheritance. VB has had *interface inheritance* since VB4, but developers wanted *real* or *implementation inheritance*. Why? What are the benefits? The main benefit of inheritance is the ability to create applications more quickly. This is an extension of the promise of component design and reusability. With implementation inheritance, you build a base class and can inherit from it, using it as the basis for new classes. For example, you could create a Vehicle class that provides basic functionality that could be inherited in both a Bicycle class and a Car class. The important point here is that Bicycle and Car inherit the *functionality*, or the actual code, from the Vehicle class. In VB4 and higher, the best you could do was inherit the structure, minus any implementation code. In VB .NET, the functionality in that base class is available to your other classes as is, or you can extend and modify it as necessary.

.NET provides you with integrated debugging tools. If you've ever debugged an ASP application that had VB COM components, you know that you had to use Visual InterDev to debug the ASPs and VB to debug the components. If you also had C++ components in the mix, you had to use the C++ debugger on those components. With .NET, there is one debugger. Any language that targets the .NET Framework can be debugged with that single debugger, even if one part of your application is written in VB .NET and calls another part written in C#, or any other language built to target the .NET Framework.

.NET supplies a standard security mechanism, available to all parts of your application. .NET provides a possible solution to DLL Hell, and removes much of the complexity of dealing with COM and the registry. .NET allows you to run components locally, without requiring the calling application to go to the registry to find components.

There are also things that VB .NET can do that you cannot do today in VB. For example, Web Applications are a new form of project. Gone is Visual InterDev with its interpreted VBScript code. Instead, you now build your ASP.NET pages with VB .NET (or C# or C++.NET), and they are truly compiled for better performance. VB .NET lets you create Windows services natively for the first time by providing a Windows Services project type. And yes, VB .NET lets VB developers build truly multithreaded components and applications for the first time.

Finally, you need to realize that the new language is actually going to have a version number on it, although the final name is undecided. It might well be called VB .NET 2002. This implies that at some point, there will be new versions of VB .NET, just as there were new versions of VB. In this book, references to previous versions of VB will be either VB or VB6. References to VB .NET 2002 will be just VB .NET.

You have decided you need to move from VB6 to VB .NET, and you picked up this book to find out about the changes. Yet, the first thing you see is a chapter about the .NET Framework. Why start with the .NET Framework? The truth is that you cannot understand VB .NET until you understand the .NET Framework. You see, the .NET Framework and VB .NET are tightly intertwined; many of the services you will build into your applications are actually provided by the .NET Framework and are merely called into action by your application.

The .NET Framework is a collection of services and classes. It exists as a layer between the applications you write and the underlying operating system. This is a powerful concept: The .NET Framework need not be a Windows-only solution. The .NET Framework could be moved to any operating system, meaning your .NET applications could be run on any operating system hosting the .NET Framework. This means that you could achieve true cross-platform capabilities simply by creating VB .NET applications, provided the .NET Framework was available for other platforms. Although this promise of cross-platform capability is a strong selling point to .NET, there has not yet been an official announcement about .NET being moved to other operating systems.

In addition, the .NET Framework is exciting because it encapsulates much of the basic functionality that used to have to be built into various programming languages. The .NET Framework has the code that makes Windows Forms work, so any language can use the built-in code in order to create and use standard Windows forms. In addition, Web Forms are part of the Framework, so any .NET language could be used to create Web Applications. Additionally, this means that various programming elements will be the same across all languages; a Long data type will be the same size in all .NET languages. This is even more important when it comes to strings and arrays. No longer will you have to worry about whether or not a string is a BStr or a CStr before you pass it to a component written in another language, which has been a common concern for VB developers calling C-based Windows APIs.

The Common Language Runtime

One of the major components of the .NET Framework is the Common Language Runtime, or CLR. The CLR provides a number of benefits to the developer, such as exception handling, security, debugging, and versioning, and these benefits are available to any language built for the CLR. This means that the CLR can host a variety of languages, and can offer a common set of tools across those languages. Microsoft has made VB .NET, C++.NET, and C# "premier" languages for the CLR, which means that these three languages fully support the CLR. In addition, other vendors have signed up to provide implementations of other languages, such as Perl, Python, and even COBOL.

When a compiler compiles for the CLR, this code is said to be *managed code*. Managed code is simply code that takes advantage of the services offered by the CLR. For the runtime to work with managed code, that code must contain metadata. This metadata is created during the compilation process by compilers targeting the CLR. The metadata is stored with the compiled code and contains information about the types, members, and references in the code. Among other things, the CLR uses this metadata to

- Locate classes
- Load classes
- Generate native code
- Provide security

If you think about it, the tasks above used to be handled by COM and the registry. One of .NET's goals is to allow applications to be distributed without the need to use the registry. In fact, .NET components can be copied into a directory and used, without the need for a registration process. .NET handles locating and loading the objects from the component, which replaces work that used to be handled by COM.

The runtime also handles object lifetimes. Just as COM/COM+ provided reference counting for objects, the CLR manages references to objects and removes them from memory when all the references are gone, through the process known as *garbage collection*. Although garbage collection actually gives you slightly less control than you had in VB, you gain some important benefits. For example, your errors should decrease because the number of objects that hang around due to circular references should be reduced or completely eliminated because .NET has logic for handling objects that are only involved in circular references. In addition, garbage collection ends up being much faster than the old way of destroying objects in VB. Instances of objects you create that are managed by the runtime are called *managed data*. You can interact with both managed and unmanaged data in the same application, although managed data gives you all the benefits of the runtime.

The CLR also defines a standard type system to be used by all CLR languages. This means that all CLR languages will have the same size integers and longs, and they will all have the same type of string—no more worrying about BStrs and CStrs! This standard type system opens up the door for some powerful language interoperability. For example, you can pass a reference of a class from one component to another, even if those components are written in different languages. You also can derive a class in C# from a base class written in VB .NET, or any other combination of languages targeted to the runtime. Don't forget that COM had a set of standard types as well, but they were binary standards. This meant that with COM, you had language interoperability at run time. With .NET's type standard, you have language interoperability at design time.

After it is compiled, managed code includes metadata, which contains information about the component itself, and the components used to create the code. The runtime can check to make sure that resources on which you depend are available. The metadata removes the need to store component information in the registry. That means moving a component to a new machine does not require registration (unless it will be a global assembly, which is described in Chapter 4, "Building Classes and Assemblies with VB .NET"), and removing components is as simple as deleting them.

As you can see, the Common Language Runtime provides a number of benefits that are not only new, but should enhance the experience of building applications. Other benefits that you will see in more detail include some of the new object-oriented features to VB .NET. Many of these new features are not so much additions to the language as they are features of the runtime that are simply being exposed to the VB .NET.

Managed Execution

To understand how your VB .NET applications work, and just how much the code differs from the VB code that Dorothy wrote in Kansas, it's important to understand managed code and how it works. To use managed execution and get the benefits of the CLR, you must use a language that was built for, or *targets*, the runtime. Fortunately for you, this includes VB .NET. In fact, Microsoft wanted to make sure that VB .NET was a premier language on the .NET platform, meaning that Visual Basic could no longer be accused of being a "toy" language.

The runtime is a language-neutral environment, which means that any vendor can create a language that takes advantage of the runtime's features. Different compilers can expose different amounts of the runtime to the developer, so the tool you use and the language in which you write might still appear to work somewhat differently. The syntax of each language is different, of course, but when the compilation process occurs, all code should be compiled into something understandable to the runtime.

NOTE

Just because a language targets the runtime doesn't mean that the language can't add features that are not understood by other languages. To make sure that your components are completely usable by components written in other languages, you must use only types that are specified by the Common Language Specification. The Common Language Specification elements will be examined in Appendix A, "The Common Language Specification."

Microsoft Intermediate Language (MSIL)

One of the more interesting aspects of .NET is that when you compile your code, you do not compile to native code. Before you VB developers panic and fear that you are returning to the days of interpreted code, realize that the compilation process translates your code into something called Microsoft Intermediate Language, which is also called MSIL or just IL. The compiler also creates the necessary metadata and compiles it into the component. This resulting IL is CPU independent.

After the IL and metadata are in a file, this compiled file is called the PE, which stands for either *portable executable* or *physical executable*, depending on whom you ask. Because the PE contains your IL and metadata, it is therefore self-describing, eliminating the need for a type library or interfaces specified with the Interface Definition Language (IDL). This metadata is so complete that any .NET language can inherit from the classes in this PE file. Remember that .NET was said to be compatible at design time, and this is why. As you develop in VB .NET, you can inherit from classes created in C#, and you will have full access to IntelliSense and other Visual Studio .NET features.

The Just-In-Time Compiler

Your code does not stay IL for long, however. It is the PE file containing the IL that can be distributed and placed with the CLR running on the .NET Framework on any operating system for which the .NET Framework exists, because the IL is platform independent. When you run the IL, however, it is compiled to native code for that platform. Therefore, you are still running native code; you are not going back to the days of interpreted code at all. The compilation to native code occurs via another tool of the .NET Framework: the Just-In-Time (JIT) compiler.

With the code compiled, it can run within the Framework and take advantage of low-level features such as memory management and security. The compiled code is native code for the CPU on which the .NET Framework is running, meaning that you are indeed running native code instead of interpreted code. A JIT compiler will be available for each platform on which the .NET Framework runs, so you should always be getting native code on any platform running the .NET Framework. Remember, today this is just Windows, but this could change in the future.

> **Note**
>
> It is still possible to call operating system–specific APIs, which would, of course, limit your application to just that platform. That means it is still possible to call Windows APIs, but then the code would not be able to run within the .NET Framework on a non-Windows machine. At this point in time, the .NET Framework exists only on the Windows platform, but this will probably change in the future.

Executing Code

Interestingly, the JIT compiler doesn't compile the entire IL when the component is first called. Instead, each *method* is compiled the first time it is called. This keeps you from having to compile sections of code that are never called. After the code is compiled, of course, subsequent calls use the compiled version of the code. This natively compiled code is stored in memory in Beta 2. However, Microsoft has provided a PreJIT compiler that will compile all the code at once and store the compiled version on disk, so the compilation will persist over time. This tool is called ngen.exe and can be used to precompile the entire IL. If the CLR cannot find a precompiled version of the code, it begins to JIT compile it on-the-fly.

After the code starts executing, it can take full advantage of the CLR, with benefits such as the security model, memory management, debugging support, and profiling tools. Most of these benefits will be mentioned throughout the book.

Assemblies

One of the new structures you will create in VB .NET is the assembly. An *assembly* is a collection of one or more physical files. The files are most often code, such as the classes you build, but they could also be images, resource files, and other binary files associated with the code. Such assemblies are known as *static* assemblies because you create them and store them on disk. *Dynamic* assemblies are created at runtime and are not normally stored to disk (although they can be).

An assembly represents the unit of deployment, version control, reuse, and security. If this sounds like the DLLs you have been creating in Visual Basic for the past six years, it is similar. Just as a standard COM DLL has a type library, the assembly has a *manifest* that contains the metadata for the assembly, such as the classes, types, and references contained in the IL. The assembly often contains one or more classes, just like a COM DLL. In .NET, applications are built using assemblies; assemblies are not applications in their own rights.

Perhaps the most important point of assemblies is this: All runtime applications must be made up of one or more assemblies.

The Assembly Manifest

The manifest is similar in theory to the type library in COM DLLs. The manifest contains all the information about the items in the assembly, including what parts of the assembly are exposed to the outside world. The manifest also lists the assembly's dependencies on other assemblies. Each assembly is required to have a manifest.

The manifest can be part of a PE file, or it can be a standalone file if your assembly has more than one file in it. Although this is not an exhaustive list, a manifest contains

- Assembly name
- Version
- Files in the assembly
- Referenced assemblies

In addition, a developer can set custom attributes for an assembly, such as a title and a description.

An End to DLL Hell?

One of the great benefits of COM was supposed to be an end to DLL Hell. If you think back for a moment to the days of 16-bit programming, you'll remember that you had to distribute a number of DLLs with a Windows application. It seemed that almost every application had to install the same few DLLs, such as Ctrl3d2.dll. Each application you installed might have a slightly different version of the DLL, and you ended up with multiple copies of the same DLL, but many were different versions. Even worse, a version of a particular DLL could be placed in the Windows\System directory that then broke many of your existing applications.

COM was supposed to fix all that. No longer did applications search around for DLLs by looking in their own directories, and then search the Windows path. With COM, requests for components were sent to the registry. Although there might be multiple versions of the same COM DLL on the machine, there would be only one version in the registry at any time. Therefore, all clients would use the same version. This meant, however, that each new version of the DLL had to guarantee compatibility with previous versions. This led to interfaces being immutable under COM; after the component was in production, the interface was never supposed to change. In concept that sounds great, but developers could, and did, release COM components that broke binary compatibility; in other words, they changed, added, or removed properties and methods within their components. The modified components then broke all existing clients. Many VB developers have struggled with this exact problem.

The .NET Framework and the CLR attempt to address this problem through the use of assemblies. Even before .NET, Windows 2000 introduced the capability to have an application look in the local directory for a DLL, instead of going to the registry. This ensured that you always had the correct version of the DLL available to the application.

The runtime carries this further by allowing components to declare dependencies on certain versions of other components. In addition, multiple versions of the same component can be run in memory simultaneously in what Microsoft calls *side-by-side instancing* or *side-by-side execution*.

The Global Assembly Cache (GAC)

Even though components in .NET do not have to be registered, there is a similar process if you have an assembly that is to be used by multiple applications. The CLR actually has two caches within its overall code cache: the download cache and the global assembly cache (GAC). An assembly that will be used by more than one application is placed into the global assembly cache by running an installer that places the assembly in the GAC. If an assembly is not in the local directory and not in the GAC, you can have a codebase hint in a configuration file. The CLR then downloads the assembly, storing it in the download cache and binding to it from there. This download cache is just for assemblies that have to be downloaded, and will not be discussed further in this book.

The GAC is where you place a component if you want multiple applications to use the same component. This is very similar to what you have with registered COM components in VB6. If the component is not found in the same directory as the executing application, the application searches the GAC, much as COM searched the registry.

Placing assemblies in the GAC has several advantages. Assemblies in the GAC tend to perform better because the runtime locates them faster and the security does not have to be checked each time that the assemblies are loaded. Assemblies can be added to or removed from the GAC only by someone with administrator privileges.

Where things get interesting is that you can actually have different versions of the same assembly loaded in the GAC at the same time. Notice that I avoided saying "registered in the GAC" because you aren't placing anything in the registry. Even if a component is running in the GAC, you can add another version of the same component running alongside it, or you can slipstream in an emergency fix. This is all based on the version number and you have control over whether an update becomes a newly running version or merely an upgrade to an existing version.

Assemblies can be placed in the GAC only if they have a shared name. Assemblies and the GAC will be discussed in more detail in Chapter 4.

The Common Type System

The Common Type System specifies the types supported by the CLR. The types specified by the CLR include

- Classes—The definition of what will become an object; includes properties, methods, and events
- Interfaces—The definition of the functionality a class can implement, but does not contain any implementation code

- Value Types—User-defined data types that are passed by value
- Delegates—Similar to function pointers in C++, delegates are often used for event handling and callbacks

The type system sets out the rules that language compilers must follow to produce code that is cross-language–compatible. By following the type system, vendors can produce code that is guaranteed to work with code from other languages and other compilers because all languages are consistent in their use of types.

Classes

Most Visual Basic developers are familiar with classes. Classes are definitions or blueprints of objects that will be created at runtime. Classes define the properties, methods, fields, and events of objects. If the term *fields* is new to you, it simply means public variables exposed by the class; fields are the "lazy way" to do properties. Together, properties, methods, fields, and events are generically called *members* of the class.

If a class has one or more methods that do not contain any implementation, the class is said to be *abstract.* In VB .NET, you cannot instantiate abstract classes directly; instead, you must inherit from them. In VB6, it was possible to create a class that was just method definitions with no implementation code. In fact, this was how you generally created interfaces in VB. If you created a class with only method definitions and no actual implementation code, you then used the Implements keyword to inherit the interface. You could actually instantiate the interface in VB6, but because it did not have any implementation code, there was no point in doing so.

In VB .NET, you can create a class that has implementation code instead of just the interface, and then mark the class as abstract. Now, other classes can inherit from that abstract class and use the implementation in it or override the implementation as needed. These are new concepts to VB developers. In the past, VB had only interface inheritance, but VB .NET has "real" inheritance, known as *implementation inheritance.*

In VB .NET, interfaces are separate from classes. In VB6, you created interfaces by creating classes with method definitions, but no implementation code inside those methods. You will see more on interfaces in the next section, but realize that although a VB .NET class can implement any number of interfaces, it can inherit from only one base class. This will be examined in more detail throughout the book.

Classes have a number of possible characteristics that can be set, and that are stored in the metadata. In addition, members can have characteristics. These characteristics include such items as whether or not the class or member is inheritable. These will be discussed in more detail in Chapter 4.

Interfaces

Interfaces in VB .NET are like the interfaces in previous versions of VB: They are definitions of a class without the actual implementation. Because there is no implementation code, you cannot instantiate an interface, but must instead implement it in a class.

There is one exception to the "no implementation code in an interface" rule: In VB .NET, you can define what are called *static* members. These can have implementation code, and you will see more about them in Chapter 4.

Value Types

In .NET languages, a standard variable type, such as an integer, is native to the language, and it is passed by value when used as an argument. Objects, on the other hand, are always passed by reference. However, a value type is a user-defined type that acts much like an object, but is passed by value. In reality, value types are stored as primitive data types, but they can contain fields, properties, events, and both static and nonstatic methods. Value types do not carry the overhead of an object that is being held in memory.

If this seems confusing, think about enums. Enumerations are a special type of value type. An enum simply has a name and a set of fields that define values for a primitive data type. Enums, however, cannot have their own properties, events, or methods.

Delegates

A delegate is a construct that can be declared in a client. The delegate actually points to a method on a particular object. Which method it points to on which object can be set when the instance of the delegate is created at declaration. This allows you to define calls to various methods in different objects based on logic in your code.

Delegates are most often used to handle events. Using delegates, you can pass events to a centralized event handler. Delegates will not be examined in more detail in this book.

The .NET Framework Class Library

The .NET Framework provides a number of types that are already created and ready for use in any language that targets the Common Language Runtime. These types include such items as the primitive data types, I/O functions, data access, and .NET Framework security.

Perhaps one of the biggest changes in the way developers will work with VB .NET is the entire area of namespaces. Namespaces will be covered in Chapter 3, "Major VB .NET Changes," but it is important to understand that the .NET Framework provides a host of utility classes and members, organized within a hierarchy called a *namespace*. At the root of the hierarchy is the System namespace. A namespace groups classes and members into logical nodes. This way, you can have the same name for a method in more than one namespace. The Left() method could therefore exist in the System.Windows.Forms namespace and the Microsoft.VisualBasic namespace.

One advantage of namespaces is that similar functions can be grouped within the same namespace, regardless of the assembly in which they are physically located. Any language targeting the runtime can use the System namespaces. For example, if you need to perform data access, you do not set a reference to the ADO.NET component. Instead, you reference, or import, the System.Data namespace. Often, you will see the following line:

```
Imports System.Data
```

This does not import all the methods and cause code bloat, however. Instead, it instructs the compiler to treat the methods and types within the namespace as part of your project's own namespace, so instead of having to write this:

```
System.Data.SQLClient()
```

You can simply make a call to

```
SQLClient()
```

There are many other System namespaces. System namespaces include the functionality for security, threading, text and binary I/O, and Web services. How to use various System namespaces is introduced throughout the book.

Don't let the term *namespaces* scare you. It is one of the most fundamental changes in VB .NET, but it is a service provided by the runtime that gives common, rich functionality to any language built on the runtime. As long as you inherit from the namespaces provided to you by the runtime, your application can run on any platform that supports .NET. In this way, you are working on learning the environment as much as you are learning the language. That's one reason why this chapter is the first in the book.

Self-Describing Components

In traditional VB, compiled components created a type library that attempted to define what was in the component as far as classes, interfaces, properties, methods, and events. Communication occurred through a binary interface at the COM level. Unfortunately, one language could expect as parameters data types or structures that are not available to other languages, or that are at least difficult to implement. For example, C++ components often expect pointers or structures to be passed in, and this could be problematic if the calling program is written in Visual Basic. The .NET Framework attempts to solve this by compiling additional data into all assemblies. This additional data is called *metadata* and allows compiled components to interact seamlessly. Couple this with a common type system so that all runtime-compatible languages share the same types, and you can see that cross-language compatibility is enhanced.

The metadata that is stored in the components is binary, and contains all types, members, and references in that file or assembly. The metadata is compiled into the PE file, but when the file is used at runtime, the metadata is moved into memory so that it can be accessed more quickly.

One of the most important things to understand is that it is the metadata that allows the runtime to find and execute your code. The metadata is also used by the runtime to create a valid binary native code version when the MSIL is compiled. The runtime also uses metadata to handle the messy details of memory cleanup and security.

When it comes to the benefits of the metadata for a developer, realize that there is so much information in the metadata that you can inherit from a PE created in a different language because the metadata provides such a rich level of detail. This means that you are actually inheriting from a compiled component, not an IDL file as was required previously. In fact, because metadata is compiled into the PE or assembly, you no longer need IDL files or type libraries. All the information is now contained in the PE.

By default, the metadata contains the following information:

- PE or assembly identity: name, version, culture, public key
- Dependencies on other assemblies
- Security roles and permissions
- Exported types

Each type has the following metadata:

- Name, visibility, base class, implemented interfaces
- Members

In addition, you can extend the metadata using attributes. These are created by the developer and allow additional information to be placed in the metadata.

Cross-Language Interoperability

If you've been building COM components for a while, you know that one of the great promises of COM is that it is language independent. If you build a COM component in C++, you can call it from VB, and vice versa. However, to reach that point, your code had to be compiled to a COM standard. Much of this was hidden from the VB developer, but your component had to implement the IUnknown and IDispatch interfaces. Without these interfaces, it would not have been a true COM component. COM is only giving you cross-language interoperability at the binary level, however. This means that you can only take advantage of this interoperability at run time.

Now, however, the CLR gives you much better language interoperability. Not only can you inherit classes from one PE written in language A and use them in language B, but debugging now works across components in multiple languages. This way, you can step through the code in a PE written in C# and jump to the base class that was written in VB .NET. This means that your cross-language interoperability is happening at design time and run time, not just the run time given to you by COM. In addition, you can raise an error (now called an *exception*) in one language and have it handled by a component in another language. This is significant because now developers can write in the language with which they are most comfortable, and be assured that others writing in different languages will be able to easily use their components.

The Catch: Use Only Common Language Specification Types

This all sounds great, and you are probably getting excited about the possibilities. There is a catch, however: To make use of this great cross-language interoperability, you must stick to only those data types and functions common to all the languages. If you're wondering just how you do that, the good news is that Microsoft has already thought about this issue and set out a standard, called the Common Language Specification, or CLS. If you stick with the CLS, you can be confident that you will have complete interoperability with others programming to the CLS, no matter what languages are being used. Not very creatively, components that expose only CLS features are called *CLS-compliant components*.

To write CLS-compliant components, you must stick to the CLS in these key areas:

- The public class definitions must include only CLS types.
- The definitions of public members of the public classes must be CLS types.
- The definitions of members that are accessible to subclasses must be CLS types.
- The parameters of public methods in public classes must be CLS types.
- The parameters of methods that are accessible to subclasses must be CLS types.

These rules talk a lot about definitions and parameters for public classes and methods. You are free to use non-CLS types in private classes, private methods, and local variables. Even if you have a public class that you want to be CLS compliant, the implementation code *inside* that class does not have to be CLS compliant; as long as the definition is compliant, you are safe.

The CLS is still in flux, but the basics are well established. See Appendix A for the basics of the CLS.

Security

If you create a VB component today, your choices for implementing security are somewhat limited. You can use NTFS to set permissions on the file itself. You can place the component in MTS/COM+ Component Services and turn on role-based security. You can call it over DCOM and use DCOMCNFG to set permissions. You can always just code your own security.

One of the runtime's main benefits is that an entire security infrastructure is built right in. In fact, two major security models are set up in the .NET Framework: code access security and role-based security. These are discussed in more detail in Chapter 12, "Performance and Security."

Code Access Security (CAS)

This security does not control who can access the code; rather, it controls what the code itself can access. This is important because it allows you to build components that can be trusted to varying degrees. If you build a VB component today and want to perform database access, you are free to call ADO and connect to a database (provided, of course, that you have a valid user ID and password). With .NET, however, you can actually specify, with the tools in the .NET Framework, what actions your component can and, more importantly, cannot perform. This has the benefit of preventing others from using the code in ways that you did not intend.

Perhaps the main benefit of CAS is that you can now trust code that is downloaded from the Internet. Security can be set up so that it becomes impossible for the code to perform any mischievous actions. This would prevent most of the macro viruses that are spread via e-mail today.

Role-Based Security

Role-based security is the same type of security you get when you use MTS or COM+ Component Services. In .NET, the Framework determines the caller, called a *principal*, and checks the principal's individual and group permissions. Unlike COM/COM+ role-based security, however, .NET cannot make an assumption that the user will have a valid NT user account and token to pass in. Therefore, .NET allows for generic and custom principals, as well as standard Windows principals. You can define new roles for each application if you want.

Summary

You have just driven by some of the most important .NET features at about 60 miles per hour. If some of the terminology seems foreign to you, do not worry. Some of it will be covered in more detail in this book. Terminology that isn't covered in more detail in this book will be covered in other books, but this book will cover the basics of what you need to know to get started using VB .NET.

For those questioning whether to move to .NET, it is important to understand the benefits .NET gives you. Having a unified debugger, gaining true multithreading, and finally having implementation inheritance are major leaps forward. The runtime also gives you a nice security framework, and you don't have to worry about registering components anymore. Web Services allows you to easily create services that are consumable over a standard HTTP connection.

As you work with VB .NET, understand that you are also working closely with the .NET Framework. It is hard to separate the two, and the more you understand about the Framework, the better VB .NET developer you will be.

Your First VB .NET Application

IN THIS CHAPTER

It's time to jump in and start working with VB .NET. First, you need to learn a little bit about the new IDE. The new VB .NET IDE might look somewhat familiar to you, but there are some significant changes that make it a more useful environment. However, these changes can be frustrating to experienced VB developers because many of the keystrokes have changed, windows have different names, and the debugging tools work differently. VB .NET is part of Visual Studio .NET (or VS .NET), which finally consolidates all the development languages into one place: VB .NET, C++.NET, and C#. You can even create a single solution, containing multiple projects, in which the individual projects are written in separate languages.

The Start Page

The very first time you start Visual Studio .NET, you are taken to a screen that allows you to configure the IDE. That screen is the My Profile page discussed later in the chapter. After your first visit to the My Profile page, all subsequent starts of Visual Studio .NET begin with the Start Page, as shown in Figure 2.1. The start page contains a number of sections, as indicated by the links along the left side. These sections are

- Get Started—This option allows you to open a recent or existing project, or create a new one. A few recent projects are listed on the Get Started area shown in Figure 2.1. As you create projects in VB .NET, this area will display the four most recently opened projects. This area also contains links to open an existing project, to create a new project, and to log a bug report. Expect this last option to disappear after the final product is released.

- What's New—This option covers new language features in Visual Studio .NET, including each individual language and the Visual Studio .NET environment. There are links to topics in the help files on new features for the VS .NET languages, the .NET SDKs, and a link to check for VS .NET upgrades.

- Online Community—This provides links to the Microsoft newsgroups. These are newsgroups accessible with any newsreader, but they are served from Microsoft's news server (msnews.microsoft.com) and not normal Usenet news servers.

- Headlines—Provides a place for links to news about .NET. This page includes a link to MSDN Online, a section for technical articles, a section for the Knowledge Base, and a number of other resources.

- Search Online—Searches the MSDN Online library.

- Downloads—Gives you access to a number of downloads. Downloads can include new tools, such as service packs, the Mobile Internet Toolkit, and code samples. Downloads can also include code samples and new documentation.

- Web Hosting—Allows you to connect directly to services that offer Web hosting for your .NET Web Services or .NET Web Applications. With one command, you can publish your .NET applications or services to these hosting companies. At least one, Brinkster, offers a free membership so that you can test your applications.

- My Profile—This screen lets you choose the overall layout of Visual Studio .NET. You can set the keyboard mappings to the same scheme as in previous versions of Visual Studio, such as Visual Basic 6. You can also set the window layout to match previous versions of Visual Studio projects, and you can automatically filter help using the profile. Throughout this book, I will assume that the profile is set to Visual Studio Developer, and that all other settings are left at their default values.

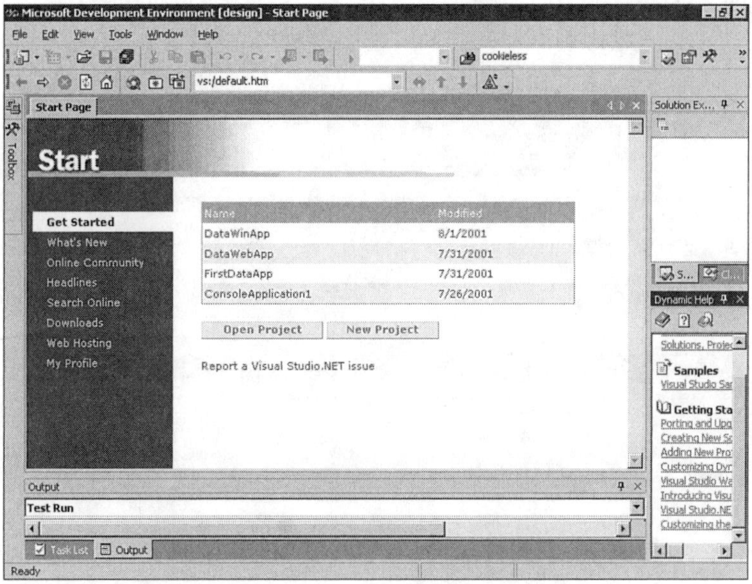

FIGURE 2.1

The Visual Studio .NET Start Page.

> **NOTE**
>
> The Start Page is HTML and will likely change by the time VS .NET is released.

Help is now more tightly integrated into Visual Studio. To see this, click on the What's New link on the Start Page. In the What's New page, there are three tabs. Click on the Product Information tab and then click on the What's New in Visual Basic link. Notice that when you do this, the help is loaded into the same window that held the Start Page, as shown in Figure 2.2. As you will see later, it is even possible to have help running continuously while you work, searching for topics associated with whatever you are working on at the moment.

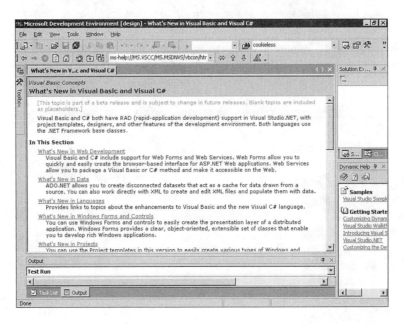

FIGURE 2.2

Help is shown within the IDE instead of as a separate window.

Creating a New Project

Return to the Start Page by clicking either the Back button or the Home button on the toolbar, and clicking on Get Started. Now, click on the New Project link. Doing so opens the New Project dialog shown in Figure 2.3. Notice that there are different languages you can use to create applications in Visual Studio .NET. This book will focus on only the Visual Basic projects.

If you examine the Visual Basic project types, you'll see that many of them are different from what you are used to with VB6. Some of the major project types are

- Windows Application—This is a *standard executable*, in VB6 terminology. It is the way to create applications with a Windows interface, using forms and controls. This is as close to "your father's VB" as you'll get in VB .NET.

- Class Library—This project type allows you to create classes that will be used in other applications. Think of it as similar to the COM components that you have been building, which VB6 called the ActiveX DLL and ActiveX EXE project types.

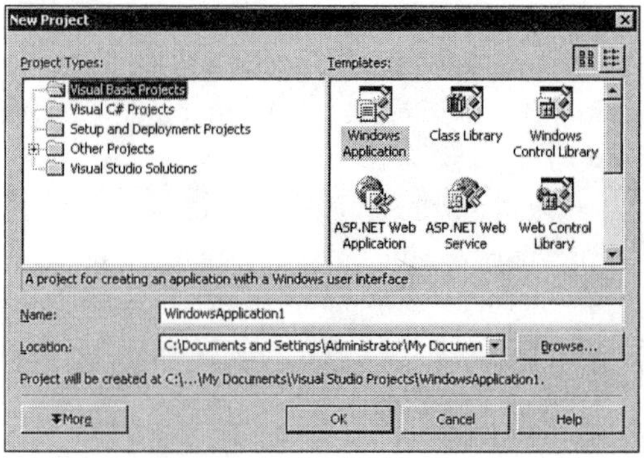

FIGURE 2.3

The New Project dialog box.

- Windows Control Library—This project type is for creating what used to be called ActiveX Controls. This type allows you to create new controls to be used in Windows applications.

- ASP.NET Web Application—Goodbye, Visual InterDev. Goodbye, server-side, interpreted scripting languages for Active Server Pages. Visual Basic .NET has Web Application projects, which use ASP.NET to create dynamic Web applications. These projects allow you to create HTML, ASP.NET, and VB .NET code files. You will now code your Web applications using a powerful, event-driven model instead of the request/response model. Of course, Web applications still use the request/response model, but you write code the same way you do for Windows applications, using an event-driven model.

- ASP.NET Web Service—If you've used VB6 to create COM components and then made them available over HTTP with SOAP, you understand the concept of Web Services. Web Service projects are components that you make available to other applications via the Web; the underlying protocol is HTTP instead of DCOM, and you pass requests and receive responses behind the scenes using XML. Some of the major promises of Web Services are that they are all standards-based and are platform independent. Unlike DCOM, which was tied to a COM, and therefore Windows-only, infrastructure, Web Service projects can be placed on any platform that supports .NET, and can then be called by any application using just the HTTP protocol.

- Web Control Library—As with Web Service projects, there's no exact match back in VB6 for the Web Control Library projects. Thanks to the new Web Application projects in VB .NET, you can add controls to Web pages just as you would in a standard Windows Application project, but VB .NET makes them HTML controls at runtime. You can design your own controls that can then be used by Web applications.

- Console Application—Many of the Windows administrative tools are still console (or command line or DOS) applications. Previously, you didn't have a good way to create console applications in VB, and instead had to rely on C++. Now, console applications are natively supported by VB .NET.

- Windows Service—As with console applications, there was no good way to create Windows services in previous versions of VB. Windows services, of course, are programs that run in the background of Windows, and can automatically start when the machine is booted, even if no one logs in. Windows services typically have no user interface, instead writing any information to the event logs. Because services are typically extremely long-running applications, be sure to include very good error handling.

Those are the basic types of applications you can create. You can also create an Empty Project (for Windows applications, class libraries, and services) or an Empty Web Project (for Web applications). A final option, New Project in Existing Folder, will create a new, empty project in a folder that already contains one or more projects.

Examining the IDE

If you are still on the New Project dialog, choose to create a Windows Application. Name it LearningVB and click the OK button. After a time, a new project will open up. Notice this adds a tab to the main window with the title Form1.vb [Design]. In this new tab, you now have what appears to be an empty form. This is commonly referred to as the Form Designer. In fact, there are various types of designers that can get loaded into the main work area. So far, VB developers should feel pretty much at home.

One difference that has occurred, perhaps without you noticing, is that the files created have already been saved on your machine. In VB, you could create a project, do some quick coding, and then exit without saving, and nothing was stored on your machine. In VB .NET, however, the files are saved at creation, so each project you create does store something on the hard drive, even if you never choose to save anything. Visual InterDev developers are used to this, but straight VB developers will see this as a change.

If you look at the right side of the IDE, you'll see a window called the Solution Explorer. This works like the Project Explorer in VB6, showing you the projects and files you have in the current *solution* (what VB6 called a *group*). The Solution Explorer currently lists the solution name, the project name, and all the forms and modules. Right now, there is just one form, named Form1.vb. In addition, the window will have a file called AssemblyInfo.vb, which is part of the metadata that will be compiled into this assembly. You also see a new node, called References, in the list. If you expand the References node, you will see all the references that are already available to your project when you start. You can see the Solution Explorer in Figure 2.4. For now, don't worry too much about the references.

FIGURE 2.4

The Solution Explorer window.

A second tab, labeled Class View, exists at the bottom of the Server Explorer window. If you click on the Class View tab, you will see the LearningVB project listed. If you expand the project node, you will see the namespaces for this project listed. It so happens that there is just one namespace at the moment, and by default, it is the same as the project name. Expand the LearningVB namespace and you will see that just Form1 is listed below it. Expand Form1 and you will see some of the form's methods, as well as a node for Bases and Interfaces. If you expand the Bases and Interfaces node and the Form node under it, you will see a long list of properties, methods, and events available to you in the form. You can see a small part of this list in Figure 2.5. Again, don't worry about these for now. Just understand that this is certainly different from anything you saw in Visual Basic 6.

If you want to know more about what one of those properties or methods can do for you, it's easy to look it up in the Object Browser. For example, scroll down the Bases and Implemented Interfaces list until you find the Load event. Right-click on it and choose Browse Definition. You will see that the Object Browser opens as a tab in the main work area, and that you are on the definition for the Load event. You can see that Load returns a System.EventHandler. Figure 2.6 shows what this should look like in the IDE. Because the Object Browser is just another tab, there's no need to close it. However, if you want to close it, the X you click is in the upper-right corner of the designer window, not under the X for all of Visual Studio .NET.

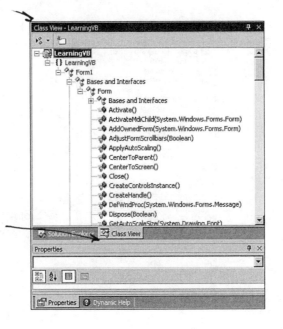

Figure 2.5

The new Class View window.

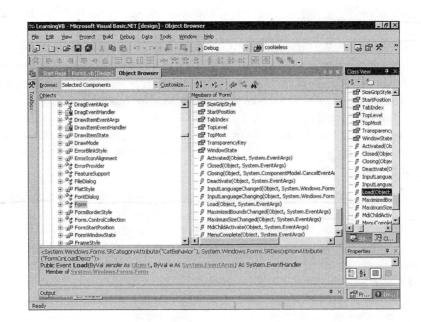

Figure 2.6

The Object Browser is now a tab in the main work area.

Below the Server Explorer/Class View windows is something that will be quite familiar to you: the Properties window. If you close the Object Browser and go back to the Form1.vb [Design] tab, you should see the properties for Form1. You might actually have to click on the form for it to get the focus. After the form has the focus, you will see the properties for the form. Most of these properties will look very familiar to you, although there are some new ones. What some of these new properties are, and what they can do for you, will be examined later in this chapter.

> **NOTE**
>
> The Properties window is sorted by category instead of alphabetically, by default. Therefore, it can be difficult to find certain properties. In the toolbar for the Properties window are buttons that let you switch between a categorized and alphabetical listing of the properties.

In the same area as the Properties window is a tab labeled Dynamic Help. This is a new Visual Studio .NET feature that allows you to have constantly updating help while you work. It monitors what you are doing in the IDE and provides a list of help topics for your current activity. For example, with only the form open and active, click on the Dynamic Help tab. You will get a list of help topics associated with the Forms Designer, how to add controls to a form, and similar topics. Figure 2.7 shows what this list will look like. Feel free to click around on various IDE windows and watch the dynamic help change. Just realize that the Dynamic Help feature does consume some resources. On more powerful computers, this will not be a big deal, but it could be a problem on machines with slow processors or too little RAM.

Along the left side of the IDE are two sideways tabs. You see only one label at a time, so one will appear as a label while the other appears as a button. The first tab/button is for the Server Explorer, and the second tab/button is for the Toolbox. To get either to appear, just hover the mouse over the tab/button, or go ahead and click on it.

The Server Explorer is a new feature to the IDE. It allows for discoverable services on various servers. For example, if you want to find machines that are running Microsoft SQL Server, there is a SQL Server Databases node under each server. In Figure 2.8, you can see that I have one server registered to my Server Explorer: culaptop. This server does have SQL Server, and you can see a list of the databases. Within Server Explorer, you can perform the actions that you used to perform with the Data View window. You can view the data in a table; you can drop or create tables; you can create, drop, and edit stored procedures; and all the other activities you performed with the Data View window in VB6. If you did much with Visual InterDev, these tools will feel even more comfortable to you.

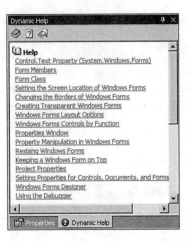

FIGURE 2.7

The Dynamic Help window.

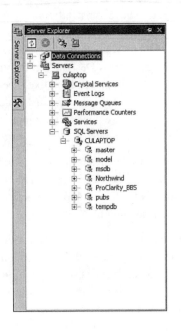

FIGURE 2.8

The new Server Explorer window.

You can also use the Server Explorer to find and connect to message queues, monitor another machine with the performance counters, and find Web services on other machines. The Server Explorer is a handy tool, with many of the administrative functions you need to perform all in one place.

The second sideways tab is Toolbox. The Toolbox is just what its name implies: It is where you find the controls that you want to put on a form. Notice, however, that this Toolbox is a little different from the Toolbox in VB6. In fact, it looks much more like the Toolbox from Visual InterDev. The Toolbox is split into horizontal tabs. Figure 2.9 shows the Windows Forms tab open, but there are also Data, Components, Clipboard Ring, and General tabs. Don't worry too much about those other tabs for now.

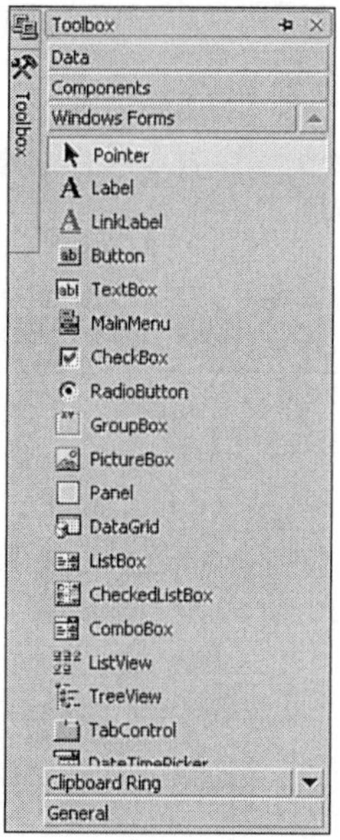

FIGURE 2.9
The improved Toolbox.

Creating Your First VB .NET Application

You have an open project with one form in it. So far, you haven't done anything to it, so you now need to create the obligatory Hello World application. I remember when Microsoft was running around showing the world how you could create a Hello World application in VB by typing just one line of code. Well, it's still that easy, but things certainly look different now.

Make sure that the form designer is the current tab in the work area, and open the Toolbox. Click and drag a button onto the form. Place it wherever you want. So far, this is just like VB6. Now, double-click on the button.

Double-clicking on the button causes the code window to open, just as it did in VB. However, in VB .NET, the code is added as a tab in the work area. The new tab is labeled Form1.vb, and has an asterisk after it, indicating it has not been saved. You have a lot of code in this window, and it's code that you haven't seen before. Some of the code is hidden from you, thanks to the fact that the VS .NET code editor lets you have code regions that allow you to collapse or expand blocks of code. If you expand the Windows Form Designer generated code section, you see a fair amount of code. In fact, before typing any code at all, you have the code shown in Figure 2.10. Notice that I have turned on line numbers just for easier referencing. If you want to turn on line numbers as well, go to Tools, Options. Expand the Text Editor node and choose Basic. Check the Line Numbers check box.

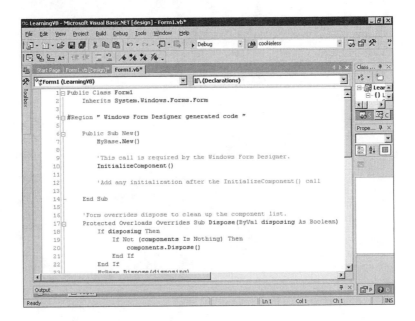

FIGURE 2.10
The code window shows a significant amount of code before you even start typing.

The first line of code shows that the form, Form1, is actually just a class. This is one of the biggest changes to VB .NET: Forms are truly classes. Why? Because forms are really just classes, and they have been forever. You might not have ever thought of it that way, but a form is just another class. When a form is displayed, you have just instantiated a class.

The next line is an `Inherits` statement. Any Windows form you create just inherits from the base `Form` class. You are calling a class in one of the .NET System namespaces; in this case, you are calling the Form class in the `System.Windows.Forms` namespace. It is this class that gives you the base functionality of forms, such as the methods and events you will access in your code. The `Inherits` statement is your first indication of true inheritance in VB .NET. You can inherit from this base class and then extend it if you want to do so.

The code located inside the normally collapsed Windows Form Designer generated code region is shown in Listing 2.1.

LISTING 2.1 Code Generated for You by the Windows Form Designer

```
#Region " Windows Form Designer generated code "

    Public Sub New()
        MyBase.New()

        'This call is required by the Windows Form Designer.
        InitializeComponent()

        'Add any initialization after the InitializeComponent() call

    End Sub


    'Form overrides dispose to clean up the component list.
    Protected Overloads Overrides Sub Dispose(ByVal disposing As Boolean)
        If disposing Then
            If Not (components Is Nothing) Then
                components.Dispose()
            End If
        End If
        MyBase.Dispose(disposing)
    End Sub
    Friend WithEvents Button1 As System.Windows.Forms.Button

    'Required by the Windows Form Designer
    Private components As System.ComponentModel.Container

    'NOTE: The following procedure is required by the Windows Form Designer
    'It can be modified using the Windows Form Designer.
    'Do not modify it using the code editor.
    <System.Diagnostics.DebuggerStepThrough()> Private Sub
    InitializeComponent()
      Me.Button1 = New System.Windows.Forms.Button()
```

LISTING 2.1 Continued

```
    Me.SuspendLayout()
    '
    'Button1
    '
    Me.Button1.Location = New System.Drawing.Point(64, 56)
    Me.Button1.Name = "Button1"
    Me.Button1.TabIndex = 0
    Me.Button1.Text = "Button1"
    '
    'Form1
    '
    Me.AutoScaleBaseSize = New System.Drawing.Size(5, 13)
    Me.ClientSize = New System.Drawing.Size(292, 273)
    Me.Controls.AddRange(New System.Windows.Forms.Control() {Me.Button1})
    Me.Name = "Form1"
    Me.Text = "Form1"
    Me.ResumeLayout(False)

End Sub
```

```
#End Region
```

The next piece inside the class is a public Sub named New, found inside the automatically generated region. Notice that it calls a Sub named InitializeComponent. The InitializeComponent routine is created for you by VS .NET. The New routine is similar to the Form_Load event procedure you got used to in VB6. Notice that you need to add any of your own code after the call to InitializeComponent.

After the New sub is a Dispose sub, much like the Form_Unload found in VB6. This is the area for the cleanup of anything you might have open. Don't worry about the Overloads and Overrides keywords for now; they will be covered when you learn more about inheritance.

As you can see, the InitializeComponent routine is in this block, and it is what sets up the controls on the form. Notice that the button has properties set, such as the location and size, and then is added to a controls collection.

Finally, below this region of code is the routine to handle the click event on the button. This looks different from what you have seen before as well. In fact, if you started a new Standard EXE project in VB6, added a button to the form, and then double-clicked the button, your entire project would show just this code:

```
Private Sub Command1_Click()

End Sub
```

However, in VB .NET, you will see a lot more code. In fact, the `Click` event is not even handled until line 57, at least in this example. The declaration of the event procedure is quite different as well. In VB .NET, the event procedure looks like this:

```
Private Sub Button1_Click(ByVal sender As System.Object, _
    ByVal e As System.EventArgs) Handles Button1.Click
End Sub
```

Again, don't worry about all the changes for now. Instead, type in the following line of code:

```
msgbox "Hello, World"
```

When you move off this line, you will notice that VB .NET automatically adds parentheses around your argument, leaving you with this:

```
MsgBox("Hello, World")
```

This is one of the first fundamental language changes: Subs and Functions require parentheses around the argument. The `MsgBox` command is a function, but in VB6, you did not need parentheses around a parameter if you were ignoring the return value. In VB .NET, you always need the parentheses, so get used to adding them or at least get used to seeing VB .NET add them for you.

Now, it is time to run this rather exciting demonstration and see whether it works. You can click the Start button on the toolbar (it should look familiar) or you can go to the Debug menu and choose Start.

Form1 should load. Click on the button, and you should get a message box to pop up, with the text `Hello, World`. In Figure 2.11, you will notice that the title of the message box is the same as the project name, just as it was in VB6. Close the application and return to the IDE.

FIGURE 2.11
The Hello World application running.

Notice that a new window is showing. At the bottom of the screen, an Output window is now open. Figure 2.12 shows this window. The Output window has a drop-down list box that can show different information. Currently, it shows you all the debug statements. You did not put any `debug.print` statements into your code, but certain actions by the compiler automatically put comments into the Debug window.

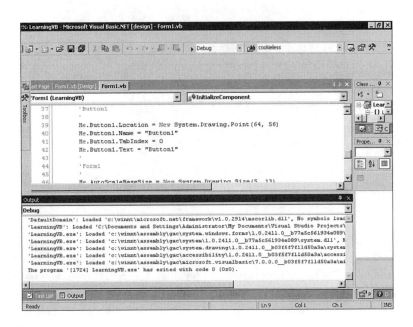

FIGURE 2.12
The new Debug window.

Before moving on, you might want to change the title of the message box. Return to the one line of code you've written so far and modify it to look like this:

```
msgbox("Hello, World", , "My first VB .NET App")
```

Now that you have added a title to the message box, run the project again, and the title of your message box will be My first VB .NET App. If you think it doesn't get any better than this, hang on.

Windows Application Enhancements

Visual Studio .NET has added a variety of features to VB .NET to make the IDE more powerful and to enhance the functionality of Windows forms. There is improved support for features such as building menus, controls that automatically resize based on the text to display, better anchoring of controls for resized windows, and a much-improved mechanism for setting the tab order.

Resizing Controls Automatically

You can set certain controls to resize automatically based on what they need to display. This is easy to examine with a simple label. Open the Toolbox and add a label to your form. Drag it over to the left side of the form, so that it is not in line with the button.

Now, change some properties of that label. Change the `BorderStyle` to `FixedSingle`, and set `AutoSize` to `True`. Change the `Text` property to `This is a test`. You might have noticed that you changed the `Text` property, and not a `Caption` property as you did in VB versions 1–6. Welcome to another one of those little changes from VB to VB .NET that might trip you up.

Now, modify the code for the `Button1_Click` event. Remove the `MsgBox` call and add the following code:

```
Label1.Text = "Put your hand on a hot stove " & _
    "for a minute, and it seems like an hour. " & _
    "Sit with a pretty girl for an hour, and " & _
    "it seems like a minute. THAT'S relativity."
```

Before you run this, realize one more thing about the code. In VB6, it would have been legal to say this:

```
Label1 = "Put your hand on a hot stove..."
```

This would run just fine in VB6 because the default property of `Label1` was the `Caption` property. Well, in VB .NET, there is no such thing as a default property. Therefore, you always have to specify the property when you write your code.

Go ahead and run the project. A form will appear that is similar to what you see in Figure 2.13. Now, click Button1 and notice that the text in the label changed, which is no big surprise. However, notice that the label has grown to try to hold all the text. If you resize the form, you will see that the label has indeed grown to show all the text. Figure 2.14 shows this to be the case.

FIGURE 2.13
A form with a small amount of text in a label.

If you're saying that this isn't a big deal, think of the code you had to write before. You had to check the length of the string, but you also had to be aware of what font was in use. A group of characters in Arial is not the same length as the same group of characters in Courier. Therefore, resizing could be a hit-or-miss proposition. The `AutoSize` property removes that guesswork for you.

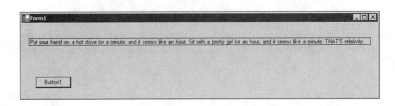

FIGURE 2.14

The same form, showing the label has grown to contain all the text.

Anchoring Controls to the Form Edges

How many times did you create a VB form and set the border style to fixed so that people couldn't resize it? If you placed a series of buttons along the bottom of the form, you didn't want people to resize the form and suddenly have this bottom row of buttons in the middle of the form.

VB .NET allows you to anchor controls to one or more sides. This can allow a control to move as the form is resized, so that it appears to stay in its proper place.

Back on Form1, delete the label you added, and remove the code inside the Button1_Click event procedure. Make the form slightly bigger and move Button1 toward the lower-right corner. Now, add a TextBox to the form. Change the TextBox's Multiline property to True and resize the text box so that it fills up most of the form, except for the bottom portion that now contains the button. Your form should now look something like the one shown in Figure 2.15.

Run the project. After the window is loaded, resize it by moving the lower-right corner down and to the right. You will end up with something that looks like Figure 2.16.

Obviously, this looks pretty strange, and it is exactly what you are used to with VB6. Your answer in VB6, short of a third-party ActiveX control, is to write a lot of code that runs when the form's Resize event is fired. You use that code to move the button and resize the text box. VB .NET has a better way of handling this, so stop the application and return to the IDE.

Make sure that you are on the Form1.vb [Design] tab and click on Button1. In the Properties window, scroll down and find the Anchor property. When you drop down this list, you get a strange box that shows a gray something in the middle, and four small rectangles around it. By default, the top and left rectangles are darkened, whereas the right and bottom rectangles are empty. The darkened rectangles indicate that right now, the button is anchored to the top and left sides of the form. As you resize the form, the button will stay the same distance from the top and left sides. That is not what you want, so click the top and left rectangles to clear them, and then click the bottom and right rectangles to select them. When you are done, the Anchor property should look like Figure 2.17. After you collapse the drop-down list, the Anchor property should be Bottom, Right.

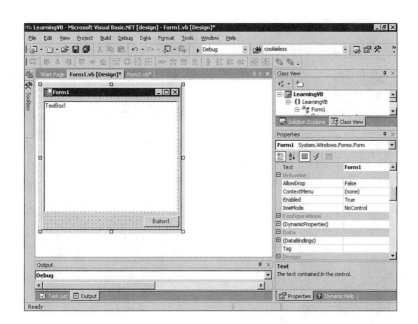

FIGURE 2.15

The form as it looks at design time.

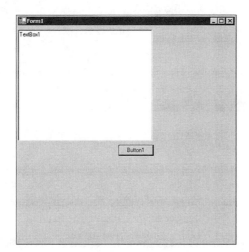

FIGURE 2.16

The form at run time, showing what happens when the form is resized.

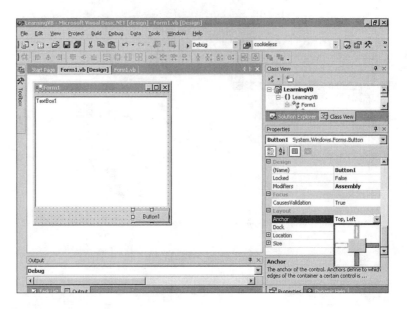

Figure 2.17

The Anchor *property tool.*

Next, click on TextBox1 and choose its Anchor property. Click on the bottom and right rectangles, but leave the left and top rectangles chosen. Now, the text box is tied to all borders, and it will remain the same distance from them. The Anchor property for TextBox1 should now be Top, Bottom, Left, Right.

Run the project again. After the form is open, resize it. Notice that the button now stays in the lower-right corner, and the text box automatically resizes with the form. You can see this behavior in Figure 2.18. The resizing and movement were accomplished without writing a line of code.

Easier Menus

If you hated building menus under previous versions of VB, you weren't alone. The VB menu editor has never won any awards for ease of use nor for user friendliness. The new Menu Editor in VB .NET might just make you enjoy building menus.

Using the same form as in the previous example, go to the Toolbox and double-click the MainMenu control. The MainMenu control is added to an area below the form, called the Component Tray, which you'll see more of later. If you click once on the MainMenu1 control in the Component Tray, you'll see a menu bar added to the form, which simply pushes down the text box. The menu shows one item that says Type Here, as shown in Figure 2.19.

FIGURE 2.18

The form showing how the controls can resize or move as the form is resized.

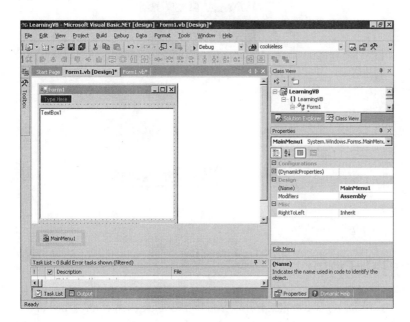

FIGURE 2.19

The new Menu Editor in action.

Click once in the box that says Type Here, and type &File. This creates a new Type Here box to the right and a new Type Here box below. Click once in the Type Here below the word &File and type &Open. Just as in previous versions of VB, the ampersand (&) is used to signify an Alt+key selection. Typing &Open creates a new Type Here box to the right and a new Type Here below. As you can see, you are graphically building a menu. Click in the box below the Open and type &Close.

You can click in the Type Here box just to the right of the File menu choice to add another top-level menu. For example, you could add &Edit to the right of the File menu. Now, the Edit menu gets new blank entries, and you could add items for copying and pasting.

Click on the Open menu choice under the File menu (on the menu you just created, not VB .NET's menus). If you look in the Properties window, you will see that the actual name of the object is MenuItem2. You can change that if you want, but don't worry about it for now. Instead, click on the drop-down for the Shortcut property. Scroll through the list until you find the Ctrl+O choice. The ShowShortcut property is set to True by default, but you won't see the shortcut at design time. Instead, run the application. Figure 2.20 shows you roughly what you should see. Notice that the underlining of the letters (signified by the ampersand) might not appear unless you hold down the Alt key.

Figure 2.20
The new menu being displayed at run time.

Setting Tab Order

If you disliked creating menus in previous versions of VB, it's a safe bet that you hated setting the tab order, especially on complex forms. You had to click each control, one at a time, and make sure that the TabIndex property was correct. Take the form you've been working with and remove the textbox. Leave Button1 in the lower-right corner.

Add three more buttons to the form. Place them in such a way as to make Button1 the last in the series. In fact, mix them up, if you prefer. If you take a look at Figure 2.21, you'll see that the buttons have been placed in such a way that you will want the tab order to be Button2, Button4, Button3, and Button1. If you start the project and run it as is, however, the order will still be Button1, Button2, Button3, and Button4.

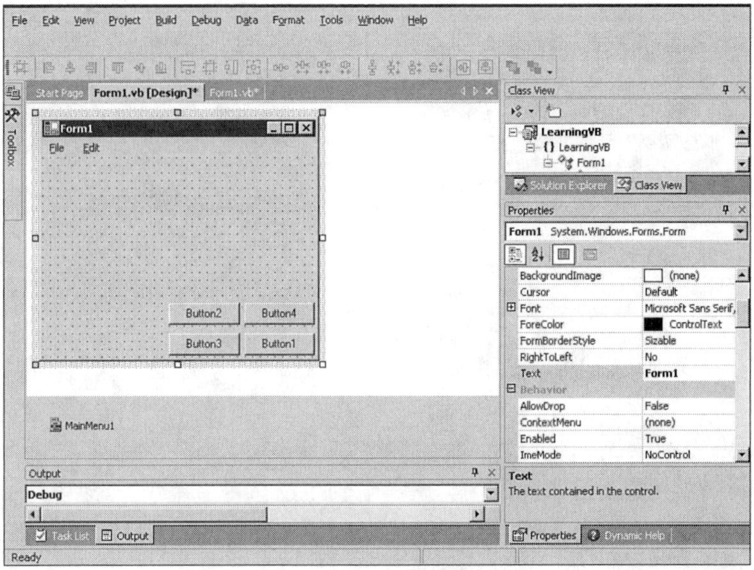

FIGURE 2.21

The form with buttons in the wrong order.

To set the tab order, click on the View menu and choose Tab Order. You now get small numbers on each control that can receive the focus, as shown in Figure 2.22. To reset the tab order, simply click on the controls in the order that you want them to receive focus. In this example, you just click on Button2, Button4, Button3, and Button1, in that order, and the tab order is set for you, as evidenced by the number in the upper-left corner of each button.

You can choose View, Tab Order again to turn off the display of the tab order. You can run the project to verify the new tab order.

Line and Shape Controls: You're Outta Here

If you examine the Toolbox, you might just find yourself searching and searching for the Line and Shape controls. They're gone. The Line and Shape controls are gone, but you do have an alternative.

Microsoft removed them because they were actually windowless controls in VB6; that is, they didn't have an associated hWnd, but were painted directly on the form. In the new VB .NET forms engine, all controls must be windowed, and you no longer have control transparency.

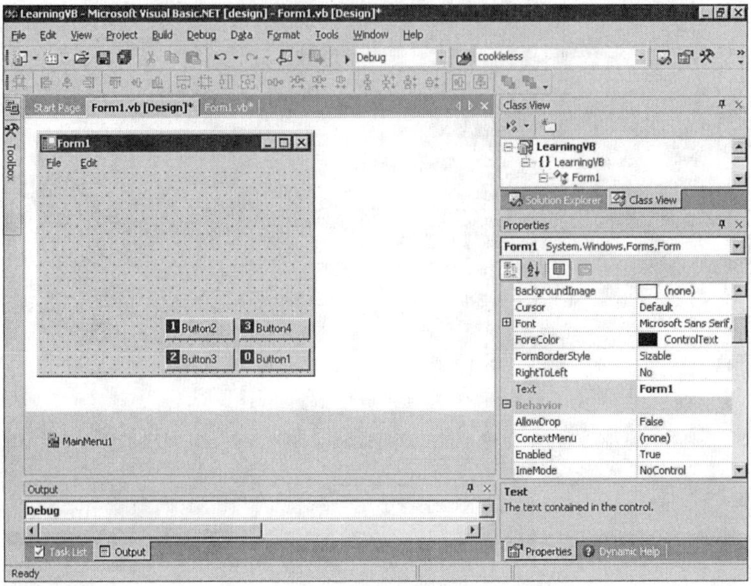

FIGURE 2.22
The new way to set the tab order.

Now that you've heard the technical explanation, what do you do about it? The easiest way to fake a line is to use a label. Turn on the border and then set the height (or width) to 1. This makes the label look like a line, and it works fine. For more complex shapes, Microsoft recommends that you use the GDI+ objects, which are very powerful. The GDI+ objects are in the System.Drawing namespace, and will be examined briefly in Chapter 3, "Major VB .NET Changes."

Form Opacity

Forms now have an Opacity property. Is it a necessary feature? Probably not, but it could be used for some useful purpose. For example, you can use it to have forms fade in or out, and you can turn forms translucent while they are being dragged.

On the Form1 you've been working with so far, find its Opacity property and change it to 50%. Now, run the project and you'll notice that the form is now quite see-through. The form still works fine (not that this current form is doing anything). You can click and drag the form; you can press the buttons. It works fine, but it is translucent at the moment. Close the project and you can add some code to take advantage of this new, if not quite critical, feature.

Go to the Toolbox and add a timer to your form. Unlike VB6, the timer doesn't actually appear on the form, in the Component Tray for the form. Click on the timer in this window and then set the timer's Enabled property to True. The interval of 100 is fine.

Now, click on the Form1.vb tab to get to the code. In the `Sub New` routine, add the following line of code right after the `Add any initialization...` comment:

```
Me.Opacity = 0
```

This merely sets the opacity to `0`, which means that the form will be completely invisible when the form loads.

Next, use the Class Name and Method Name drop-down boxes at the top of the code window to choose the `Tick` event of the Timer1 control. This adds an event procedure for the `Timer1_Tick` event. Inside that event procedure, enter the following code:

```
Me.Opacity = Me.Opacity + 0.01
If Me.Opacity >= 1 Then
    Timer1.Enabled = False
    Beep()
End If
```

This code merely increments the opacity by .01 each time the `Tick` event fires. When it finally reaches 1 (100%), the timer is shut off by setting its `Enabled` property to `False`, and the beep is called just to make a sound so that you know when it is finished.

If you are at all confused by the code, Listing 2.2 shows how the whole listing will look (with the Windows Form Designer-generated code hidden).

LISTING 2.2   Your First VB .NET Application, with All the Code Discussed So Far

```
Public Class Form1
    Inherits System.Windows.Forms.Form

#Region " Windows Form Designer generated code "

    Private Sub button1_Click(ByVal sender As System.Object, _
     ByVal e As System.EventArgs) Handles button1.Click    End Sub

    Private Sub timer1_Tick(ByVal sender As System.Object, _
     ByVal e As System.EventArgs) Handles timer1.Tick
        Me.Opacity = Me.Opacity + 0.01
      If Me.Opacity >= 1 Then
         timer1().Enabled = False
         Beep()
      End If
    End Sub
End Class
```

Run the project. You should see your form fade in slowly as the opacity is increased. You will hear a beep when the form is fully opaque.

Summary

This chapter sought to get you into the new VB .NET IDE quickly. You have created your first VB .NET application, and you have seen some of the new features presented in the IDE. It is now easier to have controls maintain their positions even when the form is resized. Help is more readily available. The Server Explorer makes it easier to locate and use resources throughout your enterprise. New project types open up a new world for VB .NET developers.

In addition to all these changes, there are some fundamental language changes as well. A few of those have been mentioned in this chapter, and if you looked at the code, you saw some others. The next chapter is dedicated to presenting some of the more important language changes.

Major VB .NET Changes

IN THIS CHAPTER

VB .NET introduces major changes to the VB language. Some are modifications to existing ways of working, whereas others are brand new. This chapter will cover some of those changes, but this is by no means an exhaustive list of all changes from VB to VB .NET. First, you'll see some of the features that have changed. Then you will see some of the new features.

General Changes

There are a number of general changes to be aware of when moving from VB to VB .NET. Among them are topics such as the removal of default properties, subs and functions requiring parentheses, and ByVal being the default method for passing parameters. These changes, and others, are detailed in this section.

Default Properties

In VB6, objects could have default properties. For example, the following code is perfectly valid in VB6, if you assume that Text1 is a text box:

```
Text1="Hello, World"
```

This code takes the string "Hello, World" and sets the default property of the text box, the Text property, to the string. The major drawback to default properties is that they require you to have a Set command in VB. For example, take a look at the following block of VB6 code:

```
Dim txtBillTo as TextBox
Dim txtShipTo as TextBox
txtShipTo = txtBillTo
```

The line of code txtShipTo = txtBillTo sets the Text property of txtShipTo to the value in the Text property of txtBillTo. But what if that isn't what you wanted? What if, instead, you wanted to create an object reference in txtShipTo that referred to the object txtBillTo? You'd have to use this code:

```
Set txtShipTo = txtBillTo
```

As you can see, default properties require you to use the Set keyword to set references from one object variable to another.

VB .NET gets around this problem by getting rid of default properties. Therefore, to copy the Text property from txtBillTo into the Text property of txtShipTo, you have to use this code:

```
txtShipTo.Text = txtBillTo.Text
```

Setting the two variables equal to each other sets a reference from one to the other. In other words, you can set an object reference without the Set keyword:

```
txtShipTo = txtBillTo ' Object reference in VB.NET
```

Default Properties Require Parameterized Properties

To be more precise, default properties *without parameters* are no longer supported. Default properties that require parameters are still valid. Default properties with parameters are most common with collection classes, such as in ADO. In an ADO example, if you assume that rs is an ADO Recordset, check out the following code:

```
rs.Fields.Item(x).Value ' OK, fully qualified
rs.Fields(x).Value ' OK, because Item is parameterized
rs.Fields(x) ' Error, because Fields is not parameterized
```

The easy solution is to fully qualify everything. This avoids any confusion about which properties are parameterized and which are not. However, as you know from your VB days, the number of dots you have should be minimized. The reason is that each dot requires an OLE lookup that slows you down. Therefore, you should code carefully when dealing with parameters.

Subs and Functions Require Parentheses

As you saw in the last chapter when you used the MsgBox function, you must now always use parentheses with functions, even if you are ignoring the return value. In addition, you must use parentheses when calling subs, which you did not do in VB6. For example, assume that you have this sub in both VB6 and VB .NET:

```
Sub foo(ByVal Greeting As String)
    ' implementation code here
End Sub
```

In VB6, you could call this sub in one of two ways:

```
foo "Hello"

Call foo("Hello")
```

In VB .NET, you also could call this sub in one of two ways:

```
Foo("Hello")

Call foo("Hello")
```

The difference between the way VB and VB .NET handle this is, of course, that the parentheses are always required in the VB .NET calls, even though you aren't returning anything. In VB .NET, the Call statement is still supported, but it is not really necessary.

Changes to Boolean Operators

The And, Not, and Or operators were to have undergone some changes in VB .NET. Microsoft originally said that the operators would short-circuit, but now they are staying the way they worked in VB6. *Short-circuiting* means that if you are examining two conditions with the And operator and the first one is false, you shouldn't need to examine the second condition. Because there is no change in VB .NET, this means that, as in VB6, if you had two parts of an And statement and the first failed, you would still examine the second part. Examine the following code:

```
Dim x As Integer
Dim y As Integer
x = 1
y = 0
If x = 2 And y = 5/y Then
...
```

As a human, you know that the variable x is equal to 1. Therefore, when you look at the first part of the If statement, you know that x is not equal to 2, so you would logically think it should quit evaluating the expression. However, VB and VB .NET examine the second part of the expression, so this code would cause a divide-by-zero error, even though the error is in the second part of the expression, and the first part has already been found to be false.

If you want short-circuiting, VB .NET has introduced a couple of new operators: AndAlso and OrElse. In this case, the following code would not generate an error in VB .NET:

```
Dim x As Integer
Dim y As Integer
x = 1
y = 0
If x = 2 AndAlso y = 5/y Then
...
```

This code does not cause an error; instead, because x is not equal to 2, VB .NET does not even examine the second condition.

Declaration Changes

You can now initialize your variables when you declare them. You could not do this in VB6. In VB6, the only way to initialize a new variable was to do so on a separate line, like this:

```
Dim x As Integer
x = 5
```

In VB .NET, you can rewrite this into one line of code:

```
Dim x As Integer = 5
```

Another significant and much-requested change is that of declaring multiple variables, and what data type they assume, on one line. For example, you might have the following line:

```
Dim x, y As Integer
```

As you're probably aware, in VB6, y would be an Integer data type, but x would be a Variant. In VB .NET, this has changed, so both x and y are Integers. If you think, "It's about time," there are many who agree. This should remove a number of bugs and strange type conversions experienced by new VB developers. It should also make the code more efficient by making variables the expected type instead of using the Object type (which replaces the Variant type, as you will see later).

Support for New Assignment Operators

VB .NET now supports shortcuts for performing certain assignment operations. In VB6, you incremented x by 1 with the following line of code:

```
x = x + 1
```

In VB .NET, you can type an equivalent statement like this:

```
x += 1
```

Not only can you use the plus sign, but VB .NET now also supports -=, *=, /=, \=, and ^= from a mathematical standpoint, and &= for string concatenation. If all this looks like C/C++, that's where it came from. However, the ++ operator is not supported. Microsoft developers made a decision not to include the ++ operator because they felt it made the code more difficult to read.

Because VB .NET is in beta, and has not yet been performance tuned, it is unclear as to whether these new assignment operators will be more efficient than their more verbose counterparts. These operators did tend to be more efficient in C/C++, due to a more efficient use of the CPU's registers. Therefore, it will be interesting to test these new operators when the final, tuned version of VB .NET is released.

ByVal Is Now the Default

In what many consider a strange decision, the default way to pass parameters in VB has always been by reference (ByRef). The decision was actually made because passing by reference is faster within the same application, but can be costly if you are calling components across process boundaries. If you're a little rusty, *by reference* means that you are passing only the memory address of a variable into the called routine. If the called routine modifies the variable, it actually just updates the value in that memory location, and therefore the variable in the calling routine also changes. Passing data by value (ByVal) means that you are actually sending a copy of the data to the called routine. The called routine must set aside a new area in memory to store that value. If the called routine changes the value, it is changed in the memory location set aside by the called routine, but the memory location of the calling routine is unaffected.

Take this VB6 example:

```
Private Sub Command1_Click()
    Dim x As Integer
    x = 3
    foo x
    MsgBox x
End Sub

Sub foo(y As Integer)
    y = 5
End Sub
```

If you run this example in VB6, the message box shows the value 5. That happens because in VB6, when you pass x to foo, you are just sending the memory address of the variable x. So, when foo modifies y to 5, it changes the value in the same memory location to which x points, and this causes the value of x to change as well.

If you tried to type this example into VB .NET, you'd see something happen. First, of course, you'd have to add parentheses around x in your call to foo. However, when you tried to type the definition of foo, VB .NET would automatically add the word ByVal into the definition, so it would end up looking like this:

```
Sub foo(ByVal y As Integer)
```

If you wanted to pass by reference, you would have to add the ByRef keyword yourself, instead of VB .NET using the new default of ByVal. This should cut down on errors like those seen by novice users who didn't understand the concept of passing by reference in previous versions of VB. So, in VB .NET, accepting the defaults results in ByVal data passing. If you run this code in VB .NET, changing y to 5 does not affect the value of x at all. Running this code in VB .NET would cause you to see 3 in the message box.

Passing data ByVal is a benefit to those of you calling procedures across process boundaries, something that is common in the world of distributed applications. The reason it is a benefit is because of how you pass parameters across boundaries. If you have two routines in the same process, and one passes a parameter to the other ByRef, both routines can access the same memory location. However, if you now move one of those routines into another process, they cannot access the same memory (at least not easily). So, even if you pass a parameter to an out-of-process routine using ByRef, the called routine has to make a copy of the data and set up memory for it. Then any changes made in the called routine have to be marshaled back to the calling routine, which requires an expensive and slow round-trip across process boundaries.

By passing parameters to out-of-process routines using ByVal, you do not have to marshal any changes back to the calling routine. Many developers built out-of-process components in VB but were passing the parameters ByRef, not realizing that it was actually slower than passing them `ByVal`. VB .NET's default of passing parameters `ByVal` should take care of many of these issues.

Block-Level Scope

VB .NET adds the ability to create variables that are visible only within a block. A *block* is any section of code that ends with one of the words `End`, `Loop`, or `Next`. This means that `For...Next` and `If...End If` blocks can have their own variables. Take a look at the following code:

```
While y < 5
   Dim z As Integer
   ...
End While
```

The variable z is now visible only within the `While` loop. It is important to realize that although z is visible only inside the `While` loop, its lifetime is that of the procedure. That means if you re-enter the `While` statement, z will have the same value that it did when you left. Therefore, it is said that the *scope* of z is block level, but its *lifetime* is procedure level.

`While...Wend` Becomes `While...End While`

The `While` loop is still supported, but the closing of the loop is now `End While` instead of `Wend`. If you type `Wend`, the editor automatically changes it to `End While`. This change finally moves the `While` loop into synch with most other VB block structures, which all end with an `End <block>` syntax.

Procedure Changes

VB .NET has changes that affect how you define and work with procedures. Some of those changes are mentioned in this section.

Optional Arguments Require a Default Value

In VB6, you could create an optional argument (or several optional arguments) when you defined a procedure. You could, optionally, give them a default value. That way, if someone chose not to pass in a value for an argument, you had a value in it. If you did not set a default value and the caller did not pass in a value, the only way you had to check was to call the `IsMissing` statement.

`IsMissing` is no longer supported because VB .NET will not let you create an optional argument that does not have a default value. `IsMissing` is not needed because an optional argument is guaranteed to have a value. For example, your declaration might look like this:

```
Sub foo(Optional ByVal y As Integer = 1)
```

Notice that the `Optional` keyword is shown, just as it was in VB6. This means a parameter does not have to be passed in. However, if it is not passed in, y is given the default value of 1. If the calling routine does pass in a value, of course, y is set to whatever is passed in.

`Static` Not Supported on Subs or Functions

In VB6, you could put `Static` in the declaration of a sub or function. Doing so made all variables in that sub or function *static*, which meant that they retained their values between calls to the procedure. For example, this was legal in VB6:

```
Static Sub foo()
    Dim x As Integer
    Dim y As Integer
    x = x + 1
    y = y + 2
End Sub
```

In this example, x will retain its value between calls. So, the second time this procedure is called, x already has a value of 1, and the value of x will be incremented to 2. The variable y would have the value of 2, and therefore the second time in it would be incremented to 4.

VB .NET does not support the `Static` keyword in front of the sub or function declaration anymore, like VB6 did, as shown in the earlier example. In fact, if you want an entire sub or function to be static, you need to place `Static` in front of each variable declaration for which you want to preserve the value. This is the only way to preserve values in variables inside a sub or function. In VB .NET, the equivalent sub would look like this:

```
Sub foo()
    Static x As Integer
    Static y As Integer
    x = x + 1
    y = y + 2
End Sub
```

The `Return` Statement

The `Return` statement can be used to produce an immediate return from a called procedure, and can optionally return a value. For example, look at this block of code:

```
Function foo() As Integer
    While True
        Dim x As Integer
        x += 1
        If x >= 5 Then
            Return x
        End If
    End While
End Function
```

In this code, you enter what normally would be an infinite loop by saying `While True`. Inside the loop, you declare an integer called `x` and begin incrementing it. You check the value of `x` and when it becomes greater than or equal to 5, you call the `Return` statement and return the value of `x`. This causes an immediate return, which means it does not wait to hit the `End Function` statement.

The old way of doing it still works, however. For example, to rewrite this procedure using the old approach to return a value, you would make it look like the following code. This sets the name of the procedure, `foo`, to the value to be returned. Then you have to exit the loop so that you'll hit `End Function`. You also could have used `Exit Function` instead of `Exit Do`.

```
Function foo() As Integer
    Do While True
        Dim x As Integer
        x += 1
        If x >= 5 Then
            foo = x
            Exit Do
        End If
    Loop
End Function
```

ParamArrays Are Now Passed ByVal

A parameter array, or `ParamArray`, is used when you do not know how many values you will pass into a procedure. A `ParamArray` allows for an unlimited number of arguments. A parameter array automatically sizes to hold the number of elements you are passing in.

A procedure can have only one `ParamArray`, and it must be the last argument in the definition. The array must be one-dimensional and each element must be the same data type. However, the default data type is `Object`, which is what replaces the `Variant` data type in VB .NET.

In VB6, all the elements of a `ParamArray` are always passed `ByRef`. This cannot be changed. In VB .NET, all the elements are passed `ByVal`. This cannot be changed. Again, `ByRef` was used in previous versions of VB because it was more efficient for passing parameters within a program all running in the same application space. When working with out-of-process components, however, it is more efficient to pass parameters `ByVal`, as explained in the earlier section entitled "`ByVal` Is Now the Default."

Properties Can Be Modified ByRef

In VB6, if a class had a property, you could pass that property to a procedure as an argument. If you passed the property `ByVal`, of course, it just copied the value. If you passed it `ByRef`, the called procedure might modify the value, but this new value was *not* reflected back in the object's property.

In VB .NET, however, you can pass a property to a procedure ByRef, and any changes to the property in the called procedure *will* be reflected in the value of the property for the object.

Take the following VB .NET example. Don't worry if the Class syntax looks strange; just realize that you are creating a class called Test with one property: Name. You instantiate the class in the Button1_Click event procedure, and pass the Name property, by reference, to foo. foo modifies the variable and ends. You then use a message box to print out the Name property.

```
Private Sub Button1_Click(ByVal sender As System.Object, _
   ByVal e As System.EventArgs) Handles Button1.Click    Dim x As New Test()
   foo(x.Name)
   MsgBox(x.Name)
End Sub

Sub foo(ByRef firstName As String)
   firstName = "Torrey"
End Sub

Public Class Test
   Dim firstName As String
   Property Name() As String
      Get
         Name = firstName
      End Get
      Set(ByVal Value As String)
         firstName = Value
      End Set
   End Property
End Class
```

When you run this example, the message box will display "Torrey". This shows that the property of the object is being passed by reference, and that changes to the variable are reflected back in the object's property. This is new in VB .NET.

Array Changes

Arrays have undergone some changes as well. Arrays could be somewhat confusing in previous versions of VB. VB .NET seeks to address any confusion by simplifying the rules and removing the capability to have nonzero lower boundaries.

Array Size

In VB6, if you left the default for arrays to start at 0, declaring an array actually gave you the upper boundary of the array, not the number of elements. For example, examine the following code:

```
Dim y(2) As Integer
y(0) = 1
y(1) = 2
y(2) = 3
```

In this VB6 code, you declare that y is an array of type Integer, and the upper boundary is 2. That means you actually have three elements: 0–2. You can verify this by setting those three elements in code.

In VB .NET, array declaration was going to change, so that the parameter was the number of elements. However, due to the possibility of breaking existing code in the upgrade process, this has been changed back to the way it worked in VB.

If you're wondering why this book points out something that *didn't* change in a chapter about changes, it is because Microsoft had announced that this would change, but then pulled back in the face of opposition from existing VB developers. Therefore, it is important to point out that it still works the same as it did before, except for the change of the lower boundary always being 0.

Lower Boundary Is Always Zero

VB6 allowed you to have a nonzero lower boundary in your arrays in a couple of ways. First, you could declare an array to have a certain range. If you wanted an array to start with 1, you declared it like this:

```
Dim y(1 To 3) As Integer
```

This would create an array with three elements, indexed 1–3. If you didn't like this method, you could use Option Base, which allowed you to set the default lower boundary to either 0 (the default) or 1.

VB .NET removes those two options from you. You cannot use the 1 to x syntax, and Option Base is no longer supported. In fact, because the lower boundary of the array is always 0, the Lbound function is not supported in VB .NET.

Array Assignment Is ByRef Instead of ByVal

In VB6, if you had two array variables and set one equal to the other, you actually were creating a copy of the array in a ByVal copy. Now, in VB .NET, setting one array variable to another is actually just setting a reference to the array. To copy an array, you can use the Copy method of the Array object.

Option Strict

Option Strict is a new statement that specifically disallows any automatic type conversions that would result in data loss. You can use only widening conversions; this means you could convert from an Integer to a Long, but you could not convert from a Long to an Integer. Option Strict also prevents conversions between numbers and strings.

Option Strict is off by default in Visual Studio .NET Beta 2. To turn it on, go to the top of the code window and type Option Strict On. Note that the default value for Option Strict has changed with almost every new build of Visual Studio .NET, and it is difficult to predict whether Option Strict will be on or off by default in the final product.

If you go to the top of a module and type Option Strict On, you can see that the IDE recognizes potential type conversion problems with the following lines of code:

```
Dim longNumber As Long
Dim integerNumber As Integer
integerNumber = longNumber
```

With this code, the IDE will underline longNumber and a tooltip will tell you the following: Option Strict disallows implicit conversions from Long to Integer.

> **NOTE**
>
> For what it's worth, I strongly recommend that you use Option Strict On and Option Explicit On. In VS .NET Beta 2, Option Explicit is on by default, but again there is no guarantee this will be the case in the final product. Turning on both Option Explicit and Option Strict can help reduce errors that can occur only at runtime.

Data Type Changes

There are several changes to data types that are important to point out. These changes can have an impact on the performance and resource utilization of your code. The data types in VB .NET correspond to the data types in the System namespace, which is important for cross-language interoperability.

All Variables Are Objects

Technically, in VB .NET, all variables are subclassed from the Object base class. This means that you can treat all variables as objects. For example, to find the length of a string, you could use the following code:

```
Dim x As String
x = "Hello, World"
MsgBox(x.Length)
```

This means that you are treating x as an object, and examining its Length property. Other variables have other properties or methods. For example, an Integer has a ToString method that you can use, which you will see in a moment.

Short, Integer, and Long

In VB .NET, the Short data type is a 16-bit integer, the Integer is a 32-bit integer, and the Long is a 64-bit integer. In VB6 code, the Integer was a 16-bit integer and the Long was a 32-bit integer. It became common for VB developers to use the Long in place of the Integer, because the Long performed better on 32-bit operating systems than Integer, which was just 16-bit. However, on 32-bit operating systems, 32-bit integers perform better than 64-bit integers, so in VB .NET, you will most likely want to return to using the Integer data type instead of the Long data type.

Automatic String/Numeric Conversion Not Supported by Option_Strict

In VB6, it was easy to convert from numbers to strings, and vice versa. For example, examine this block of code:

```
Dim x As Integer
Dim y As String
x = 5
y = x
```

In VB6, there is nothing wrong with this code. VB will take the value 5 and automatically convert it into the string "5". VB .NET, however, disallows this type of conversion if Option Strict is turned on. Instead, you would have to use the CStr function to convert a number to a string, or the Val function to convert a string to a number. You could rewrite the preceding code for VB .NET in this manner:

```
Dim x As Integer
Dim y As String
x = 5
y = CStr(x)
y = x.ToString ' This is equivalent to the previous line
```

Fixed-Length Strings Not Supported

In VB6, you could declare a fixed-length string by using a declaration like the one shown here:

```
Dim y As String * 30
```

This declared y to be a fixed-length string that could hold 30 characters. If you try this same code in VB .NET, you will get an error. All strings in VB .NET are variable length.

All Strings Are Unicode

If you got tired of worrying about passing strings from VB to certain API calls that accepted either ANSI or Unicode strings, you will be happy to hear that all strings in VB .NET are Unicode.

The Value of True

Since Visual Basic 1.0, the value of True in VB and Access has been equal to –1. The .NET Framework declares that True should be equal to 1. This is an apparent disconnect between VB .NET and the underlying .NET Framework.

In reality, 0 is False and any nonzero is True in VB .NET. However, if you ask for the value of True, you will get -1 inside of VB .NET. You can verify that any nonzero is True by using this code:

```
Dim x As Integer
x = 2
If CBool(x) = True Then
    MsgBox("Value is True")
End If
```

If you make x any positive or negative integer, the CBool function will return True. If you set x equal to 0, CBool will return False. Even though True is actually shown as -1 in VB .NET, if you pass it out to any other .NET language, it is seen as 1. This means that all other .NET languages see it as the correct value.

Just as it had said it was changing how arrays were dimensioned, Microsoft originally said that the value of True in VB .NET was going to be 1. However, enough VB developers complained, and Microsoft decided to leave True as -1. This is a shame, but not because True should be 1. It is a shame because it means a number of developers have written code that looks for the value -1 instead of the constant True. The important thing to understand is this: Do not code for the value (1 or -1). Just use the keyword True and you will avoid any problems.

The Currency Data Type Has Been Replaced

The Currency data type has been replaced by the Decimal data type. The Decimal data type is a 12-byte signed integer that can have up to 28 digits to the right of the decimal place. It supports a much higher precision than the Currency data type, and has been designed for applications that cannot tolerate rounding errors. The Decimal data type has a direct equivalent in the .NET Framework, which is important for cross-language interoperability.

The Variant Data Type Has Been Replaced

The Variant data type has been replaced. Before you start thinking that there is no longer a catch-all variable type, understand that the Variant has been replaced by the Object data type. The Object data type takes up only four bytes because all it holds is a memory address. Therefore, even if you set the variable to an integer, the Object variable holds four bytes that point to the memory used to store the integer. The integer is stored on the heap. It will take up 8 bytes plus 4 bytes for the integer, so it consumes a total of 12 bytes. Examine the following code:

```
Dim x
x = 5
```

In this case, x is a variable of type Object. When you set x equal to 5, VB .NET stores the value 5 in another memory location and x stores the address of that memory location. When you attempt to access x, a lookup is required to find that memory address and retrieve the value. Therefore, just like the Variant, the Object data type is slower than using explicit data types.

According to the VB .NET documentation, the Object data type allows you to play fast-and-loose with data type conversion. For example, look at the following code:

```
Dim x
x = "5" ' x is a string
x -= 2
```

In this example, x will now hold the numeric value 3. The only way you can run this example is if you set Option Strict Off in the file. If you change the code to use string concatenation, the conversion also works fine. For example, the following code will run without an error, and x will end up holding the string "52":

```
Dim x
x = "5" ' x is a string
x &= 2
```

An Object data type can be Nothing. In other words, it can hold nothing, which means it doesn't point to any memory address. You can check for Nothing by setting the Object variable equal to Nothing, by using the IsNothing function, or asking if an object Is Nothing. All three checks are shown in the following code:

```
Dim x
If x = Nothing Then MsgBox("Nothing")
If IsNothing(x) Then MsgBox("Still nothing")
If x Is Nothing Then MsgBox("And Still Nothing")
```

Structured Error Handling

Error handling has changed in VB .NET. Actually, the old syntax still works, but there is a new error handling structure called Try...Catch...Finally that removes the need to use the old On Error Goto structure.

The overall structure of the Try...Catch...Finally syntax is to put the code that might cause an error in the Try portion, and then catch the error. Inside the Catch portion, you handle the error. The Finally portion runs code that happens after the Catch statements are done, regardless of whether or not there was an error. Here is a simple example:

A PROGRAMMER'S INTRODUCTION TO VISUAL BASIC .NET

```
Dim x, y As Integer ' Both will be integers
Try
    x \= y ' cause division by zero
Catch ex As Exception
    msgbox(ex.Message)
End Try
```

> **NOTE**
>
> The ex As Exception part of the Catch statement is optional.

Here, you have two variables that are both integers. You attempted to divide x by y, but because y has not been initialized, it defaults to 0. That division by zero raises an error, and you catch it in the next line. The variable ex is of type Exception, which holds the error that just occurred, so you simply print the Message property, much like you printed Err.Description in VB6.

In fact, you can still use Err.Description, and the Err object in general. The Err object will pick up any exceptions that are thrown. For example, assume that your logic dictates that an error must be raised if someone's account balance falls too low, and another error is raised if the balance drops into the negative category. Examine the following code:

```
Try
    If bal < 0 Then
        Throw New Exception("Balance is negative!")
    ElseIf bal > 0 And bal <= 10000 Then
        Throw New Exception("Balance is low; charge interest")
    End If
Catch
    MessageBox.Show("Error: " & Err.Description)
End Try
```

In this case, your business logic says that if the balance drops below zero, you raise an error informing the user that the balance is below zero. If the balance drops below 10,000 but remains above zero, you notify the user to start charging interest. In this case, Err.Description picks up the description you threw in your Exception.

You can also have multiple Catch statements to catch various errors. To have one Catch statement catch a particular error, you add a When clause to that Catch. Examine this code:

```
Dim x As Integer
Dim y As Integer
Try
    x \= y ' cause division by zero
```

```
Catch ex As Exception When Err.Number = 11
   MsgBox("You tried to divide by zero")
Catch ex As Exception
   MsgBox("Acts as catch-all")
End Try
```

In this example, you are looking for an `Err.Number` of 11, which is the error for division by zero. Therefore, if you get a division-by-zero error, you display a message box that says `You tried to divide by zero`. However, if a different error were to occur, you would drop into the `Catch` without a `When` clause. In effect, the `Catch` without a `When` clause acts as an "else" or "otherwise" section to handle anything that was not handled before.

Notice that the code does not fall through all the exceptions; it stops on the first one it finds. In the preceding example, you will raise an `Err.Number` of 11. You will see the message `You tried to divide by zero`, but you will skip over the catch-all `Catch`.

If you want to run some code at the end, regardless of which error occurred (or, indeed, if no error occurred), you could add a `Finally` statement. The code to do so follows:

```
Dim x As Integer
Dim y As Integer
Try
    x \= y ' cause division by zero
Catch ex As Exception When Err.Number = 11
    MsgBox("You tried to divide by zero")
Catch ex As Exception
    MsgBox("Acts as catch-all")
Finally
    MsgBox("Running finally code")
End Try
```

In this code, whether or not you hit an error, the code in the `Finally` section will execute.

Exiting a `Try...Catch...Finally` Early

Sometimes you want to exit a `Try...Catch...Finally` early. To exit early, use the `Exit Try` statement. `Exit Try` can be placed in any `Catch` block or in the `Try` block, but not in the `Finally` block. `Exit Try` is supposed to break you out of the `Try` immediately, ignoring any `Finally` code. However, in Beta 2, `Exit Try` drops immediately to the `Finally` block. Expect this to be fixed in the final version of VS .NET. The syntax would look like this:

```
Dim x As Integer
Dim y As Integer
Try
    x \= y ' cause division by zero
Catch ex As Exception When Err.Number = 11
    msgbox("You tried to divide by zero")
```

```
    Exit Try
Catch ex As Exception
    msgbox("Acts as catch-all")
Finally
    msgbox("Running finally code")
End Try
```

Structures Replace UDTs

User-defined types, or UDTs, were a way to create a custom data type in VB6. You could create a new data type that contained other elements within it. For example, you could create a `Customer` data type using this syntax:

```
Private Type Customer
    Name As String
    Income As Currency
End Type
```

You could then use that UDT in your application, with code like this:

```
Dim buyer As Customer
buyer.Name = "Martha"
buyer.Income = 20000
MsgBox(buyer.Name & " " & buyer.Income)
```

The `Type` statement is no longer supported in VB .NET. It has been replaced by the `Structure` statement. The `Structure` statement has some major changes, but to re-create the UDT shown earlier, the syntax is this:

```
Structure Customer
    Dim Name As String
    Dim Income As Decimal
End Structure
```

Notice that the only real difference so far is that you have to `Dim` each variable inside the structure, which is something you did not have to do in the `Type` statement, even with `Option Explicit` turned on. Notice also that `Dim` is the same as `Public` here, meaning that the variables are visible to any instance of the structure.

Structures have many other features, however. One of the biggest differences is that structures can support methods. For example, you could add a `Shipping` method to the `Customer` structure to calculate shipping costs based on delivery zone. This code adds a `DeliveryZone` property and a `DeliveryCost` function:

```
Structure Customer
    Dim Name As String
    Dim Income As Decimal
```

```
    Dim DeliveryZone As Integer

    Function DeliveryCost() As Decimal
        If DeliveryZone > 3 Then
            Return 25
        Else
            Return CDec(12.5)
        End If
    End Function
End Structure
```

Here, you have a built-in function called `DeliveryCost`. To use this structure, your client code would look something like this:

```
Dim buyer As Customer
buyer.Name = "Martha"
buyer.Income = 20000
buyer.DeliveryZone = 4
msgbox(buyer.DeliveryCost)
```

In this case, the message box would report a value of 25.

If you think this looks like a class, it certainly is similar. In fact, structures can have properties, methods, and events. They also support implementing interfaces and they can handle events. There are some caveats, however. Some of those stipulations include the following:

- You cannot inherit from a structure.
- You cannot initialize the fields inside a structure. For example, this code is illegal:
  ```
  Structure Customer
      Dim Name As String = "Martha"
  End Structure
  ```
- Properties are public by default, instead of private as they are in classes.

Structures are value types rather than reference types. That means if you assign a structure variable to another structure variable, you get a copy of the structure and not a reference to the original structure. The following code shows that a copy is occurring because an update to `seller` does not update `buyer`:

```
Dim buyer As Customer
Dim seller ' Object data type
seller = buyer
seller.Name = "Linda"
MsgBox(buyer.Name)
MsgBox(seller.Name)
```

Note that the preceding code will not work if you have `Option Strict` turned on. If you want to test this, you'll have to enter `Option Strict Off`.

New Items

In addition to changes to the core language and some of the tools, there are some completely new features to VB .NET. The major new items include such features as constructors and destructors, namespaces, inheritance, overloading, free threading, and garbage collection. This is not an exhaustive list by any means, but these six features are worth discussing to one degree or another. One feature that should be mentioned as well is something you've been seeing all along: auto-indention. As soon as you create a block, such as a Sub or If block, the IDE indents the next line of code automatically.

Constructors and Destructors

Constructors and destructors are potentially new concepts for VB programmers. They are similar to the Class Initialize and Class Terminate events you have in VB classes. At their simplest level, constructors and destructors are procedures that control the initialization and destruction of objects, respectively. The procedures Sub New and Sub Finalize replace the VB6 Class_Initialize and Class_Terminate methods. Unlike Class_Initialize, Sub New runs only once, when the object is first created. Sub New cannot be called explicitly except in rare circumstances.

Sub Finalize is called by the system when the object is set to Nothing or all references to the object are dropped. However, you cannot ensure exactly when Sub Finalize actually will be called, thanks to the way VB .NET does garbage collection, which is discussed in the next few sections.

One of the reasons for constructors is that you can create an object and pass in some initialization parameters. For example, assume that you want to create a class dealing with a training course, and you want to initialize the class with a course number so that it can retrieve certain information from a database. In your class, you create a Sub New method that accepts an argument for the course ID. The first line inside the Sub New is a call to another constructor, usually the constructor of the base class on which this class is based. Fortunately, VB .NET gives you an easy way to call the constructor of the base class for your current class: MyBase.New.

If you want to create a class for a training course and initialize it with a course ID, your class would look something like this:

```
Class Course
    Sub New(ByVal CourseID As Integer)
        MyBase.New()
        FindCourseInfo(CourseID)
        ...
    End Sub
End Class
```

To call this class from the client code, your call would look something like this:

```
Dim TrainingCourse as Course = New Course(5491)
```

How `Sub Finalize` works will be covered in the section on garbage collection, where you will also see `Sub Dispose`.

Namespaces

Perhaps one of the most confusing aspects of VB .NET for VB developers is the concept of a namespace. A *namespace* is a simple way to organize the objects in an assembly. When you have many objects, such as in the `System` namespace provided by the runtime, a namespace can simplify access because it is organized in a hierarchical structure, and related objects appear grouped under the same node.

For example, say you wanted to model the objects, properties, and methods for a pet store. You might create the `PetStore` namespace. You could then create some subnamespaces. For example, you might sell live animals and supplies as two major categories. Within the live animals category, you might sell dogs, cats, and fish. If this sounds like an object model, it can be thought of as similar. However, none of these are actual objects. You could have a namespace called `PetStore.Animals.Dogs`, and in this namespace you'd find the classes and methods necessary for dealing with dogs. If you wanted to handle the inventory, you might find that in `PetStore.Supplies`. If you wanted to look at the kinds of dog food you have in stock, you might look in `PetStore.Supplies.Dogs`. Where the physical classes exist is up to you; they all can be in one big assembly, but logically separated into these various namespaces.

If you want to use the objects in an assembly without having to fully qualify them each time, use the `Imports` statement. Doing so allows you to use the names of the objects without fully qualifying their entire namespace hierarchy.

For example, when you created your first VB .NET project in Chapter 2, "Your First VB .NET Application," you saw some `Imports` statements at the top of the form's code module. One of those statements was `Imports System.WinForms`. That statement made all the classes, interfaces, structures, delegates, and enumerations available to you without you having to qualify the full path. That means the following code is legal:

```
Dim x as Button
```

Without the `Imports System.WinForms` statement, your line of code would have to look like this:

```
Dim x as System.WinForms.Button
```

In fact, the `MsgBox` that you know and love can be replaced by the `System.WinForms.MessageBox` class. `MsgBox` still works for compatibility, but it is actually part of the `Microsoft.VisualBasic.Interaction` namespace, which contains a number of methods that approximate functions in previous versions of VB.

If you're wondering why Microsoft pulled out some language elements and made them part of the runtime, it should be fairly obvious: so that any language targeting the runtime, on any platform, would have access to common functionality. That means that you can go into C# and have a message box, just by importing `System.WinForms` and calling the `MessageBox` class. `MessageBox` is quite powerful—the `Show` method has twelve variations made available thanks to overloading. You'll learn about overloading in a moment.

Creating Your Own Namespaces

You are free to create your own namespaces inside your assemblies. You can do this simply by inserting your own `Namespace...End Namespace` block. Inside the namespace block, you can have structures, classes, enums, interfaces, and other elements. You must name the namespace and it becomes what someone would import. Your code might look like this:

```
Namespace VolantTraining
    Public Class Customer
        'code here
    End Class

    Public Class Student
        'code here
    End Class
End Namespace
```

Namespaces can be nested within other namespaces. For example, your namespace might look something like this:

```
Namespace VolantTraining
    Namespace Customer
        Class Training
            ...
        End Class
        Class Consulting
            ...
        End Class
    End Namespace
    Namespace Student
        ...
    End Namespace
End Namespace
```

Here one namespace, `VolantTraining`, holds two other namespaces: `Customer` and `Student`. The `VolantTraining.Customer` namespace holds the `Training` and `Consulting` classes, so you could have customers who have used your training services and customers who have used your consulting services.

If you choose not to create explicit namespaces, all your classes and modules still belong to a namespace. This namespace is the default namespace and is the name of your project. You can see this namespace, and change it if you want, by viewing the Project Properties dialog box for your project. The text box labeled `Root Namespace` represents the root namespace for your project. If you declare a namespace within your project, it is subordinate to this root namespace. Therefore, if the root namespace of your application is `Project1`, the full namespace for `VolantTraining` is `Project1.VolantTraining`.

Inheritance

The most-requested feature to have added to VB for years has been inheritance. Microsoft often countered that VB already supported inheritance; VB supported *interface* inheritance, which meant that you could inherit (what VB called *implement*) an interface. However, the interfaces you implemented in VB did not have any code in them, or if they did, the code was ignored. Therefore, the class implementing the interface had to provide methods for all the methods in the interface. If you had more than one class that implemented the same interface, you had to rewrite the code in each class that implemented the interface. VB developers wanted to be able to write that implementation code once, in a base class, and then to inherit that class (instead of an interface) in other classes, which would then be called *derived classes*. The derived classes would be able to use the existing code in the base class. With VB .NET, developers have their wish.

Not only does your derived class inherit the properties and methods of the base class, it can extend the methods and, of course, create new methods (in the derived class only). Derived classes can also override any existing method in the base class with a new method of the same name, in a process called *overriding*. Forms, which are really just classes, can be inherited to create new forms.

There are many concepts to inheritance, and seeing it in practice is important enough to make it a chapter unto itself. Chapter 5, "Inheritance with VB .NET," is all about inheritance and how to use it in VB .NET.

Overloading

Overloading is another feature that some VB developers have been requesting for a long time. In short, overloading allows you to define the same procedure multiple times. The procedure has the same name but a different set of arguments each time.

You could fake this in an ugly way in VB6. You could pass in an argument as a Variant, and then use the VarType command to check the type of variable that was passed in. This was cumbersome, and the code could get nasty if your procedure had to accept an array or a collection.

VB .NET gives you a nice way to handle this issue. Imagine that you have a procedure that can accept a string or an integer. The functionality inside the procedure would be quite different depending on whether what is passed is a string or an integer. Your code might look something like this:

```
Overloads Function FindCust(ByVal psName As String) As String
    ' search name field for %psName%
End Function

Overloads Function FindCust(ByVal piCustNo As Integer) As String
    ' search CustID field
End Function
```

You now have a function called FindCust that can be passed either an integer or a string. Your calls to it could look like this:

```
Dim x As String
x = FindCust("Smith")
x = FindCust(1)
```

As long as Option Strict is turned on (which is not the default, at least in Beta 2), you cannot compile an invalid call. For example, there is no overloaded FindCust that accepts a floating-point value of any kind. VB .NET would not let the following code compile:

```
x = FindCust(12.5)
```

Multithreading

For the first time, VB .NET has given VB developers the ability to write truly multithreaded applications. If your application is going to perform a task that could take a long time, such as parsing through a large recordset or performing a complex series of mathematical calculations, you can push that processing off to its own thread so that the rest of your application is still accessible. In VB6, the best you could do to keep the rest of the application from appearing to be locked was to use the DoEvents method.

Examine this code, which is written for VB .NET. Here you have some code for Button4. This code calls the BeBusy routine, which has a loop in it to just to take up time. However, while in this loop, you are consuming the thread for this application, and the UI will not respond while the loop is running.

> **CAUTION**
>
> This takes about eight seconds to run on my machine. It might run a significantly longer or shorter time on your machine. The good news is the VB .NET IDE runs on a separate thread, so if you find yourself waiting forever, just click on the IDE and choose Stop Debugging from the Debug menu.

```
Private Sub Button4_Click(ByVal sender As System.Object, _
   ByVal e As System.EventArgs) Handles Button4.Click    BeBusy()
End Sub

Sub BeBusy()
   Dim i As Decimal
   For i = 1 To 10000000
      'do nothing but tie up app
   Next
   Beep()
End Sub
```

If you run this code and try to click on the form before BeBusy is done running, you'll find that the form doesn't respond to any events. For example, other buttons can't be clicked while BeBusy is running. For the form to continue to respond while BeBusy is running, you can run BeBusy on a separate thread.

To create a new thread, you must use the System.Threading.Thread class. In the creation of the class, you pass in the name of the procedure or method you want to run on that thread. You preface the procedure or method name with the AddressOf operator. Your code would look like this:

```
Dim busyThread As New System.Threading.Thread(AddressOf BeBusy)
```

To fix the code and keep BeBusy from consuming the main program thread, you have now created a new thread and will run BeBusy on that thread. However, that line of code isn't enough. Next, you must call the Start method on that new thread. With VB .NET, calling BeBusy on its own thread would look like this:

```
Private Sub Button4_Click(ByVal sender As System.Object, _
   ByVal e As System.EventArgs) Handles Button4.Click
      Dim busyThread As New System.Threading.Thread(AddressOf BeBusy)
   busyThread.Start()
End Sub
```

No changes are required to the BeBusy procedure. If you now run this code, the interface will remain active while BeBusy is running. The Beep in BeBusy will let you know when the procedure has finished running.

There are some caveats to using free threading. They seem significant, but each one has a fairly reasonable workaround. Some of those caveats and workarounds are as follows:

- The procedure or method you run on a new thread cannot accept any arguments. To get around this problem, you have a couple of choices. You could use global variables, but that is not an elegant solution. Instead, create properties or fields in the class whose method you are calling, and set those properties after the object is created. Obviously, that wouldn't help you in the earlier example because the call was simply to a sub in the same program.

- The procedure or method you run on a new thread cannot return a value. To get around that issue, you could use global variables, but again, this is not an elegant solution. One major problem is that your application would have to keep checking the thread to see when it was done, before you would be safe in using that global variable. Instead, you should consider raising an event with the return value as a parameter in the event.

Synchronization is also an issue with multithreaded applications. If you are performing a complex series of calculations on one thread, other parts of your application must wait until that thread is finished before they can use the results. You can monitor threads to see when they are finished or you can have the methods on those threads raise events to notify you when they are done. VB .NET provides an IsAlive property for each thread, so you can check to see when the thread is running.

There is much more to multithreading, and it will be covered in detail in Chapter 11, "Multithreading in VB .NET."

Garbage Collection

Garbage collection is now being handled by the runtime. In VB6, if you set an object to Nothing, it was destroyed immediately. This is no longer true in VB .NET. Instead, when you set an object to Nothing or it loses all its references, it is marked for garbage collection. It's still in memory, taking up resources. The garbage collector runs on a separate thread, and it passes by occasionally looking for objects to clean up (destroy). The garbage collector comes by only when you start running low on resources and need to clean up objects. However, if the system is under a heavy load, the time it takes the garbage collector to come by and clean up objects could be many seconds—an eternity in CPU terms.

Because objects do not get destroyed when you set them to Nothing, Microsoft calls this "no deterministic finalization" because the developer is no longer truly in control of when the object will be destroyed. The Sub Finalize method is called when the object is truly destroyed by the garbage collector.

It is important to understand that even though an object has been marked for garbage collection, any resources it has opened are still open, including any data or file locks that it might have obtained. Because the object is still in memory, holding open references, you might want to explicitly call the garbage collector by using the `Collect` method of the `GC` class in the `System` namespace. A simple call to `GC.Collect` forces the garbage collector to come by and clean up any objects that have been marked for collection.

When an object is cleaned up, `Sub Finalize` is called automatically. However, a convention being used by .NET developers is to have a `Sub Dispose` in a class. The `Sub Dispose` is called specifically, and it frees up any resources. As long as the code in `Sub Dispose` properly closes all the open resources, it acts similarly to deterministic finalization in VB6. Following this convention, your `Sub Dispose` would specifically close all open resources, such as files, database connections, and other objects. Then, you don't have to specifically call the garbage collector because all the object's resources have been closed.

To see garbage collection in action, create a new Windows Application and name it GCtest. On the form, add two buttons. Add a component to the project and name it `Garbage`. Inside the `Garbage` component, add the following code:

```
Protected Overrides Sub Finalize()
    Beep()
End Sub
```

This just adds a beep sound when the object is finally taken out of memory by the garbage collector.

Back in the form, add the following code:

```
Dim oGarbage As New Garbage()

Private Sub Button1_Click(ByVal sender As System.Object, _
 ByVal e As System.EventArgs) Handles Button1.Click
    oGarbage = Nothing
End Sub

Private Sub Button2_Click(ByVal sender As Object, _
 ByVal e As System.EventArgs) Handles Button2.Click
    GC.Collect()
End Sub
```

Now, run the project. When you click on Button1, you set the object to Nothing. However, you don't hear a beep because the object hasn't actually been taken out of memory. Now, click Button2, and you'll hear the beep. You have forced the garbage collector to come by and clean up the object, which causes the `Sub Finalize` code to run.

3

MAJOR VB .NET
CHANGES

IDE Changes

There are numerous IDE changes. Several of those were addressed in Chapter 2: the lack of the Line and Shape controls, the new menu builder, the new way of setting the tab order, and the Dynamic Help window.

One area that is interesting is the changes available thanks to the GDI+ library. As mentioned earlier, the Line and Shape controls are gone. You can replace the lines with a label with a height of one and borders turned on. Or, you can use the System.Drawing namespace. For example, System.Drawing has a Graphics class that contains such methods as DrawCurve, DrawEllipse, DrawLine, and DrawRectangle. There is actually quite a bit of code required to draw a line. You need to place code in the OnPaint sub to have the code called automatically. Just create a new form and add the following code, but don't forget to add an Imports System.Drawing to the top of the form:

```
Protected Overrides Sub OnPaint(ByVal e As PaintEventArgs)
    Dim LineMaker As Graphics
    LineMaker = e.Graphics
    Dim RedPen As New Pen(Color.Red, 3)
    Dim Point1 As New Point(30, 30)
    Dim Point2 As New Point(Me.Size.Width - 30, 30)
    LineMaker.DrawLine(RedPen, Point1, Point2)
End Sub
```

You can see the results of this code in Figure 3.1.

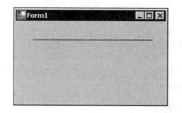

FIGURE 3.1

A form with a line drawn, thanks to GDI+.

Just drawing lines in GDI+ isn't that exciting. With VB .NET, you can actually create forms that are not rectangular. To create a circular form, create a form and add one button to it. Type Imports System.Drawing.Drawing2D at the top, and add the following code to the form:

```
Private Sub Button1_Click_1(ByVal sender As System.Object, _
 ByVal e As System.EventArgs) Handles Button1.Click
    Dim graPath As GraphicsPath = New GraphicsPath()
    graPath.AddEllipse(New Rectangle(0, 0, 200, 200))
    Me.Region = New [Region](graPath)
End Sub
```

Run the project and click on the button. The form turns into a circle, as shown in Figure 3.2.

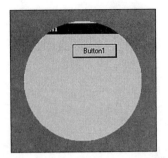

FIGURE 3.2

A circular form, also thanks to GDI+.

Summary

There are a number of changes to the VB language in the move to VB .NET. It is important to understand them as you move forward. Some changes are minor, such as the requirement to use parentheses and the lack of default properties. More significant changes on the list are features such as the new `Try...Catch...Finally` error handling.

Finally, there are some critical new features. Namespaces are the most dramatic change that will affect every VB .NET developer. Inheritance and free threading will also make major changes in the way applications are written.

Now that you have seen many of the significant changes in the language itself, each of the next chapters covers a single topic, showing either new functionality (such as Windows Services and Web Services) or changes to how things are done (such as building classes and assemblies).

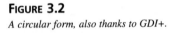

Building Classes and
Assemblies with VB .NET

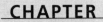

IN THIS CHAPTER

During the last three or so years, many VB developers have spent a great percentage of their time building COM components. These components are used as the middle-tier components in n-tier systems. The benefits of building n-tier applications are well known, and include

- Code reuse

- Elimination of many or all distribution headaches

- Encapsulation of business logic to control business processes and access to databases

Not surprisingly, VB .NET lets you build components, but they are no longer COM components. COM components have certain elements such as class IDs (CLSIDs), type libraries, and interface IDs (IIDs). Each class in a COM component has to support IUnknown and IDispatch.

VB .NET refers to one or more classes compiled into a file as a *class library*, rather than a COM component. Class libraries are compiled into an assembly, which often has a .DLL extension. You can use the classes from the class library much like you would the classes from a COM component: You instantiate the objects in the client application and then call properties and methods and respond to events. However, assemblies are *not* COM components; instead, they are .NET assemblies.

Creating Your First Class Library

To see how to build your first class library, start Visual Studio .NET and from the Start Page, click Create New Project. From the New Project dialog box, choose Visual Basic Projects in the Project Types list box, and then choose Class Library in the Templates list box. Name the project Healthcare and click the OK button.

At this point, a new class is created for you. The first thing you might notice is that the class does not have a designer, which is the "form" on which you can drop controls. This lack of a designer makes the class different from most other VB .NET file types, such as Forms, Web Forms, and even a Web Service. Instead, you start with basically the same thing you had in VB6: an empty class. You don't even have a block of code generated by Visual Studio .NET, as you do in most of the other file types.

Right now, you have one class, named Class1. Here is where things start to diverge from VB6. In VB6, you had one class per class module, and these were compiled into a single component. VB6 class modules had a .CLS extension. In VB .NET, your module has a .VB extension, and a single .VB source code file can contain more than one class. You can create a new class at any time using the Class...End Class block. Finally, one or more source code files can be compiled into an assembly.

In the code window, change the class definition line to name the class Patient. In other words, change this line:

```
Public Class Class1
```

to this:

```
Public Class Patient
```

You have now changed the class name, but if you look in the Solution Explorer window, or just look at the tab on the current code window, you see the filename is still `Class1.vb`.

Right-click on the Class1.vb icon in the Solution Explorer and choose Rename. Name the file `Healthcare.vb`. You should see the tab in the main code window change to reflect the new filename. What you have done is change the name of the file that holds one or more classes.

Adding a "Souped-Up" Class

You already have your first class, which was created for you when you created the class library. This class is now called `Patient`, but it does not have a constructor (`Public Sub New`) as most new files in VB .NET do. You can add your own constructor if you want your class to have one.

Not only doesn't this class have a constructor already built for you, neither does it have a designer. It is possible to create a new class that comes with a designer and a constructor already created. In the Solution Explorer, right-click on the project name, choose Add, and then choose Add Component. From the dialog that opens, choose Component class and click Open. This adds a new file to the project, which has only a class in it. This class, however, includes a designer, as shown in Figure 4.1.

The new class includes a designer, so you can perform actions such as dragging database connections to the designer to make it easier to create data components.

Double-clicking on the designer opens the code window. You can see that there is more code in this class than in the class that was created with the class library project. If you examine the code, you'll notice the following line:

```
Inherits System.ComponentModel.Component
```

This line makes the class inherit from the base `Component` class in `System.ComponentModel`. If you added that line to your `Healthcare` class, you would have access to the designer there.

For now, you'll return to the generic `Healthcare` class you created earlier.

Creating Properties

You can now start adding properties to your class, but be aware that the syntax for creating properties has changed.

4

BUILDING CLASSES
AND ASSEMBLIES
WITH VB .NET

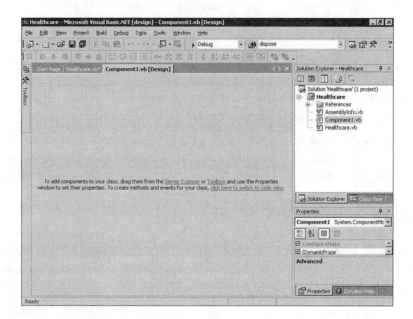

FIGURE 4.1

A new class created with a designer and a constructor already created.

Add a `FirstName` property by first creating a private variable. Inside the class, add the following code:

```
Dim msFirstName as String
```

Now, add the following code. Realize that as soon as you type the first line, most of the rest of the code will be filled in for you by the IDE. You'll still have to add the `Return` and the assignment.

```
Public Property FirstName() As String
    Get
        Return msFirstName
    End Get
    Set(ByVal Value As String)
        msFirstName = Value
    End Set
End Property
```

Notice the new syntax for creating properties. No longer do you create matching `Public Property Get`/`Public Property Let` procedures. Instead, you create a `Public Property` block and then add a `Get` and a `Set` section to it. There is no `Let` anymore, which makes life easier.

Also notice that you do not have to add an argument to the definition of the property, as you have to do in the `Public Property Let` in VB6. This means that you no longer have to specifically create an argument to accept the incoming value; instead, if the user passes in a value, it is put in the `Value` variable automatically.

Building a Test Client

Now, it is time to test this class. True, it has only one property, but you need to see how to call this class in a client application. From the File menu, choose New and then Project. This time, add a Windows Application. Name it HealthcareClient, but before you click OK, make sure that you select the Add to Solution radio button. The default is to close the current solution and open a new one. By choosing to add this new project to the current solution, you have the equivalent of a VB6 group.

After you click the OK button, the new project is loaded into the Solution Explorer, as shown in Figure 4.2. As in VB6, the project name that appears in bold in the Solution Explorer is the project that will start when you start the application. Simply right-click on the HealthcareClient project and choose Set as StartUp Project from the pop-up menu.

FIGURE 4.2

The Solution Explorer showing two projects loaded at once.

In the Solution Explorer, right-click on the References node for the HealthcareClient project and choose Add Reference. The Add Reference dialog box will appear. Click on the Projects tab and you should see your Healthcare project. It is already highlighted, but the OK button is disabled, as you can see in Figure 4.3. Click the Select button to move Healthcare into the Selected Components box, and then click the OK button.

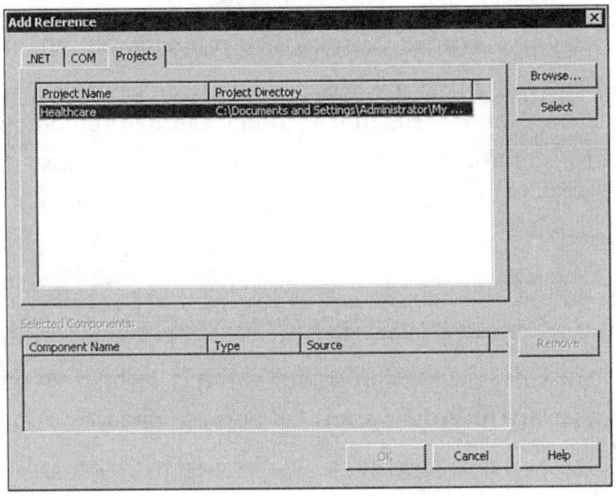

Figure 4.3
The Add Reference dialog box.

Now, on the form in HealthcareClient, add a button. Double-click the button to get to the code window, and enter the following code for the Button1_Click event procedure:

```
Protected Sub button1_Click(ByVal sender As Object, _
  ByVal e As System.EventArgs) Handles button1.Click
    Dim myPatient As New Healthcare.Patient()
    myPatient.FirstName = "Bob"
    MsgBox(myPatient.FirstName)
End Sub
```

This code should look very familiar to VB6 developers. After adding a reference, you instantiate the object by setting the variable myPatient to a New Healthcare.cPatient. If you are used to VB6, you might be tempted to try this shortcut and type this line of code:

```
Dim myPatient As New Patient()
```

If you type the line this way, however, you'll get an error that says User-defined type not defined: Patient. This shows that you need to have the name of the component fully qualified. The word Healthcare in this case is not the assembly name; instead, it is the namespace.

To get around this problem, you can import the namespace containing the Patient class. As you read in Chapter 3, "Major VB. NET Changes," all projects have a default namespace, and the name of the default namespace is the same as the project. Therefore, if you go to the top of the code module and add an `Imports` statement, the shortcut reference to the `Patient` class will work. Your `Imports` statement must go at the top of the module, and it will look like this:

```
Imports Healthcare
```

You might have noticed in the code that you used the `New` keyword to create the object. In VB6, you could use the `New` keyword in two ways. Here is the first way:

```
Dim myPatient as New Healthcare.Patient
```

In VB6, this code works, but it is not the best way to create objects. When you use this method, the object is not actually created until you call the first property or method. In fact, each call to a property or method requires a check to see whether the object has already been instantiated. To avoid this overhead, you should have been using this method in VB6:

```
Dim myPatient as Healthcare.Patient
Set myPatient = New Healthcare.Patient
```

In VB .NET, however, the following two methods are considered equivalent:

```
Dim myPatient As New Patient()
```

```
Dim myPatient As Patient = New Patient()
```

In both of these lines, the object is created in memory immediately. This means that with VB .NET, you will have the object in memory, and you avoid the overhead of having to check whether the object is in memory. With VB6, this overhead could occur with every call to the object if you instantiated it using the shortcut syntax. With VB .NET, you completely avoid this because VB .NET knows the object is instantiated immediately and does not need to check whether the object exists.

Read-Only and Write-Only Properties

Returning to the class library you are creating, you should notice that the property you created, `FirstName`, has both a `Get` and `Set` section in the `Property` block. In VB6, to make a property read-only, you simply did not create a `Public Property Let` statement. To create a write-only property, you did not create the `Public Property Get`.

You might be tempted to try to create a read-only property by simply leaving out the `Set...End Set` block. However, VB .NET handles read-only and write-only properties differently: You must add a keyword to the property declaration. To create a read-only property named `Age` (you can assume that it's calculated from the person's date of birth), your code would look like this:

```
Public ReadOnly Property Age() As Single
    Get
```

```
            'get Date of Birth (DOB)
            'calculate age from DOB
            'return age
        End Get
End Property
```

Creating a write-only property is equally simple. Just put the keyword WriteOnly in the property declaration, and have only a Set...End Set block in the property procedure.

Parameterized Properties

It is possible to create a parameterized property. Using the example of a patient, consider that a patient is likely to have several physicians attending to him at any one time. Therefore, although your Healthcare class library might have a Physician class, the Patient will likely hold a collection of Physician objects. You would be able to access this collection through a parameterized property and walk through this collection.

Creating a parameterized property is fairly straightforward: You simply add a parameter to the property procedure. If you have a Physicians property that walks through a collection of Physician objects, the code would look something like this:

```
Dim PhysiciansList As New Collection()
Public ReadOnly Property Physicians(ByVal iIndex As Integer) _
  As Physician
  Get
      Return CType(PhysiciansList(iIndex), Physician)
  End Get
End Property
```

You might notice several unusual things in this code. First of all, the basic functionality is there, in that you pass in an index value and get back a particular object in a collection. Notice also that even though the PhysiciansList is defined as a Collection data type, Option Strict will prevent an automatic conversion from a Collection type to a Physician type. Therefore, if Option Strict is on, you must run the CType function and pass both the object you want to convert and the type of the class (or object) into which it should be converted. Only then will the return actually succeed.

Default Properties

At the beginning of Chapter 3, you learned that default properties were gone, with the caveat that default properties *without parameters* were gone. However, if a property has one or more parameters, it can be the default property. Therefore, the Physicians property in Patient could be a default property.

Making a property the default property is as simple as adding the word `Default` in front of the property declaration. To make the `Physicians` property the default, your declaration would look like this:

```
Default Public ReadOnly Property _
    Physicians(ByVal iIndex As Integer) As Physician
```

Now, in your client program, you could call the default property on the `Patient` object. The last two lines of this code snippet are equivalent:

```
Imports Healthcare
...
Dim Patient As New Patient()
Dim Phys As New Physician()
Phys = Patient.Physicians(1)
Phys = Patient(1) 'equivalent to line above
```

Constructors in Your Classes

The one class you have built so far, `Patient`, did not come with a constructor; in other words, there was no `Sub New` available when you first created the class library. Constructors can be quite useful because they allow you to instantiate an object with some values already in it.

For example, assume that you wanted the `Patient` to allow you to pass in a `PatientID` when you instantiated the object. That means you could write code that would create the object and, at creation time, read a database and fill in the properties for a particular patient. Your new definition for the `Sub New` would look like this:

```
Public Sub New(Optional ByVal iPatientID As Integer = 0)
```

Your client code could now instantiate the object and pass in a value at instantiation. Either of the following lines would allow you to create an instance of the object with a value already set:

```
Dim Patient As New Patient(1)

Dim Patient As Patient = New Patient(1) 'equivalent to line above
```

Classes Without Constructors

Obviously, your classes do not have to have constructors. If you just use the `Class...End Class` block to create a new class, you will not be provided with a `Sub New`. Whether or not a class has constructors or implements `System.ComponentModel.Component`, the class can still have properties and methods, and can be created just like any other class. The `Physicians` class that has been mentioned in previous examples could look something like this:

```
Public Class Physician
    Dim miPhysID As Integer
```

```
Public Property PhysicianID() As Integer
    Get
        Return miPhysID
    End Get
    Set
        miPhysID = Value
    End Set
End Property

Public ReadOnly Property Age() As Single
    Get
        'get Date of Birth (DOB)
        'calculate age from DOB
        'return age
    End Get
End Property
End Class
```

Adding Methods to Classes

Adding a method to your class is done the same way it was done in VB6. If you want to create an `Admit` method in the `Patient` class, your code might look something like this:

```
Public Function Admit() As Boolean
    'add patient to database, notify billing, etc.
    Return True
End Function
```

The call to this from the client is equally simple:

```
If Patient.Admit Then...
```

Before you begin thinking that there aren't any changes in methods, understand that there are major changes in defining methods. However, the changes are specific to inheritance, and they will be covered in Chapter 5, "Inheritance with VB .NET."

Adding Events

To add an event to your class, use the `Event` keyword. Imagine that you wanted to add an event to the class that notified you when you had pending lab results. You could create the event using code like this inside the class that needs to fire the event:

```
Event LabResult(ByVal LabType As String)
```

This just creates the event definition in your code. To actually cause the event to fire, you'll have to add a `RaiseEvent` statement elsewhere in the code. For example, if you set a

PatientID property, you can go check a database for any new lab results for that patient. If there are new lab results, you could raise an event. Your code would look similar to this:

```
Dim miPatientID As Integer
Public Property PatientID() As Integer
    Get
        Return miPatientID
    End Get
    Set
        miPatientID = Value
        'check labs database for this patient
        'if there are new lab results
        RaiseEvent LabResult("CBC")
    End Set
End Property
```

If this were a real procedure, you wouldn't hard-code "CBC" into the event, but would instead pull the lab type from the database.

Handling the Event Using WithEvents

You have two options for handling this event in the client. The first way to handle the event is using the WithEvents keyword. The second way is to use the AddHandler statement.

To use the WithEvents keyword, you need to declare the object and include the WithEvents keyword. Notice that if you are using the WithEvents keyword, the declaration cannot be local to a sub or function. Therefore, this code will go outside any sub or function, at the module level in your client:

```
Dim WithEvents Patient As New Patient
```

This line assumes that you have imported the HealthCare namespace. This line is at the module level of your class because you cannot use the WithEvents keyword in a declaration inside a procedure. Therefore, you have to declare the object using the WithEvents keyword outside of any procedure.

Now, to add an event procedure, click on the Class Name drop-down list box at the top of the code window and choose Patient. In the Method Name drop-down list box, choose LabResult. This creates an event procedure named Patient_LabResult that looks like this:

```
Public Sub Patient_LabResult(ByVal LabType As System.String) _
  Handles Patient.LabResult
    ...
End Sub
```

Handling the Event with `AddHandler`

The second way to handle events is to use the `AddHandler` statement. You now do not have to define the class using the `WithEvents` keyword. Instead, you define it as you did before. You must also have a sub or function that will act as the event procedure.

Next, you use the `AddHandler` statement to tie a particular event from the object to the procedure you created to handle the event.

For example, assume that you wanted to create an event handler sub called `LabHandler`. This procedure would be defined as a standard sub. It would have to take as arguments any parameters defined in the `LabResult` event back in the Patient class. In the example here, the event named `LabResult` passes along a lab parameter with a data type of `string`. Therefore, your procedure would have to accept a string as an argument.

When you use `AddHandler`, you specify the name of the event in the `Patient` class you want it to handle (`LabResult`), but you must also refer to the procedure; in this case, `LabHandler`. However, you don't refer directly to `LabHandler`; instead, you refer to the address of `LabHandler`, using the `AddressOf` operator. Your code to set up event handling with the `AddHandler` statement would look like this:

```
Protected Sub Button1_Click(ByVal sender As Object, _
   ByVal e As System.EventArgs) Handles Button1.Click
     Dim Patient As New Patient()
     AddHandler Patient.LabResult, AddressOf Me.LabHandler
     ...
End Sub

Private Sub LabHandler(ByVal LabType As String)
   ...
End Sub
```

Notice that in the `AddHandler`, you refer to the object variable (`Patient`) and the event name (`LabResult`) using the *Object.Event* syntax.

Why might you want to use the `AddHandler` keyword instead of using `WithEvents`? The advantage of using `AddHandler` is that you can create one procedure that can handle multiple events, even if the events are being fired from different components. You can also handle events from objects that you create at runtime. For example, you might get a collection of objects passed to you, but still be able to handle their events using the `AddHandler` keyword.

The "Final" Code

The following code doesn't actually do anything, and some earlier changes are undone in this code. Still, if you are trying to keep up with the code, and want to make sure that the compilation works in the next section, here is how your code inside the Healthcare project should look:

```
Public Class Patient
    Dim msFirstName As String
    Dim PhysiciansList As New Collection()
    Dim miPatientID As Integer

    Public Property FirstName() As String
        Get
            Return msFirstName
        End Get
        Set(ByVal Value As String)
            msFirstName = Value
        End Set
    End Property

    Default Public ReadOnly Property Physicians _
    (ByVal iIndex As Integer) As Physician
        Get
            Return CType(PhysiciansList(iIndex), Physician)
        End Get
    End Property

    Public Function Admit() As Boolean
        'add patient to database, notify billing, etc.
        Return True
    End Function

    Event LabResult(ByVal LabType As String)

    Public Property PatientID() As Integer
        Get
            Return miPatientID
        End Get
        Set(ByVal Value As Integer)
            miPatientID = Value
            'check labs database for this patient
            'if there are new lab results
            RaiseEvent LabResult("CBC")
        End Set
    End Property
End Class

Public Class Physician
    Dim miPhysID As Integer
```

```
    Public Property PhysicianID() As Integer
        Get
            Return miPhysID
        End Get
        Set(ByVal Value As Integer)
            miPhysID = Value
        End Set
    End Property

    Public ReadOnly Property Age() As Single
        Get
            'get Date of Birth (DOB)
            'calculate age from DOB
            'return age
        End Get
    End Property
End Class
```

Compiling the Assembly

Now that you have created a class library with two classes (Patient and Physician), it is time to compile your assembly. In VB6, you would compile a COM component, but you aren't in VB6 anymore. Instead, you are writing for the .NET Framework, and that means you will be compiling an assembly. The assembly might have a .DLL extension, but it is not a traditional DLL in the Windows API sense, nor is it a COM DLL in the VB6 sense.

Building the assembly is fairly easy. The build option is no longer on the File menu, but is now a separate menu labeled Build. If you click on the Build menu, you will see several choices. Because you have a solution in this example, with a class library (Healthcare) and Windows application (HealthcareClient), you will see options to build or rebuild the solution. You also have an option to deploy the solution. In the next section of the Build menu, you have the option to build or rebuild one of the projects in the solution, depending on which project is highlighted in the solution explorer when you click the menu. Finally, there is a choice for a batch build and one for the Configuration Manager.

In .NET, you can compile your assemblies in either Debug or Release mode, or you can create your own custom modes. Debug mode compiles in symbolic debug information and does not use any compiler optimizations. Release mode does not compile in any of the symbolic debug information, and it applies code optimizations. Obviously, you will use Debug mode while developing and debugging your application. After you have the bugs worked out and are ready to deploy the application, you switch to Release mode and recompile your assembly. Realize that you can modify these modes or add your own. For example, you could add debug information into projects compiled under Release mode, if you choose to modify Release mode in that fashion.

You can see that the Debug option is set if you look at the toolbar. The Solutions Configuration drop-down list box allows you to choose Debug or Release, and to open the Configurations Manager. You can see this in Figure 4.4.

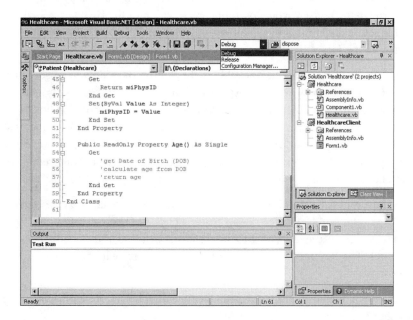

FIGURE 4.4

The Solutions Configuration option on the toolbar.

For now, just click on the Healthcare project one time in the Solution Explorer window. This will select it as the project to build if you choose not to build the entire solution. Now, click on the Build menu and choose Build Healthcare. The Output window at the bottom of the IDE should report when the build is done, and show how many projects succeeded, how many failed, and how many were skipped. In this case, the HealthcareClient is not counted as skipped, so you should see that one project succeeded, with no failures and no projects skipped.

The compilation process creates two files. The default location for the project is My Documents\ Visual Studio Projects\Healthcare. If you look in that folder, you'll see a bin folder below it. Inside the bin folder are two files: Healthcare.dll and Healthcare.pdb. The .DLL is the assembly, and the .PDB is the debug file that goes along with the .DLL because you compiled it with the Debug configuration. .PDB stands for *program database*. The .PDB extension is a bit unfortunate for many users because .PDB is also used as a common format for files used by the Palm operating system. This means that .PDB files get associated with the Palm's Desktop application.

Reusing the Assembly in Other Applications

One of the other big differences from this and VB6 is that VB .NET assemblies do not use the registry. In fact, VB .NET does not put any information about the assembly in the registry. If you search through the registry, you won't find any mention of the Healthcare assembly. You will find information about the project and solution, but that's just so that Visual Studio .NET can show them in the recent files list.

Given that there is nothing about the assembly in the registry, how do you reuse it in another application? If you start a new Windows Application project in VB .NET and right-click on the References node in the Solution Explorer window, the Add Reference dialog box is shown. However, the Healthcare component is not listed. This shouldn't be too surprising; it showed up earlier because `HealthcareClient` was part of the same solution. Now, however, you have started a new project, which creates a new solution. This solution is in a different directory, and therefore has no knowledge of the Healthcare component.

To have the new project use the Healthcare component, make sure that you are on the .NET Framework tab of the Add Reference dialog box and click the Browse button. Navigate to the `My Documents\Visual Studio Projects\Healthcare\bin` folder and choose `Healthcare.dll`. The References node in the Solution Explorer window now shows the Healthcare component.

Your application can now use the Healthcare component. You can create objects by typing the following code:

```
Dim Patient As New Healthcare.Patient()
```

You can always use the `Imports` command to import the `Healthcare` namespace, so you could instantiate objects with just this code:

```
Dim Patient As New Patient()
```

How .NET Locates Assemblies

Think back to COM: When a program makes a call to a component, the Service Control Manager goes to the registry, looks up the component information, locates the object, creates it, and returns to the calling application a pointer to the newly created object. .NET doesn't use the registry, so it has to use a different mechanism for locating assemblies that are referenced in an application (or in another assembly). The full details are not critical to understanding how to develop components, but a basic understanding of the process is important for troubleshooting.

Step 1: Getting the Reference Information

Your application attempts to call a referenced assembly. The reference contains the following information about the assembly:

- Name
- Version
- Culture
- Public Key (for strongly named assemblies)

The runtime uses this information to try to locate the assembly, using the following steps.

Step 2: Looking at the Configuration File

The configuration file is a powerful concept. You can create a configuration file to handle any reference information that might change. For example, if you think you will need to update the particular version of an assembly used by your application, you can store that information in a configuration file. You can also force an application to bind to only the versions of components that were available when the application was built. This is called *Safe Mode*. The configuration file is an XML file.

Step 3: Using CodeBases or Probing

If you want to prevent probing, you can specify a CodeBase value in the configuration file. When the runtime loads the file pointed to by the CodeBase, it checks the version information to make sure it matches what is in the application's reference. By default, if the assembly pointed to by the CodeBase is the same version or higher, the binding will occur.

If there is no CodeBase, the probing process is initiated. *Probing* is simply the runtime looking for the assembly by following a search criteria. First, the runtime looks in the GAC if the assembly is strongly named. If the assembly is private, the search is performed only in the application's root directory, referred to as the *AppBase*. The runtime sees a reference to an assembly in the application, such as Healthcare, and looks for the assembly by first searching for `Healthcare.DLL`.

If the assembly is not found in the AppBase directory, the probing continues, and the runtime searches based on the path set up in the configuration file. This path is specified with the `<AppDomain>` tag, as such:

```
<probing privatePath="MyAssemblies"/>
```

The runtime automatically appends some other information to the search path. For example, if the assembly you are searching for is `Healthcare`, the runtime looks in `AppBase\Healthcare`. It also looks in the `bin` directory, so it searches `AppBase\bin`. Because you specified `MyAssemblies` in the `<AppDomain>` tag, the runtime searches `AppBase\MyAssemblies`.

4

BUILDING CLASSES AND ASSEMBLIES WITH VB .NET

Finally, the search includes any localization information. Therefore, if you are creating multi-lingual, or localized, applications, it appends the locale. If the locale is de, the search path will include AppBase\Bin\de, AppBase\Healthcare\de, and AppBase\MyAssemblies\de.

Step 4: The GAC

Recall that the Global Assembly Cache is a cache for assemblies to be used by multiple applications on the same machine. Even if an assembly is found through probing or CodeBases, the runtime looks for updated versions in the GAC, provided you have not turned off this functionality. If a higher version exists in the GAC, it is used.

If no assembly was found using a CodeBase or probing, the runtime searches the GAC for a match. If a matching assembly is found, it is used.

To add assemblies to, remove assemblies from, or view assemblies in the GAC, use the gacutil.exe console application, provided by the Framework. The GAC is also a directory, so you can add assemblies to the GAC merely by copying them into the directory.

Step 5: The Administrator Steps In

It is possible for the administrator to create a file that specifies a particular version of an assembly to be used. If an application is searching for version 2.1.4.0 of Healthcare, the Administration policy file can point the application to another version, forcing an upgrade or downgrade.

Working with Assemblies and the GAC

NOTE

You must have administrator privileges on your computer to complete the examples in this section. Only an administrator can delete files from the GAC.

Often, when you create an assembly, you will want it to be shared by multiple applications. This is not really a problem because multiple applications can point to the same DLL. However, when you set a reference to a DLL inside a project, it records the path to the DLL. What if the path later changes? Or what if you don't know the final path on the eventual production machine?

As you've already read, the Global Assembly Cache, or GAC, allows you to place components into a cache that can be accessed by any application. Therefore, you could take the Healthcare.DLL and add it to the GAC, allowing applications to access it regardless of the physical location of the DLL.

Setting the Strong Name

To see this in action, the first thing you need to do is set a strong name for the component. A strong name is a way to positively identify a component. It includes some standard information, such as the assembly's name, version number, and culture information if provided. It also adds a public key and a digital signature.

Strong names are a way for the client to verify that a component is unchanged from the component referenced by that client when it was built. This means that the client can be assured that the assembly is unchanged and that it was, in fact, generated by the proper party. The use of a strong name follows this procedure:

1. The assembly is compiled with a strong name set for it. The digital signature is created with the developer's private key, and the signature is stored in the portable executable file of the assembly. This combination of the name and a key ensures uniqueness in much the same way a GUID (Globally Unique ID) did in the world of COM.

2. The client references the assembly. Setting this reference adds the assembly's public key as part of the reference. Technically, only a portion of the assembly's public key is added to the reference in order to save space.

3. At runtime, the client verifies the strong name by using the public key to check the digital signature. Proper negotiation indicates that the assembly has not been tampered with, and the person owning that public key did create the assembly.

Setting a strong name also ensures that no one else can create a new version of your component. Because your component is signed with your unique key, no one else can create a new version because he does not have your key. Clients can be assured that new versions come from the original author only. Finally, strong names are used to verify that a component has not been modified since it was built, much like Authenticode technology and ActiveX controls that are downloaded and used in a browser.

To set the strong name for your Healthcare assembly, make sure that the Healthcare project is chosen in the Solution Explorer window. Click on Project, Properties to open the Healthcare property pages. Click on Strong Name in the left-hand navigation window.

You have two ways to create a strong name: You can use a key file or a key container. The key file method is not as secure as the key container method. With a key file, you include the file in the project, which means it could be shared inadvertently, and you are warned of this fact on the dialog box. The key container actually accesses the key from the runtime, and therefore does not have to store the key file in the project. For now, you'll keep it simple and use the key file.

Click Generate Key under the Key File text box, and `KeyFile.snk` appears in the text box. You can see this in Figure 4.5.

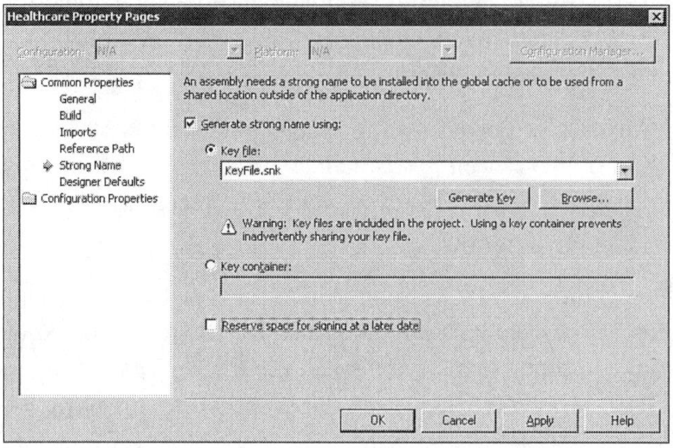

FIGURE 4.5

The Strong Name tab of the Project Properties dialog box.

After clicking the OK button, you can see that the `KeyFile.snk` file has been added to your project if you look in the Solution Explorer.

The next few steps will seem odd at first, but I'll explain what is happening as you go. Understand that you are about to test using the component from a specified path, and then from the GAC.

Adding the Assembly to the GAC

Now that you have set a strong name for the assembly, go ahead and build the assembly again by choosing Build Healthcare from the Build menu. Recall that, by default, you have just built the assembly in `My Documents\Visual Studio Projects\Healthcare\bin` (if you used the default directory to create the application). Now, however, copy the `Healthcare.dll` you just created and drop it in another directory; for my examples, I'll assume that it has been copied to the root of the C: drive, but you are free to copy it elsewhere. The point is you want it in a different, and easily accessible, directory.

Now, create a new Windows Application project, and call it NewHealthcareClient. Right-click on the References node in the Solution Explorer window and choose Add Reference. Click on the Projects tab, and then click the Browse button. Navigate to the root of the C: drive and point to the `Healthcare.DLL` you copied there, and then click OK.

You have now added a reference in your new client application to the assembly you created earlier. If you expand the References node in the Solution Explorer, click on Healthcare, and look at the Properties window, you'll notice the `Path` property is set to `C:\Healthcare.dll`. This might seem to be exactly what you did in the previous example, and so far it is; in fact, the only difference so far is that the assembly has a strong name.

Now, on the form in your NewHealthcareClient project, add a button and add the following code:

```
Private Sub Button1_Click(ByVal sender As System.Object, _
  ByVal e As System.EventArgs) Handles Button1.Click
    Dim myPatient As New Patient()
    myPatient.FirstName = "Sue"
    MsgBox(myPatient.FirstName)
End Sub
```

You can go ahead and run this application in order to test it, but you will want to actually build it before continuing with the testing. Click on the Build menu and choose Build. Your `NewHealthcareClient.exe` file will be in `My Documents\Visual Studio Projects\ NewHealthcareClient\bin` by default. If you look in that directory, you will see something strange: a copy of `Healthcare.dll`! This was automatically copied into the directory in which you compiled the application.

It isn't always desirable to have the DLL in the execution directory for each application. First, a single application might reference dozens of assemblies, and you don't want them all in the application directory. Further, you might want the component to be shared by multiple applications, so you can slipstream fixes in without having to worry about copying into a multitude of directories.

In the directory in which your EXE was compiled, run NewHealthcareClient to see whether it works. It should work flawlessly. Now, in that directory, delete the `Healthcare.DLL`. Run the application again, and click on the button you added. Now, you get a nasty error message, as shown in Figure 4.6.

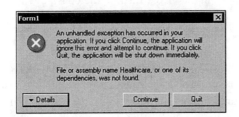

FIGURE 4.6

An error indicating that an assembly could not be found.

If you click the Details button on the error message box, you will see the following information:

```
System.IO.FileNotFoundException: File or assembly name Healthcare, or one
 of its dependencies, was not found.
```

You might now be scratching your head. You referenced an assembly in the root of the C: drive, and that assembly still exists. However, your application is apparently only looking in the local directory for the file. Now that the local copy of that file is gone, the application gets all confused and indicates it cannot locate the assembly.

However, the application is also searching the GAC, and of course it is not finding the assembly there, either. You must first add the assembly to the GAC in order for the application to be able to see it.

Open a console window and go to the root of the C: drive. You are going to use `gacutil` to install the assembly into the GAC. However, you need to locate `gacutil` and either type in the full path or, as in this case, just copy it into a directory in the path. After you have located `gacutil`, type the following command:

```
gacutil /i healthcare.dll
```

This installs the assembly into the GAC. If you had not created a strong name, you would have received a message that you could not install an assembly without a strong name into the GAC. Because you did create a strong name for this assembly, it installs into the GAC without problems.

Now, return to your NewHealthcareClient application and run it again. This time, it runs normally. You haven't made a single change to the client application, but when it looks for the assembly, it checks not only the local directory (which no longer contains a copy of the assembly), but it also checks the GAC. In this case, of course, it finds the assembly in the GAC and uses it.

Now, remove the assembly from the GAC. Back in the console window, type the following command:

```
gacutil /u healthcare
```

Notice that you do not include the .DLL extension on the name of the assembly to remove. After you have removed the assembly, run your client again. Now, two things can happen. If you did not shut down your client before uninstalling the assembly from the GAC, the client continues to run fine. However, if you did shut down the client and now restart it, it will not run. This is because the client has cached the information about the assembly in memory, and does not notice it has been removed from the GAC unless the client is stopped and restarted.

Versioning and .NET Assemblies

Understanding how .NET assemblies are versioned is important. The first rule to remember is simple: Only assemblies with strong names have the version policies applied to them. Therefore, if you aren't using strong names, this won't be something you have to worry about.

Assume that you are going to use strong names. Maybe you want strong names because you want to use the GAC, or you'll just use strong names for a little extra security. Regardless, it is important to understand how versioning works with strongly named assemblies.

.NET Version Numbers

The .NET version number consists of four parts:

```
<major number>.<minor number>.<build>.<revision>
```

Assume that you are working on a project, and that you are building a new version on a regular basis, such as daily. Each day that you build the application, you will increment the build version. If you have to make multiple builds in one day, you can increment the revision number. Regardless of how you actually use the four parts of the version to track your projects, they become very important when you begin changing them.

The first two numbers are often referred to as the *logical version number* of an assembly. For example, in the COM world, it is often common to ask, "What version of ADO are you using?" with common answers being "2.5" or "2.6."

Although the first two numbers might be the logical version, however, the client applications of strongly named assemblies care about all the numbers. The runtime sees assemblies with different version numbers as different assemblies, and this means your client, by default, will see these as different assemblies. It is actually possible for an administrator to override this default behavior if necessary.

Setting the version number can be accomplished in a couple of ways. If you look in the `AssemblyInfo.vb` file that is created as part of your project, you will see the following line:

```
<Assembly: AssemblyVersion("1.0.*")>
```

This will allow you to set the version for the application. Or, you can enter the following lines in the code module for your classes:

```
Imports System.Reflection
<Assembly: AssemblyVersionAttribute("2.3.4.6")>
```

These lines have to go outside the classes you have created.

Summary

Creating classes (or objects) is one of the most common things for a VB developer to do. Class creation is different in VB .NET, as you can tell from this chapter. It changes much more when you start looking at inheritance, as you will in the next chapter.

The main differences are how you create properties, how you handle read-only, write-only, and default properties, and how you can handle events. There is also a big difference in the fact that you compile assemblies instead of COM components. Finally, the way files are located is also very different.

Finally, you looked at sharing files using the GAC, and you took a look at how versioning is handled in .NET. Throughout the rest of the book, you will see class libraries used occasionally to encapsulate some of the functionality in your applications.

Inheritance with VB .NET

IN THIS CHAPTER

Inheritance is here! Inheritance is here!

Are you excited? Perhaps the most requested feature in Visual Basic since version 1.0 has been inheritance. Finally, inheritance has arrived, and it is good. Most VB .NET developers will want to rush out and inherit themselves silly, but it should be noted that inheritance is very powerful, and with that power comes responsibility. Namely, you must make sure that you should be using inheritance when you actually use it.

If you haven't been on the inheritance bandwagon before, you might be unsure about just what inheritance is, or at least what it can do for you. This chapter seeks to introduce you to inheritance, .NET style.

What Is Inheritance?

For years, one of the most requested features from Visual Basic developers has been inheritance. Microsoft has had one form of inheritance, *interface inheritance*, available in VB since VB first started supporting object creation in VB4. Developers, however, wanted to have what is known as *implementation inheritance*. With VB .NET, developers finally get their wish, thanks to the CLR. If you're unclear on what interface and implementation inheritance are, read on.

Inheritance is a very powerful form of code reuse. With inheritance, you write one class that contains some properties and methods. That class becomes the basis for other classes, and is known as the *base class*. Classes that then use this base class are known as *derived classes*. Most often, the derived classes extend the functionality of the base class.

Imagine if you wanted to create an application to model part of a university. As part of your application, you wanted to create two objects, representing students and professors. Students and professors both have a number of things in common: Each has a name, an address, and so forth. However, each also has some differences. Students have declared majors, whereas professors have classes they can teach. Students are charged tuition, whereas professors are paid for their work. Professors submit grades, whereas students receive them.

As you can see, there are similarities and differences that must be taken into account when these objects are built. The goal of inheritance is to write the code for the similarities once, and then use it in both the Student and Professor objects.

Interface Inheritance in VB6

In VB6, you had what was called *interface inheritance*. With interface inheritance, you could create the interface (or shell, or definition) of a reusable component. Suppose that you wanted to create a Person object that had all the shared attributes of both students and professors. In the case of VB6, you would create a class module that contained the definitions of those attributes, but no actual implementation code. Your interface class might be named iPerson and look like this:

```
Public Property Get Name() As String
End Property
Public Property Let Name(psName As String)
End Property

Public Property Get Address() As String
End Property
Public Property Let Address(psAddress As String)
End Property

Public Function Enroll() As Boolean
End Function
```

In VB6, you could create an interface using a class module. Technically, VB could not create interfaces, but you could use the hack of creating a class module with only definitions for properties and methods, and then implement it in another class. This was actually just creating a class, but there would be no implementation code in it, so it "looked like" an interface. For example, the Enroll method does not have any code to actually handle the enrollment. And if you are curious why there is an Enroll function in the iPerson interface, it is because professors can also take courses at the university, which some do because they can do so for free at most institutions.

To use this interface in other classes in VB6, you had to put this line of code in your class:

```
Implements iPerson
```

This line set up your new class to inherit the interface from the iPerson class. In VB6, you could actually put implementation code into the interface class, but it was ignored when you implemented the interface in your derived class.

Imagine that you have used the Implements keyword in a class named Student. This class must now implement every public property, method, and event found in iPerson. Therefore, your code in Student would include code similar to the following:

```
Public Property Get iPerson_Name() As String
    iPerson_Name = msName
End Property

Public Property Let iPerson_Name(psName As String)
    msName = psName
End Property
```

```
Public Property Get iPerson_Address() As String
    iPerson_Address = msAddress
End Property

Public Property Let iPerson_Address(psAddress As String)
    msAddress = psAddress
End Property

Public Function iPerson_Enroll() As Boolean
    'open database
    'check to see if class is filled
    'if not, add student
End Function
```

The code in Student contains the implementation of the interface designed in iPerson.

Looking at this, you'll probably realize that most of the time, the Student implementation code will end up being the same in a Professor class, at least for these class members. Wouldn't it be easier to create this implementation code in iPerson and then just have that code brought into both Student and Professor? That's what implementation inheritance is all about.

VB .NET's Implementation Inheritance

In VB .NET, you don't have to create a separate interface, although you can. Instead, you can just create a class with implementation code and inherit that in other classes. This means you could add the code for the Name and Address properties and the Enroll method in a Person class. Then, the Professor and Student classes could both inherit from the base class Person. Student and Professor would both have access to the code inside of Person, or they could replace it with their own code if needed.

One thing to realize is that in VB .NET, all classes are inheritable by default. This includes forms, which are just a type of class. This means you can create a new form based on an existing form. You will see an example of inheriting forms later in this chapter.

Even though VB .NET provides true implementation inheritance, interfaces are not gone. In fact, they are greatly improved in VB .NET; together, inheritance and interfaces give you the ability to use polymorphism. This will be examined at the end of this chapter.

A Quick Inheritance Example

Create a new VB .NET Windows Application project and name it InheritanceTest. Add a button to the form and go to the code window. In the code, add the following class. Make sure that you add it *outside* the class for the form!

```
Public Class Person

    Dim msName, msAddress As String

    Property Name() As String
        Get
            Name = msName
        End Get
        Set(ByVal Value As String)
            msName = Value
        End Set
    End Property

    Property Address() As String
        Get
            Address = msAddress
        End Get
        Set(ByVal Value As String)
            msAddress = Value
        End Set
    End Property

    Public Function Enroll() As Boolean
        'check class enrollment
        'if enrollment < max. class size then
        'enroll person in class
        Enroll = True
    End Function
End Class
```

This code creates a Person class with two properties, Name and Address, and an Enroll method. So far, there is nothing about this class that you haven't seen before.

Now, add a second class, called Student. Your code should look like this:

```
Public Class Student
    Inherits Person
End Class
```

As you can see, there isn't any implementation code in Student at all. There are no properties or methods defined. Instead, all you do is inherit from Person.

Now, in the Button1_Click event handler on the form, add the following code:

```
Private Sub Button1_Click(ByVal sender As System.Object, _
 ByVal e As System.EventArgs) Handles Button1.Click
    Dim myStudent As New Student()
    MsgBox(myStudent.Enroll)
End Sub
```

Your form is creating an instance of the `Student` class. The only code in the `Student` class is an `Inherits` statement that inherits the `Person` class. However, because VB .NET supports implementation inheritance, you'll be able to call the `Enroll` method of the `Person` class from within the `Student` class, even though the `Person` class does not explicitly define an `Enroll` method. Instead, the `Enroll` method is present because `Student` is inheriting the method from `Person`. Go ahead and run the project to verify that the message box does report back a value of `True`.

Is it possible to instantiate `Person` directly? In this case, yes. For example, you could modify the `Button1_Click` event handler to look like this:

```
Dim myStudent As New Student()
Dim myPerson As New Person()
MsgBox(myStudent.Enroll)
MsgBox(myPerson.Enroll)
```

Both these calls to the `Enroll` method will work fine.

This might raise a host of questions. For example, could `Student` redefine the `Enroll` method so that it is not using the code in `Person`? The answer is yes. Could `Person` refuse to let someone instantiate it directly, instead forcing people to instantiate other classes that inherit it? Again, the answer is yes. You will see this and more as you examine more that you can do with inheritance.

Shared Members

VB .NET introduces the concept of shared members. *Shared members* are a way of creating a member (a property, procedure, or field) that is shared among all instances of a class. For example, you could create a property for a database connection string. This will be the same for each class, so you can fill it in for one class and all classes can then see that one property. Shared properties are most often used in inheritance, so that all objects created from derived classes can share the same member across all instances of the class. However, shared members also can be used regardless of whether you are using inheritance.

To see how shared properties work, suppose that you wanted to create a logging mechanism to record any kind of message created by the application (informational messages, error messages, and so on). You want to record the message into a log file, and keep a total count of the number of messages, regardless of the type of message.

Start Visual Studio .NET and create a new Windows Application and name it MessageLogTest. Create a new project, but keep it in the same solution. This new project should be a class library, and name it MessageLogger.

In the code for MessageLogger, rename the class `Logger`, and enter the following code:

```
Imports System.IO
Public Class Logger
    Public Function LogMsg(ByVal psMessage As String)
        Static iCount As Integer
        iCount += 1
        Dim file As TextWriter = New StreamWriter("c:\output.txt", True)
        file.WriteLine(psMessage & ". " & iCount)
        file.Close()
    End Function
End Class
```

In this application, you are creating one method called LogMsg that accepts a string from the client. The method then has a static integer called iCount. iCount keeps track of the number of messages that the logger has written, and is appended to each message so you can see its value.

Return to the MessageLogTest application. Right-click on the References node in the Solution Explorer window and choose Add Reference. Go to the Project tab and you will see the MessageLogger project. Click the Select button and then click OK. This now adds a reference from the Windows application to the class library you are creating.

On the form, add two buttons. Go to the code window and enter the following code (the Windows Form Designer–generated code is hidden):

```
Imports MessageLogger
Public Class Form1
    Inherits System.Windows.Forms.Form

#Region " Windows Form Designer generated code "

    Dim infoLogger As New MessageLogger.Logger()
    Dim errorLogger As New MessageLogger.Logger()

    Private Sub Button1_Click(ByVal sender As System.Object, _
      ByVal e As System.EventArgs) Handles Button1.Click
        infoLogger.LogMsg("Informational message")
    End Sub

    Private Sub Button2_Click(ByVal sender As Object, _
      ByVal e As System.EventArgs) Handles Button2.Click
        errorLogger.LogMsg("Error message")
    End Sub
End Class
```

Now, run the application (make sure that MessageLogTest is the startup application, which it should be if you created it first). Click each button one time. If you look at the output.txt file, it looks like this:

```
Informational message. 1
Error message. 1
```

You will notice that both objects created (infoLogger and errorLogger) successfully wrote to the text file. However, the static count of the number of messages shows both messages as number one. Why?

You have created two separate objects in memory. They are completely separate, so each object has its own LogMsg method, meaning that each has its own copy of the static iCount. Therefore, one message sent using the infoLogger gets the value of 1, but a message sent with errorLogger goes to the other object in memory, and also gets 1.

To avoid this situation, you could share the LogMsg method. This allows you to share the method across multiple instances of the object, meaning that all the objects will call through the same copy of the method.

To share the LogMsg function, return to the MessageLogger application and, in the Logger class, modify the definition of the function to look like this:

```
Public Shared Function LogMsg(ByVal psMessage As String)
```

By adding the keyword Shared, this method will now be shared across multiple instances of the object. To test this, delete the output.txt file. Now, run the application again, and press each button once. If you examine the output.txt again, you will see the following output has been produced:

```
Informational message. 1
Error message. 2
```

Now, you can see that regardless of which object you call, the count of the number of messages is incremented properly. This means that the same LogMsg method was called from two different objects because it has been shared between the two objects.

Inheritance Keywords

There are a number of keywords associated with inheritance. Remember that by default, all classes you create are inheritable. You inherit from classes using the Inherits keyword. The class from which you inherit is then known as the *base class*. The Inherits keyword can be used only in classes and interfaces. It is important to point out that a derived class can only inherit from one base class.

Forcing or Preventing Inheritance

The `NotInheritable` modifier is used to mark a class as not inheritable; in other words, it cannot be used as a base class. If you were to modify the `Person` class in your `InheritanceTest` project, it would look like this:

```
Public NotInheritable Class Person
```

If you change the `Person` definition to look like the preceding line, `Student` will no longer be able to inherit from `Person`.

In contrast to the `NotInheritable` modifier, there is also a `MustInherit` modifier. `MustInherit` says that a class cannot be instantiated directly. Instead, it must be inherited by a derived class, and the derived class can be instantiated.

If you changed `Person` to include the `MustInherit` keyword, it would look like this:

```
Public MustInherit Class Person
```

Now, you would not be able to use the following line of code in the client:

```
Dim myPerson As New Person
```

However, you would still be able to inherit `Person` in your `Student` class, and your client could instantiate `Student`.

Overriding Properties and Methods

When you inherit a base class, the properties and methods cannot be overridden, by default. Given your earlier example in `InheritanceTest`, you could not have created a function named `Enroll` in `Student` because one existed in `Person`.

There is a modifier, `NotOverridable`, that says a particular property or method cannot be overridden. Although methods are normally not overridable, you can use this keyword only in a unique case: If you have a method that is already overriding a base method, you can mark the new, derived method as `NotOverridable`.

If you want to allow a property or method to be overridden, you can mark it with the `Overridable` modifier, as shown here:

```
Public Overridable Function Enroll() As Boolean
```

Now, your `Student` can create its own `Enroll` method. To do so, your client will have to use the `Overrides` modifier, so it would look like this:

```
Public Overrides Function Enroll() As Boolean
```

What happens if the Enroll function is marked as Overridable in the base class, but you don't override it in the derived class? In this case, it acts like any other method in the base class, and calling from the derived class will actually call the implementation of the function in the base class.

In the VB .NET IDE, it is also possible to use the drop-down lists at the top of the code window to override methods or implement interfaces. As you can see in Figure 5.1, there are two classes in the file. Class Student is inheriting class Person, and in so doing, is able to override the Enroll method. If you change the Class Name drop-down to (Overrides), Enroll shows up in the Method Name drop-down, and can be used to create the stub of the derived Enroll method in Student.

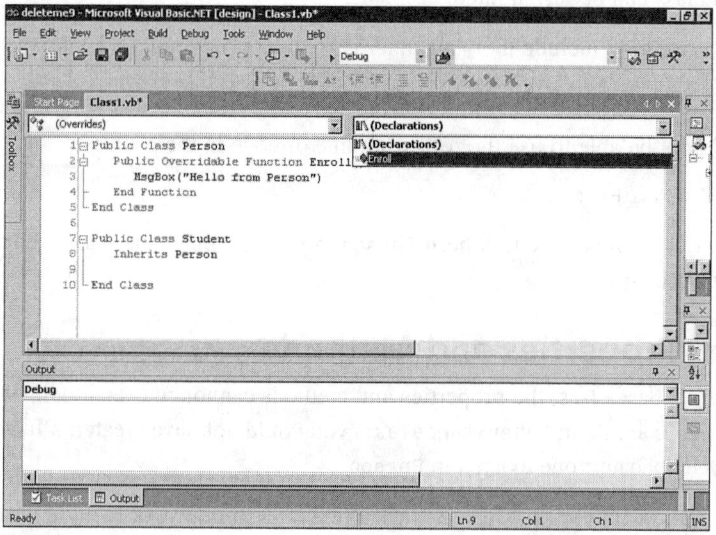

FIGURE 5.1
Overridable methods are shown in the Method Name drop-down when you inherit within VB .NET.

There is also a MustOverride modifier. This forces a derived class to override the property or method. The MustOverride modifier changes the structure of the property or method. Because the property or method must be overridden, you do not put any implementation code in it. In fact, there is not even an End Property or End Sub or End Function when using the MustOverride modifier. If a class has even a single property or method with the MustOverride modifier, that class must be marked as MustInherit because the method can be used only if it is overridden in another class. Therefore, the class must be inherited to be used.

For example, here you have a base Transportation class that has a method, Move, that is marked as MustOverride. This means that Transportation must be marked as MustInherit. The Train class inherits from Transportation, and then overrides the Move method.

```
Public MustInherit Class Transportation
    MustOverride Function Move() As Boolean
End Class

Public Class Train
    Inherits Transportation
    Public Overrides Function Move() As Boolean
        'code goes here
    End Function
End Class
```

MyBase and MyClass

Although you can override a base class property or method in your derived class, you can still access the properties or methods in the base class using the MyBase keyword. This allows you to call base class members even though you have overridden them in your derived class.

For example, assume that you wanted to have a Transportation class, with an overridable function called Move. Train then inherits from Transportation, and implements its own Move method, overriding the one in Transportation. Now, from within Train, you can call the Move method in Train or the one in Transportation.

The method CallMethods calls first the Move in Train, and then the Move in Transportation. The user will see two message boxes. The first will have the text Hello from the Train class, whereas the second will have the text Hello from the Transportation class.

Figure 5.2 shows a diagram of how the code works. The Move in CallMethods uses the Move in the Train class, but MyBase.Call executes the code in the base class, Transportation.

```
Public Class Transportation
    Overridable Function Move() As Boolean
        MsgBox("Hello from the Transportation class")
    End Function
End Class

Public Class Train
    Inherits Transportation
    Public Overrides Function Move() As Boolean
        MsgBox("Hello from the Train class")
    End Function

    Public Sub CallMethods()
        Move()
        MyBase.Move()
    End Sub
End Class
```

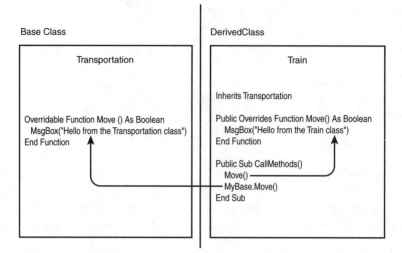

Figure 5.2

MyBase *allows derived methods to call the implementation in the base class, even if the derived class overrides that method.*

Related to MyBase is MyClass. Assume that, in your base class, you have method A calling an overridable method B. If you want to verify that the method B you call is the one you wrote in the base class, and not the derived, overridden method B in the derived class, call method B with the MyClass qualifier, as in MyClass.B.

For example, assume that you have a Transportation class that has two methods: MakeReservation and BuyTicket. MakeReservation calls BuyTicket. MakeReservation and BuyTicket are both overridable. Your Train class can inherit Transportation, and create a BuyTicket method that overrides the BuyTicket in Transportation. If you don't create a MakeReservation in Train, your call to MakeReservation will use the code in the Transportation class. However, if the code in Transportation.MakeReservation calls BuyTicket, by default you'll call the BuyTicket you've created in Train. Here is the code:

```
Public Class Transportation
    Overridable Function MakeReservation() As Boolean
        'CheckSchedule
        BuyTicket()
        'etc
    End Function
    Overridable Function BuyTicket() As Boolean
        MsgBox("Generic Transportation implementation")
    End Function
End Class
```

```
Public Class Train
   Inherits Transportation

   Public Overrides Function BuyTicket() As Boolean
      MsgBox("Train-specific implementation")
   End Function
End Class
```

Now, suppose that you want the MakeReservation to call the BuyTicket method in Transportation, even if Train overrides BuyTicket. To accomplish this, just change Transportation.MakeReservation to this:

```
Public Class Transportation
   Overridable Function MakeReservation() As Boolean
      'CheckSchedule
      MyClass.BuyTicket()
      'etc
   End Function
```

Figure 5.3 shows this in action. First, a client instantiates Train, which is derived from Transportation. The client then calls Train.MakeReservation. Because Train does not override MakeReservation, the MakeReservation in Transportation is called. The first line in MakeReservation calls BuyTicket. However, because Train does override BuyTicket, that method is used. The next line in Transportation calls MyClass.BuyTicket, which calls the BuyTicket method in the same class in which MakeReservation is running.

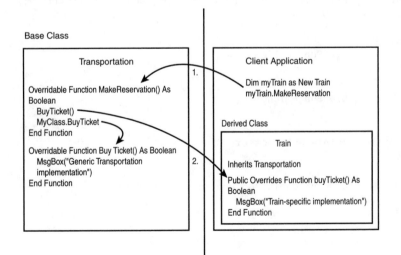

FIGURE 5.3

MyClass *can call implementation code in the same class running the current routine, regardless of whether the client has overridden that method elsewhere.*

5

INHERITANCE WITH
VB .NET

It's important to note that if your Train class overrides MakeReservation, MyClass will not come into play. The reason is that the implementation of the base MakeReservation is gone, so the MyClass.BuyTicket is overridden and will not be called (unless Train calls MyBase.BuyTicket for some reason).

Understanding Accessibility and Inheritance

Accessibility can be a bit complicated when using inheritance. There are several modifiers used to set the accessibility. They are:

- Public—Accessible throughout the project and any project that references it
- Friend—Accessible within the project but not outside it
- Protected—Accessible within the class in which it was created, or any class that is derived from the base class containing the protected element
- Protected Friend—Accessible within the same project, in a derived class, or both
- Private—Not accessible outside the module or class containing the element

To see this in an example, take the following code. You have three classes in the class library: Person, Student, and Foo. Person is a base class, containing one Sub of each accessibility type mentioned above. Student is a derived class of Person. Foo is a class in the same project, but it does not derive from Person.

Next, you have a client application that instantiates the Student class only. Notice what Subs from Person make it to Student, to Foo, and to the client. The code for the class library follows:

```
Public Class Person
    Public Overridable Sub PublicSub()
    End Sub

    Friend Overridable Sub FriendSub()
    End Sub

    Protected Overridable Sub ProtectedSub()
    End Sub

    Protected Friend Overridable Sub ProtectedFriendSub()
    End Sub

    Private Sub PrivateSub()
    End Sub
End Class
```

```
Public Class Student
    Inherits Person

    Public Overrides Sub PublicSub()
    End Sub

    Friend Overrides Sub FriendSub()
    End Sub

    Protected Overrides Sub ProtectedSub()
    End Sub

    Protected Friend Overrides Sub ProtectedFriendSub()
    End Sub
End Class

Public Class Foo
    Dim myStudent As New Student()
    Public Sub Test()
        myStudent.PublicSub()
        myStudent.FriendSub()
        myStudent.ProtectedFriendSub()
    End Sub
End Class
```

Notice that Student, which is derived from Person, can see everything but Person's PrivateSub method because it is marked as private and is therefore only visible to Person.

Foo, on the other hand, can only see the PublicSub, FriendSub, and ProtectedFriendSub. ProtectedSub can be seen only by the class in which it exists and any class derived from that base class.

Finally, take the following client code that instantiates a Student object:

```
Imports AccessibilityTest

Public Class Form1
    Inherits System.Windows.Forms.Form

    Private Sub Button1_Click(ByVal sender As System.Object, _
ByVal e As System.EventArgs) Handles Button1.Click
        Dim myStudent As Student
        myStudent.PublicSub()
    End Sub
End Class
```

Notice that in the client, the only method that is accessible is the PublicSub method. Figure 5.4 shows each Sub and how far it is visible in each case.

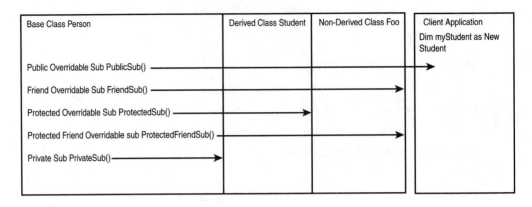

FIGURE 5.4

The accessibility of various methods, based on the accessibility modifiers.

Polymorphism

Polymorphism is the ability to change the implementation of a base class for different objects. For example, if you have a bicycle and a car, both can move, but they do so in very different ways. They use different mechanisms for movement, and the distance that each can move in an hour is significantly different. Yet, both a `Car` and a `Bike` class might inherit from a base `Transportation` class, which could also be used as the basis for a `Plane` class, a `Train` class, a `HotAirBalloon` class, and so on.

Polymorphism with Inheritance

Polymorphism was possible in VB6 using interfaces, which will be examined in a moment. VB .NET allows you to perform polymorphism using inheritance. The difference from what you have done so far is that you can actually use the base class as a variable type, and you can handle any derived class with that new variable.

For example, examine the following code. The `Transportation` class contains just one method, `Move`. Two classes inherit the `Transportation` class: `Car` and `Bicycle`. Both have overridden the `Move` method. The code looks like this:

```
Public MustInherit Class Transportation
    Public MustOverride Function Move() As Boolean
End Class

Public Class Bicycle
    Inherits Transportation
    Overrides Function Move() As Boolean
        'code here
```

```
        Move = True
    End Function
End Class

Public Class Car
    Inherits Transportation
    Overrides Function Move() As Boolean
        'different code here
        Move = True
    End Function
End Class
```

So far, this looks similar. However, notice now what your client can do. It cannot directly create an instance of Transportation because it is marked as MustInherit. But, you can declare a variable of type Transportation. You can be assured that any object that inherits Transportation has a Move method, and you don't have to worry about what kind of object it is. Your client code might look like this:

```
Protected Sub Button1_Click _
    (ByVal sender As Object, ByVal e As System.EventArgs)
    Dim MyCar As New Car()
    Dim MyBike As New Bicycle()

    PerformMovement(MyCar)
    PerformMovement(MyBike)
End Sub

Public Sub PerformMovement(ByVal Vehicle As Transportation)
    If Vehicle.Move() Then
        'do something
    End If
End Sub
```

You'll notice that the PerformMovement Sub accepts an argument of type Transportation. This Sub doesn't care if you pass it an object of Car or Bicycle type. Because the object being passed in inherits from Transportation, it is guaranteed to support the Move method, so the code will run without problems.

Polymorphism with Interfaces

Interfaces still exist in VB .NET. In VB6 and COM, they were most often used when you needed to be able to modify your code without breaking existing clients. You could actually modify the structure of your classes, but provide an interface that looked like the old version of the component. This kept existing client applications happy while at the same time you were able to modify the classes to enhance functionality.

In VB .NET, you can still use interfaces this way. However, interfaces are best used when you want to be able to use different object types in the same way, and the objects don't necessarily share the same base type. For example, the IEnumerable interface is used to expose an enumerator for a class. Using this interface, you can move through a class using For Each, even if the class is not based on a Collection object.

You'll see an example of polymorphism with interfaces using the same example of the Car and the Bicycle. First, Transportation will be created as an interface instead of a base class, which might make more sense: The Move method is most likely to be quite different between a car and bicycle. Then, you'll implement the Transportation interface. Finally, you'll call the objects from the client.

```
Interface Transportation
    Function Move() As Boolean
End Interface

Public Class Bicycle
    Implements Transportation
    Function Move() As Boolean Implements Transportation.Move
        'code here
        Move = True
    End Function
End Class

Public Class Car
    Implements Transportation
    Function Move() As Boolean Implements Transportation.Move
        ' different code here
        Move = True
    End Function
End Class
```

You'll notice that now, when you implement from an interface, you don't have to use the Overrides modifier. In addition, the method definition is followed by an Implements keyword that specifies which method in the interface the current method is implementing. This allows you to have different names for the methods in the class that is implementing the interface. The client code here will be the same as it is when you use inheritance polymorphism.

A Visual Inheritance Example

You have been reading quite a bit about inheritance, and it has been in the form of non-GUI classes so far. However, forms are classes, so you can inherit from forms as easily as you can any other class. VB developers have been requesting form inheritance for many years, and now you have your wish, thanks to the .NET Framework.

It is sometimes easier to see inheritance at work in forms, and there are a few caveats when inheriting forms. You'll get started with a simple example and then extend it as you work with it.

Creating the Base Project

Start a new Windows Application project in Visual Studio, and name it baseVisual. In reality, you could create this as a different project type, but starting as a Windows Application is usually the easier way to get started.

Your baseVisual project will start with a form in the designer window. To keep things simple, add two buttons to the form. For ease of the demo, just leave things named as they are. Change the Text property of the first button to Run Code and the Text property of the second button to Close. Move the buttons to the left side of the form, as shown in Figure 5.5.

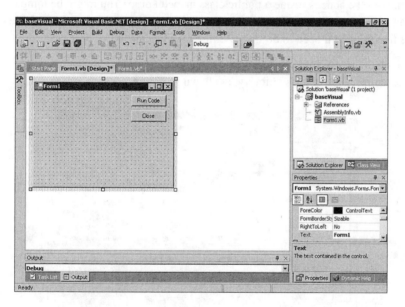

FIGURE 5.5

Your very simple base form.

Go to the code window and, for Button1, add the following code:

```
Private Sub Button1_Click(ByVal sender As System.Object, _
 ByVal e As System.EventArgs) Handles Button1.Click
   MsgBox("This is the code in the base form")
End Sub
```

Now, add the following code to Button2:

```
Private Sub Button2_Click(ByVal sender As Object, _
 ByVal e As System.EventArgs) Handles Button2.Click
    Me.Close()
End Sub
```

NOTE

The code assumes that you have used Button1 for the Run Code and Button2 for the Close functionality.

At this point, all the code is inside a public class named Form1. You might be tempted to create a new form in the project that inherits from Form1, but inheriting forms works a little differently. The first thing you need to do that is different is change the project type.

Right-click on the baseVisual project in the Solution Explorer window and choose Properties. Change the Output Type to Class Library, as shown in Figure 5.6.

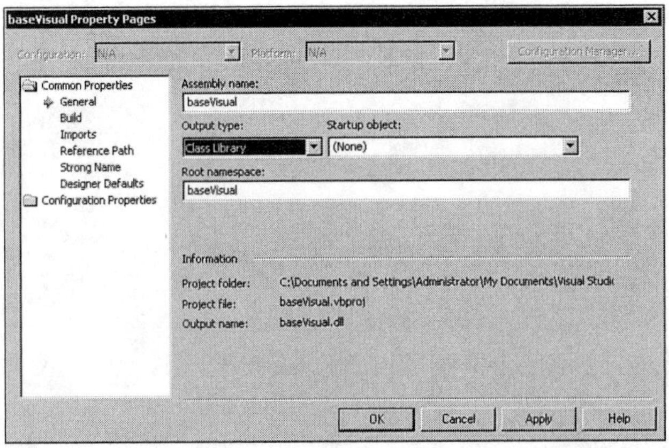

FIGURE 5.6
Changing the project type from Windows Application to Class Library.

baseVisual will now compile as a DLL, but it has your form in it.

Add a new project into the solution. Make the project a Windows Application and name it derivedVisual. Your new derivedVisual project will automatically come with a new form, named Form1. Delete Form1 from derivedVisual.

You might be tempted to inherit the base form from baseVisual now, but there is one additional step: You can't derive the form in another project until the assembly is built. Therefore, right-click on baseVisual in the Solution Explorer and choose Build. Note that you could derive a new form in the same project, based on Form1, without having to first build the project.

After the assembly is built, right-click back on the derivedVisual project in Solution Explorer. Choose Add, and notice one of the choices on the menu is Add Inherited Form. Choose to add an inherited form, and a dialog box appears. It will ask for the name of the form you want to create. The name doesn't matter, so you can leave it as Form1.VB .Click the Open button.

Now, a new dialog box pops up, which you can see in Figure 5.7. This is the Inheritance Picker, and will let you find a compiled assembly from which to inherit. The Inheritance Picker already sees Form1 in baseVisual, because it is in the same solution. Click on Form1 in baseVisual to enable the OK button, and click OK.

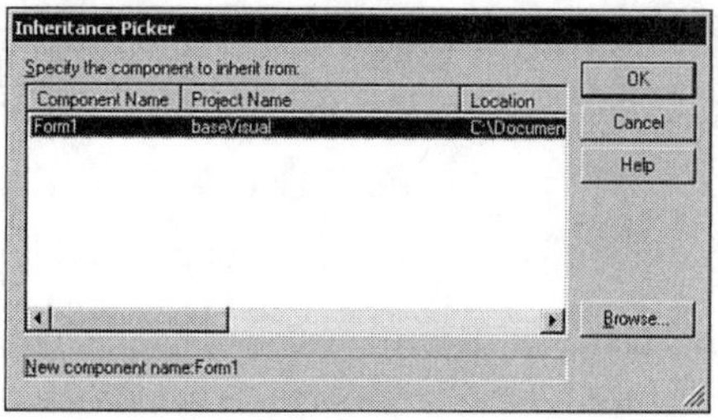

FIGURE 5.7
The Inheritance Picker showing the forms you can inherit.

After you click OK, two things happen. For one, baseVisual appears under the References node for the project. More noticeably, a new form is created in derivedVisual. Surprise! It looks just like the form you created in baseVisual, except for those funny symbols on the two buttons. Those funny symbols, shown in Figure 5.8, indicate that the buttons are inherited controls from the base form.

Add a new button to the form. Notice that it does not have the symbol indicating inheritance because, of course, it is not inherited. Set derivedVisual as the startup project and run the application. Clicking the button you just added doesn't do anything, because you didn't add any code to it. However, clicking the Run Code button displays a message box, indicating that the code from the base class was inherited. The Close button closes the form and stops the application.

After the application has stopped running, double-click on the Close button. Nothing happens. That's because, by default, you cannot change the properties of the objects on a form, or write code against them. You could, of course, write code against the button you just added, but not the buttons provided by the baseVisual form.

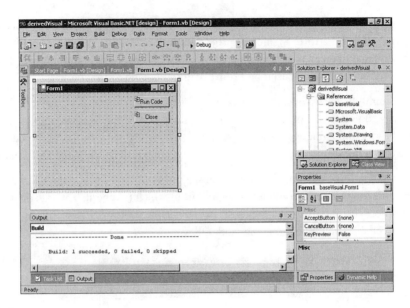

FIGURE 5.8

Your new, derived form.

However, you can change this behavior. Return to Form1 in the baseVisual project. Click on the Close button and notice that the Modifiers property is set to Assembly. Change the Modifiers to Family. Family is similar to the Protected accessibility keyword you saw earlier, which means it can be modified by classes inheriting this class. Assembly, the default, is visible to all classes in the assembly in which it resides. However, your derivedVisual is a separate project, and therefore a separate assembly. Now, also change the Modifiers property for the Run Code button to Family.

Rebuild the baseVisual project because you have made some changes to the form. Return to Form1 in derivedVisual. You may have to close the form designer and reopen it to get it to see the changes you made to the base class. Double-click on the Run Code button (Button1); this time, you are taken to the code window. Add the following code:

```
Private Sub Button1_Click(ByVal sender As System.Object, _
 ByVal e As System.EventArgs) Handles Button1.Click
   MsgBox("This is the code in the derived form")
End Sub
```

Now, run the project again, and click on the Run Code button. Something very strange happens: You get two message boxes. The first is from the base form, whereas the second is from the derived form. If you're curious as to what's happening, understand that with forms, you are not overriding the base class functionality; you're adding to it, extending it in a pseudo-polymorphic sense.

It is possible to return to the baseVisual class and mark Button1 as Public Overridable, and then, in derivedVisual, create a Button1 as Public Overrides. Only the code in derivedVisual runs then, but it runs twice. It is unknown whether this is the planned behavior, or a bug in Visual Studio .NET Beta 2. For now, follow this simple rule: If you want to override function-ality of a base control, don't put any implementation code in the base form for that control.

Cross-Language Inheritance

You hear a lot about .NET's cross-language inheritance, so now you can examine it for your-self. Add a new project to the current solution, but this time make it a C# Windows Application. Name it derivedVisualCs.

Your new project, derivedVisualCs, will start with a form, Form1.cs. Delete this form from the project. Now, add an inherited form to derivedVisualCs. Don't worry about the name, but once again choose Form1 from baseVisual in the Inheritance Picker.

Add a new button to the form. You can double-click on the button and add some code. However, you'll also have to add some additional code because the form doesn't have the necessary code for C# to start it as the startup object. Therefore, make sure that you enter all this code:

```
[STAThread]
static void Main()
{
        Application.Run(new Form1());
}
private void button3_Click(object sender, System.EventArgs e)
{
        Windows.Forms.MessageBox("Hello from C#!");
}
```

Make derivedVisualCs your startup project and then run the application. When the form loads, click on the button3 you added. You should see a message box that says, "Hello from C#!" Now, click on the Run Code button. You get a message box that says, "This is the code in the base form," which you know is written in VB .NET! As you can see in Figure 5.9, you have VB .NET code running in a C# application. You can now see some of the power of .NET's cross-language inheritance. Your GUI programmers could build the base forms in one language and developers in other languages could inherit from those forms, extending them as needed.

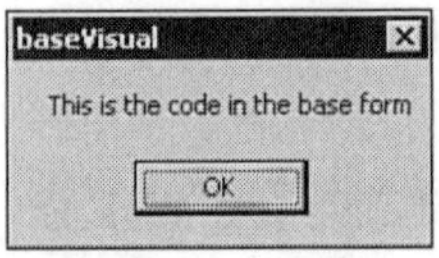

Figure 5.9
Code, inherited from VB .NET, running in a C# application.

When to Use and When Not to Use Inheritance

When inheritance was first introduced into some other languages, it caused problems as users went too far, creating deep and overly complex inheritance trees. Inheritance is powerful and useful, but should not be overdone. I remember working with a developer. He spent an entire day working on the design of objects and finally said, "I can't figure out where to use polymorphism." My suggestion was that if he couldn't find where to use it, maybe he didn't need to.

There are actually three ways to build an object model:

- Encapsulation—If you want to use functionality from an object, but not really look like the object or override its functionality, don't inherit; instead, encapsulate an instance of the object. Example: You have a calculator application, and you want to show the number display in red when it is negative. You could define a new type of control from the TextBox or Label controls that show the number in red when negative, or you could just hook onto the Change event of the text box, and perform the functionality there.

- Interface implementation—If the derived objects don't share very much in terms of implementation, use an interface instead of a common base class. There is not much point in having a base class for which all the methods must be overridden; an interface would probably be a better way to go. Classes can also implement multiple interfaces, so a car may implement both `iGasPowered` and `iDrivable`, whereas an airplane might implement `iGasPowered` and `iFly`. A bird, on the other hand, implements `iEatWorms` and `iFly`, but does not implement `iGasPowered` or `iDrivable`.

- Inheritance—Use inheritance if you want to utilize functionality in the base class and extend it while trying to look like the base class. If some of the methods in the base class are not appropriate for your derived class, it is probably a good indication that inheritance was not the right move. In some cases, merely encapsulating another class instance and proxying calls to it might be a cleaner solution.

Summary

As you can see, starting with inheritance is not difficult. However, the challenge comes when you design your components and your object model. Inheritance is quite powerful, but you must intelligently define your base classes to make them broad enough to be inheritable, but general enough to be useful to many derived classes.

Inheritance is available across .NET languages, as you saw in the visual inheritance section. Visual inheritance is a powerful technique for gaining a common set of functionality across all the forms in your application. Gone are the days of having to fake form inheritance by creating new class modules that controlled the appearance of the forms, and using control arrays to create new controls programmatically. Although you can still use this approach, things are much simpler because you can actually inherit forms and extend them through the form designer.

With the introduction of implementation inheritance, VB .NET moves into the realm of object-oriented (OO) languages for the first time. VB6 had some OO constructs, but the addition of implementation inheritance, one of the most basic OO concepts, greatly strengthens VB .NET's OO portfolio.

Getting Started with ADO.NET

IN THIS CHAPTER

ADO.NET is Microsoft's new technology for accessing data. Microsoft has long been at the forefront of the universal data access movement, starting with the original Open Database Connectivity (ODBC) almost nine years ago. There's really no disputing the importance of data access to modern applications, but how you access the data has a significant impact on the performance and scalability of the application. Add to this the fact that applications are growing increasingly distributed, and passing large amounts of data from one place to another becomes an even more critical part of designing and building applications.

Microsoft has had a long time to work on data access. It has gone through a number of major changes in data access technology, and ADO.NET is no different. Developers will discover a whole new way to create scalable data-driven applications. By combining the power of data access, XML, and the .NET Framework, Microsoft has introduced its most powerful data access technology to date.

The Importance of ADO.NET

The world of applications has been evolving for some time. Originally, applications were centralized, and they were accessed via dumb terminals. All the code ran on the mainframe, and the information technology (IT) professionals controlled everything.

Along came the PC and everything changed. The computing power moved to the desktop, and people ran spreadsheets, databases, word processors, and the like. However, no PC can be an island for long. Soon, people were tying their PCs together with umbilical cords back to servers and, of course, those mainframes.

Given that PCs were often connected to servers, you saw the rise of client/server computing. Unlike the centralized approach of mainframe/dumb terminal applications, you had a distributed approach in which the data was on the server, and much of the functionality ran on the client.

Next came n-tier development, in which the business rules were placed into centralized objects running on a server. This meant that the client application was used for such tasks as accepting input, viewing data, printing, and so forth. Business rules and data access were encapsulated in shared, reusable components, which accessed the data in a mid-range or mainframe database.

At the next stage of evolution, Web applications became all the rage, and soon enough, development had returned to the centralized model of the mainframe days. The browser was acting as nothing more than a dumb terminal, accepting user input and displaying screens. All the processing occurred under the control of the IT department, although it was often scattered among Web servers, application servers, and database servers.

Although Web applications are still common, many of them are being developed using the n-tier model. More importantly, the rise of a new class of components, called *Web Services*, is driving changes in how applications are developed. With Web Services, you can use the Internet as a distributed operating system, with components located anywhere in the world, and accessed via HTTP. You will see more about Web services in Chapter 9, "Building Web Services with VB .NET."

It is into this world that ADO.NET arrives, ready to address the challenge of having components that, although spread across the Internet, still need to pass data to each other. ADO.NET also addresses some scalability concerns. Some parts of ADO.NET are much simpler than their counterparts in previous data access technologies. Some facets of ADO.NET might seem more complex, but this is usually due to a level of indirection aimed at making data access more logical in today's environment.

To better understand ADO.NET, it is useful to understand how it evolved. Prepare for a brief history lesson, and you'll better understand why ADO.NET came to be.

The ADO.NET Family Tree

ADO.NET is the latest in a line of data access technologies from Microsoft. Even though it is an evolutionary step, it is a *large* evolutionary step forward; it is arguably the largest change in Microsoft's data access since Microsoft's first object model was released ten years ago. ADO.NET represents the first time Microsoft has attempted to separate the concept of accessing the data from the concept of working with the data, as you will see in the following sections.

In the Beginning: Embedded SQL and APIs

At first, applications accessed data by simply embedding SQL statements into the program, along with all the information to get to the database. Most mainframe applications built before the 1990s had direct access to the database built right in. They contained connection information, SQL statements to retrieve and manipulate data, and the code to display that data. These were very tightly coupled applications, relying on the name of the server and database never to change. In addition, any change in the table structure usually required that the client applications be recompiled.

To open up databases to some form of alternative access, database-specific APIs were created, such as DB-Lib and OCI. These APIs were designed to allow developers, almost always using C, to access the data from a Unix or Windows machine. These libraries were typically fast because they were optimized for a specific back-end database. They were typically challenging to use, however; they were low-level APIs, and not object-based as later technologies would be. In addition, because they were database-specific, it became very hard to move from one database to another. To make the move, a large portion of your application had to be rewritten to use a completely different library.

ODBC, DAO, and RDO

When Microsoft released Access 1.0 in the early 1990s, it was its first Windows-based database program. Access contained the JET database engine, which is just Microsoft's desktop database engine (as SQL Server is its server database engine). Microsoft realized that although JET was good for building applications based on data stored on the PC, not all data was stored on a PC. Instead, most companies already had data stored in server-based databases such as SQL Server, Oracle, and DB2. Microsoft, therefore, wanted people not only to have access to this back-end data, but also to be able to use it as easily as they used data stored in JET. To accomplish this, in 1993, Microsoft released Open Database Connectivity, or ODBC.

ODBC, unlike the database-specific APIs, allowed the developer to program in such a way that the physical database became less important than the logical structure of the schema. You could write your SQL statements and, if they were just standard SQL, you could change the back-end database engine without having to rewrite any of your code. This was because ODBC was a layer of indirection between your application and the database. You pointed to something called a *data source name*, or DSN. The DSN determined what database you were accessing (by loading the appropriate ODBC driver) and the location of the database.

ODBC was designed to let you not only access back-end data, but to make that back-end data look like local data. The remote tables looked just like local JET tables to the point that you could perform SQL joins between local JET tables and remote tables. Or, you could perform joins between tables in different back-end databases, such as joining SQL Server tables to Oracle tables, using ODBC and JET as the intermediate layer.

In JET, Microsoft also included an object model called *Data Access Objects*, or DAO. DAO contained a set of classes that allowed you to easily access databases, tables, records, and other schema objects. For any table, you could examine the columns, including the column names, types, and so on. You could use DAO to programmatically access data and perform data inserts, updates, and deletions. You could issue data definition language (DDL) commands to create or drop tables, create or drop indexes, add constraints, and so forth.

JET was a boon to developers because it presented the developer with an easy-to-use, rich set of objects with which to access and manipulate data. Developers using Access or Visual Basic could use DAO to work with any data in a JET database, including those tables linked into the JET database via ODBC. This meant that the developer had easy access to the data regardless of the actual database in which it was stored.

The problem with DAO, however, was that it was built on top of JET. What if all your data was in SQL Server, or Oracle, or some other back-end database? You could link all the tables into a JET database via ODBC and use DAO, but then you had JET sitting between you and your data. JET was relatively fat for its time, taking up about 1MB of memory in an era when machines typically had 4–16MB RAM. In addition, JET included a query optimizer, which was already available in the back-end databases. All queries to the back-end database had to pass through this fat JET layer, and each query got optimized by JET and again by the back-end. The result was that going through DAO and JET could be slow.

An alternative to using DAO was to program directly against ODBC. This was typically a much faster way of accessing the data, but it was much more challenging. ODBC was not object-based, as was DAO. Therefore, programming against the ODBC API required significantly more code, and such items as database cursors, and even memory, had to be managed by the developer.

For a long time, developers accessing back-end data had these two options: use DAO, which was easy but (relatively) slow, or program against the ODBC API, which was fast but difficult.

Microsoft realized that there must be a better way, so when Visual Basic 4.0 was released in 1995, Microsoft also released a new object model, built on top of ODBC, called *Remote Data Objects* or RDO. RDO was very similar in structure to DAO, but most of the object names were just different enough to require DAO code to be rewritten. Still, the basic concepts were the same, as far as connecting to a database, and then having access to a collection of the tables, and then a collection of the columns, and so on. The actual accessing of the data was similar in both DAO and RDO, but RDO didn't go through the JET database engine, so you had nearly-ODBC speeds with the ease of programming that had previously existed only in DAO.

Microsoft had DAO and RDO, both based on ODBC. These were the two object models that developers were using with great success. However, Microsoft saw a shift coming in the market, and decided to address it with a new underlying technology: OLE DB.

OLE DB and ADO

Microsoft had built ODBC with a particular bias: It assumed a relational database. Understand that although there were ODBC drivers available for Excel files, text files, and other nonrelational sources, these drivers actually made the sources look relational. DAO and RDO were designed with a relational structure in mind; when you connected to a database, it automatically populated a collection of available tables. Each table had a collection of available columns that was automatically populated. These collections and objects were available because the back-end was assumed to be a relational database.

Microsoft knew that not all corporate data was stored in relational databases. For example, corporate data could be stored in Exchange or the Active Directory, neither of which uses a relational engine. Data could be stored in Excel, or text files, or a variety of other formats. Microsoft wanted to design a way to read data, both relational and nonrelational, using one consistent methodology. OLE DB was born.

OLE DB is a low-level API, like ODBC. However, OLE DB does not assume a relational back-end. Instead, OLE DB uses its own drivers, called *providers*, to access the data. Native OLE DB providers allow you to access relational or nonrelational data using the same API.

Although OLE DB is a low-level API, Microsoft had learned from its ODBC and RDO experience, so OLE DB shipped with ActiveX Data Objects, or ADO. ADO is the easy-to-use object model built on top of OLE DB. Using ADO, you can make a connection to the database and access the records. ADO allows you to use a single set of objects to access the back-end data, regardless of the format of the data.

Unlike DAO and RDO, however, the ADO object model is quite small. DAO and RDO both contain dozens of objects, whereas ADO contains fewer than ten major objects. DAO and RDO can automatically fill out collections of tables, columns, and relationships. ADO has no such objects because ADO, being based on OLE DB, cannot automatically assume a relational database as its source. Therefore, with ADO, you have to know how to query the system tables in order to examine the structure.

> **NOTE**
>
> Microsoft actually released a companion object model to ADO, called *ADOX*. ADOX does assume a relational back-end, and has the necessary objects to work with tables, columns, relationships, and the like. Despite this, few people ever use ADOX.

Given the fact that OLE DB does not assume a relational back-end, ADO has a small number of objects, and therefore has a small memory footprint. It is also quite fast; OLE DB providers tend to outperform ODBC drivers for a given database.

ADO, in some of its more recent incarnations, also adds some XML features. For example, you can use ADO to create disconnected recordsets. These recordsets are stored on disk, and you can open them with ADO without the need to first connect to a database. These recordsets can be persisted in either a binary, advanced data tablegram (ADTG) format or in XML format. These disconnected recordsets can be used to boost application performance because with them, you do not have to make an expensive database connection and then retrieve the records from the database and stream them across the wire. It is even possible to make inserts, updates, and deletes to these disconnected recordsets and later synchronize the changes with the underlying database.

Despite this capability to create disconnected recordsets, ADO typically assumes a connected environment, where you stream records from the database to the client, using one of several cursor types. As different as ADO is from DAO and RDO, all three are built on a connected

6

model and combine both *accessing* data with *working with* data. The distinction is important, and will be examined in the next section.

In addition, data is typically retrieved and stored in memory in such a way that it is easy to access and manipulate when it is in-process to the client application. However, if the data is retrieved into a middle-tier COM component and needs to be transferred to a client to be displayed, it is a constant struggle to determine the best way to pass the data from one tier to another. Cross-process data passing is always a challenge with n-tier applications. ADO.NET attempts to address the question of separating data access from data viewing and manipulation, and also how to pass data across tiers. You can see the evolutionary timeline of Microsoft's data access technologies in Figure 6.1.

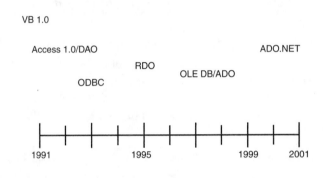

FIGURE 6.1
The timeline of Microsoft's data access technologies.

Why ADO.NET Exists

Just as Microsoft saw a need to move from ODBC to OLE DB, it saw the need to move beyond OLE DB. Although there is nothing inherently wrong with either ODBC or OLE DB, Microsoft saw that much of today's development efforts were spent building n-tier systems. Not only were these n-tier applications built inside the company, but also these applications might want to reuse a specific type of component—Web services—that was exposed on the Web via HTTP.

Thanks to an initiative called the *Simple Object Access Protocol*, or SOAP, it is possible to call components anywhere on the Web via HTTP. SOAP is an XML-based protocol built for sending and receiving information in a distributed environment, enabling remote procedure calls over HTTP. With SOAP and Web services, you have the added advantage of platform independence; the Web service could be written in C# and running on a Windows XP server, whereas the client that calls it could be a Web service written in C++ running on Linux, or could be a Web-enabled cell phone or PDA. The point is, the call is simply an HTTP request, and the results are sent back in an HTTP response, with the actual request and response calls containing XML.

Passing data from a Web service to some form of client shows one reason ADO.NET exists. Passing an ADO `Recordset` object from a Web service to a client is possible, but there are certain caveats. First, you have to create a static cursor. Then, you have to save the `Recordset` in XML format and send that back to the client. The default ADTG format of ADO `Recordsets` is typically not transferable across firewalls or through proxy servers; even if it is, the binary ADTG format will have little meaning to a non-Windows client application. Therefore, ADO.NET, as you will see, speaks XML natively.

A further reason for ADO.NET's existence is the fact that Microsoft wanted to separate data access from working with data. This provides yet another layer of indirection, and allows you to separate the objects that let you work with data from the objects that allow you to access the data. This new layer also makes it quite easy to work with disconnected data as the default, which can lead to huge scalability gains.

Further, ADO.NET exists because of the .NET Framework. In the past, ODBC and OLE DB, along with their associated object models, were independent of any specific tool. With the .NET Framework, Microsoft put ADO.NET into the standard set of services available to any language using the Framework. Now, data access becomes one of the base services provided by the underlying application services infrastructure, ensuring a consistent database access technology across all the .NET languages.

By being built into the .NET Framework, this means that ADO.NET takes advantage of all the services provided by the Framework, such as automatic memory management, garbage collection, and so forth. This makes ADO.NET easy to work with, and means that those of you writing C++ managed code should not have to worry about handling the memory used by ADO.NET.

ADO.NET is different from DAO, RDO, and ADO in that it does not have an underlying API like OLE DB and ODBC. Instead, ADO.NET can use native drivers, called *managed providers*, written for each database, or it can use a generic OLE DB managed provider that uses OLE DB providers. Because there is an OLE DB provider for ODBC, this means that ADO.NET can use its managed providers, OLE DB, or ODBC. The highest performance comes from the managed providers, as you can imagine. The only managed providers available with the first release of the .NET Framework are for SQL Server 7.0/2000 and OLE DB. Previous versions of SQL Server, or any other database, will need to use the ADO.NET managed provider for OLE DB.

ADO.NET's Disconnected Architecture

Much ado has been made about ADO.NET's disconnected architecture, and it is important. Before diving into this disconnected architecture, however, it is important to understand that ADO.NET can operate in a connected mode as well. ADO.NET uses different objects depending on whether you are operating in a connected or disconnected mode, and this paradigm allows you to more easily identify when you are using a connected versus a disconnected mode.

In Microsoft's previous data access technologies, you made a connection to the server and kept it open while you retrieved and manipulated the data. This worked fine as long as the number of clients was small, but it did not tend to scale very well. In addition, you opened a connection to the data and were sometimes able to scroll through the data, depending on the cursor you chose. With some of the cursor options of ADO, you actually read the values for each record from the underlying tables as you accessed that record. That meant a lot of communication back and forth to the database, and also meant that the only way to achieve good performance was to maintain an open connection.

One trick that some people employed to improve performance was to create a disconnected recordset in ADO. This could be accomplished by reading all the records at one time, and storing them in memory at the client, in what was called a *static cursor*. You could then write the entire recordset to disk to persist it over time. You then used this local copy of the data instead of going back to the database for the data. This approach worked very well for data that did not change often.

ADO.NET stores data in memory in an inherently disconnected fashion. Recall that ADO.NET separates the data access from the data usage, which means that the concepts of moving through data in a fully scrollable fashion, and performing inserts, updates, and deletes, has nothing to do with the physical act of connecting to the database itself. Consider the act of buying and driving an automobile. Every morning, when you need to drive to the office, you get in your car and drive. You do not have to go to the dealer first to get your car. Instead, you got the car one time, and then you took it home, and now you drive it from there. Occasionally, you have to return to the dealer to have maintenance done on the car, but by and large, you use the car disconnected from the dealer from which you bought the car.

In the same vein, ADO.NET allows you to connect to the database and retrieve records, and then disconnect from the database. You continue to work with the records, performing such actions as scrolling through the records, sorting and filtering records, and performing inserts, updates, and deletions.

You might be saying to yourself, "Big deal. I could do all that with ADO's disconnected recordsets." You are partially correct, but as you will see later, ADO.NET provides a new object, called the *DataSet*, that allows an unprecedented level of disconnected support. For example, if you were using a disconnected ADO recordset and you inserted a record that violated some foreign key constraint, you would not know about this foreign key violation until you attempted to resynchronize your disconnected recordset with the underlying data source. ADO.NET's DataSet, on the other hand, can enforce referential integrity constraints in the disconnected mode, ensuring that you are following the rules and making valid data changes.

ADO and other connected models can also face challenges when moving data from tier to tier. If a middle-tier component opened a connection and began retrieving data, it needed to feed the records to the client in a string, in a collection of objects, in a variant array, by passing a recordset object, or with some other method. Each method tended to have its own benefits and pitfalls, and no one method was right for every situation. Disconnected records in ADO.NET, on the other hand, can be much easier to pass from one tier to another (or across process boundaries in the same tier).

By not maintaining an open connection, and making it easier to pass data efficiently across process boundaries, ADO.NET achieves a new level of scalability.

Performance and Scalability Considerations

One of the primary questions with ADO.NET is, "Yes, but how does it perform compared to ADO?" The answer so far is, "Quite well." ADO.NET is being tested by the ADO.NET product team, and even in its beta form, it is meeting or exceeding ADO performance when compared on an apples-to-apples basis. The reasons for this vary, but one reason is that the managed provider for SQL Server is faster and more efficient than the OLE DB provider for SQL Server. Another reason is that the objects are more finely tuned for specific tasks than those in ADO.

Performance and scalability are tightly coupled. As performance increases, scalability increases. Because tasks are completing faster, the same resources can handle more events in the same amount of time. Therefore, by tuning the performance, you can make the applications more scalable.

In addition to just trying to speed up the actual access time, the fact that ADO.NET can work in a disconnected mode has huge scalability implications. If you create an application that connects to a server for some of its data, you have a connection to the database. If you have five clients, this might not be an issue. However, if you have five thousand clients, this connection load could overwhelm your server, either from a resource standpoint, or a licensing (in other words, legal) standpoint. By building ADO.NET to connect, retrieve the data, and then disconnect, you achieve maximum scalability.

Consider what most people do with an application: They retrieve data and then examine that data. This examination, or "think time," is often significantly longer than the time it takes to retrieve the data. Assume that you retrieve data from a database, and the process takes one second. You then display the data to the user and the user ponders it for the next 29 seconds. This means that in the total 30 seconds the data is being used, the connection is only needed one-thirtieth of the time, or for one second. Maintaining the connection the other 29 seconds would be a waste of time.

You might be thinking, "No big deal. I can do this with ADO. I only build Web applications, and by the time the data has rendered in the browser, my page has fallen out of scope and the connection is closed." That is true, but what if you needed to pass that data from one component to another? How do you do this in the most efficient manner? What if the same component is to be used by a Windows client that does not have the object fall out of scope? What if part of the processing requires a fully scrollable cursor, which requires the connection to stay open when using ADO?

ADO.NET addresses many of these issues by storing the data in a disconnected mode, and by storing it in such a way that it is easy to pass from one component to a client, regardless of what that client happens to be. The passing mechanism is based on XML, which means that you do not have to manipulate the data types as you did when using COM marshaling with ADO disconnected recordsets.

The XML Basis of ADO.NET

XML, if you believe the hype, is the answer to everything. From the problems of world hunger to world peace to the meaning of life, XML is the answer. People get upset when you say it, because they want to think XML is magical, but XML is text. Before you have a fit, realize that HTML is text. Active Server Pages are text. There's no binary information in XML, HTML, or ASPs. They are all text files. However, it's the tags and formatting of XML and HTML that make them special, and XML is an incredibly powerful technology because it combines the data with the definition of the data, all in one neat package that is accessible to any XML-speaking application on any platform. Think of electronic data interchange (EDI) without having to look up in a book to discover what the 42nd position in a string represents. In a way, XML is the Esperanto of the computer world.

The good news about ADO.NET is that it natively speaks XML. When you retrieve data from a data source, or when you transmit data from one component to another component or a client, the format of the data is XML. If you happen to write data to a file in order to persist it, the format is XML. You could persist data in ADO using XML, but it was not the default; in ADO.NET, XML is the native tongue.

Not only can ADO.NET speak XML, it can read XML. If you have an XML file, ADO.NET can use that to create an in-memory data store that appears to you to be just like any other dataset. The data inside the `DataSet` object is not in XML format, but any time you transmit data, it is automatically sent as XML. The receiving application sees this incoming data as XML and can process it as it chooses.

Being able to natively read and write XML is important for several reasons. First, XML is an open standard that is supported on a variety of platforms. There are standards for how XML is structured, and for how the schema information is stored. This means that XML can be read by any number of clients, and that the schema of the data can be transmitted as well, obviating the need to predefine the schema and have the data in a fixed format, such as is the case with EDI. By basing data on XML, you allow your data to be transmitted to applications other than just .NET or COM programs. Instead, you can now interoperate with clients on any platform, written in any language, as long as they understand XML.

By being all text, XML is very easy to transfer via HTTP. As mentioned earlier, the binary format of an ADO recordset has no meaning on a Unix box, and the binary information is often not transferable over a proxy server or through a firewall. Text, on the other hand, flows freely through most corporate systems, using HTTP as the protocol.

Having now read a bit about what ADO.NET is and what its goals are, it is time to jump into a quick example and build some simple data access applications.

Building Simple ADO.NET Applications

It is tempting to go through some of the objects that make up ADO.NET before actually creating an application, but chances are you're ready to get your hands dirty with some code. Also, chances are you've already built a few applications that use ADO.NET, so some of this will look familiar to you. Therefore, you'll start by creating a simple application by coding the ADO.NET by hand, and then you'll use the controls given to you by the Visual Studio .NET environment in order to make life easier.

Creating a `DataReader` in Code

Open VS .NET and create a new ASP.NET Web Application and name it DataWebApp. Choose Visual Basic or C#, depending on your preference. To start, you'll create some very simple code, and you'll build on that a bit as you work this example.

The first thing to do is open the code view of the WebForm. You'll be adding a Connection object first, and which Connection object you use will depend on what database you are using. If you are using SQL Server 7.0 or SQL Server 2000, you will create a `SqlConnection` object. If you are using another database, you will need to use the `OleDbConnection` object. Because a free evaluation copy of SQL Server can be downloaded from Microsoft, this book will use SQL Server as a back-end database, and most examples will therefore use the `SqlConnection` object.

The `SqlConnection` object, like most of the objects in .NET, is fairly flexible. You can create it and initialize it at creation, or you can create it empty and then set properties. To initialize it at creation, you pass the connection string as an argument when you use the `New` keyword.

The connection string is also fairly flexible. For now, understand that in this sample string, the data source might be all you need to change. In fact, if you are running this Web application on the same machine that has SQL Server installed, you won't need to change anything. The data source is the name of the server on which SQL Server resides, and the name `localhost` just means the machine on which the code is running. Of course, if you are like most of the world, the user ID can be left as sa and there is no password. However, if you have actually turned on some security, feel free to use any user ID and password you choose.

Open the code view of the page; at the top, you need to reference the namespace you are using. Technically, you don't need to reference the namespace, but it will save you a tremendous amount of typing if you do. To have the least amount of typing when using the SQL Server–managed provider, enter the following line at the top of your code window (before the class):

```
Imports System.Data.SqlClient
```

Now, scroll down to the `Page_Load` subroutine, and add the `Connection` object by entering the following line of code:

```
Dim cn As New SqlConnection("data source=localhost;" & _
    "initial catalog=pubs;user id=sa;password=;")
```

If you had not added the `Imports` statement to the top, you would have had to refer to the class name as `System.Data.SqlClient.SqlConnection`, a rather long name to type. You will also notice from the connection string that the initial catalog is Pubs, which is the name of the database. Throughout this book, examples will use either the Pubs or the Northwind databases, both of which ship with SQL Server as sample databases.

Next, you need to create a `Command` object. In ADO, the `Connection` object could execute SQL statements using the `Execute` method. This is not true in ADO.NET, however, so you will need to explicitly create a `Command` object in order to execute SQL statements. The type of `Command` object you will create is the `SqlCommand` object, so add this line of code under the `SqlConnection` line you just added:

```
Dim cm As New SqlCommand("Select * from Authors", cn)
```

You have now created a `SqlCommand` object that uses the `SqlConnection` you created, called cn, and also has a SQL statement set that will retrieve all the rows and all the fields from the Authors table.

Next, you need to create a `DataReader` object. Understand that what the `DataReader` will do is allow us to access the data, one record at a time. It is a forward-only method of access, which means it is not a fully scrollable cursor. This is ADO.NET's connected model, if you will. To create the `DataReader`—in this case, a `SqlDataReader`—you must declare the variable and then use a method on the `SqlCommand` object in order to generate a `DataReader`. In the following three lines of code, you declare the `SqlDataReader`, open the `SqlConnection` created in the earlier lines, and create the `SqlDataReader` object by calling the `ExecuteReader` method of the `SqlCommand`. The code looks like this:

```
Dim dr As SqlDataReader
cn.Open()
dr = cm.ExecuteReader
```

You might be tempted to think that you could now start accessing the data in the `DataReader`. In reality, however, the data isn't quite ready to be read; instead, you have to call the `Read` method of the `DataReader`. The `Read` method works like `MoveNext`, advancing you to the next record. It also returns a `Boolean` indicating whether there are more records. When the `DataReader` is created, it defaults to a position prior to the first record, so you have to call the `Read` method even to access the first record.

After calling the `Read` method the first time, you are sitting on the first record. You can access the fields of the record using several methods, such as the index number of the field or the field name. Although not the most efficient method, using the field name will make this example as clear as possible.

You want to print out the name of the first person in the Authors table. If you have examined the Authors table, you know that the first name is stored in the `au_fname` field and the last name is stored in the `au_lname` field. Therefore, you can concatenate these two fields to display the person's name. In this example, you will use `Response.Write` to output something to the HTML stream. Your code would end up looking like this:

```
dr.Read()
Response.Write("Name: " & dr("au_fname") & " " & dr("au_lname"))
```

You have now taken the first record in the Authors table and displayed it in the browser. Your final code, minus the hidden region of Web Form Designer Generated Code, should look like the code in Listing 6.1.

LISTING 6.1 A Simple Web Page with One Record

```
Imports System.Data.SqlClient

Public Class WebForm1
    Inherits System.Web.UI.Page

#Region " Web Form Designer Generated Code "

    Private Sub Page_Load(ByVal sender As System.Object, _
        ByVal e As System.EventArgs) Handles MyBase.Load
        'Put user code to initialize the page here
        Dim cn As New SqlConnection("initial catalog=pubs;" & _
            "data source=localhost;user id=sa;password=;")
```

LISTING 6.1   Continued

```
    Dim cm As New SqlCommand("Select * from Authors", cn)
    Dim dr As SqlDataReader
    cn.Open()
    dr = cm.ExecuteReader
    '*** Lines below will be changing ***
    dr.Read()
    Response.Write("Name: " & dr("au_fname") & " " & _
        dr("au_lname"))
    '*** Lines above will be changing ***
    dr.Close()
    cn.Close()
  End Sub

End Class
```

You'll notice that the code contains comments around a section of code. That is because the code in between the comments will be changing as more features are added to the example. You'll also notice the addition of `Close` commands on the `DataReader` and `Connection` objects. This is not just a good idea, but closing the `DataReader` is the only way to free up the `Connection` object for more processing. You'll read more about the `Close` method throughout the chapter.

If you execute this code, the result might not appear to be very exciting, as shown in Figure 6.2. However, realize what you have done: You have retrieved a record from a database and displayed it on a Web page, in a few lines of code. Granted, this is nothing original, but it does work and it is all done using the .NET tools, so feel happy that you have your first ADO.NET example under your belt.

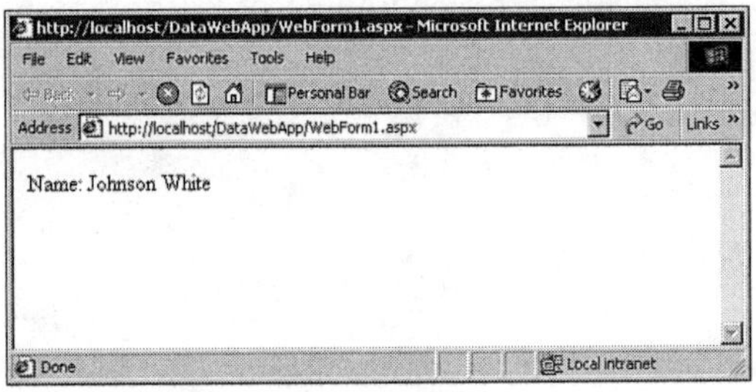

FIGURE 6.2

The first author's name is displayed in the ASP.NET page.

Displaying the first author's first and last names isn't exactly the most exciting thing you can do. Instead, you could list all of the fields for the authors, in an HTML table. You'll now modify the code between the commented lines in order to loop through all the records and build an HTML table that displays the results. Don't worry if you aren't an HTML wizard; that is not as important in this example as understanding what is happening with the data.

In this next example, you will loop through all the records coming back into the DataReader. In the past, you would have used a Do...Loop in order to determine the end-of-file (EOF) marker in a stream of data. With the DataReader, you simply check the Read method. It returns True as long as there are additional records, and returns False when no records are left. Therefore, your loop will look something like this:

```
While dr.Read...
' display code goes here
End While
```

This code will effectively loop you through all the records in a forward-only pass through the data. Within the loop, you will have code to display the individual fields. If you know the names of the fields, you can use the names as you did in the previous example. Or you can use the index numbers of the fields, starting at zero. In fact, you can use a For...Next loop to loop through the fields, from zero to the number of fields minus one. Your code would look something like this:

```
For iField = 0 To dr.FieldCount - 1
    Response.Write(dr(iField))
Next
```

Just running the code as shown so far won't produce very nice results inside a Web page. Instead, you can place the data in an HTML table, where each field is placed in its own cell, and each record is a separate row in the table. To accomplish this, change the code inside the comments so that the end result looks like Listing 6.2.

LISTING 6.2   A Simple Web Page Displaying All Records from the Authors Table

```
'*** Lines below will be changing ***
Response.Write("<table border=1><tr>")
While dr.Read
    Dim iField As Integer
    For iField = 0 To dr.FieldCount - 1
        Response.Write("<td>" & dr(iField) & "</td>")
    Next
    Response.Write("</tr><tr>")
End While
Response.Write("</tr></table>")
'*** Lines above will be changing ***
```

If you run this page, your results should look something like those seen in Figure 6.3.

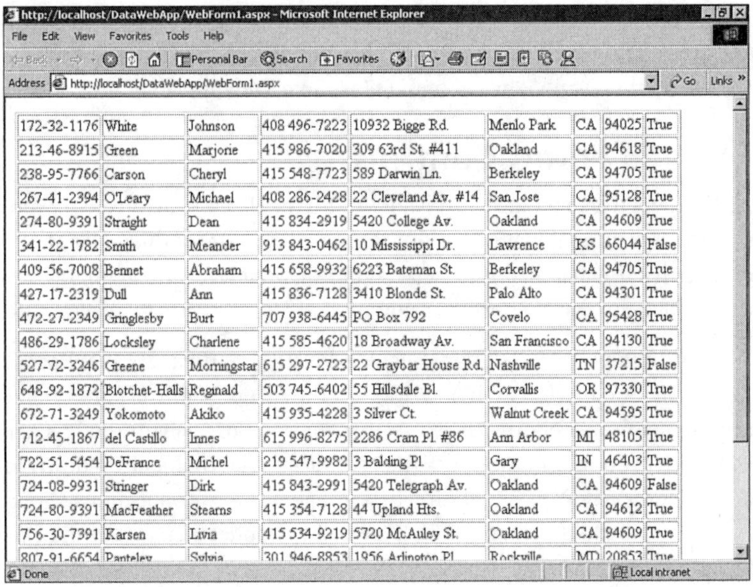

FIGURE 6.3
All the authors displayed in an HTML table.

Using the `DataReader` to quickly scroll through the records is a common approach to dealing with data in a Web page. After all, Web pages are processed on the server and then displayed on the client. You rarely need to have a fully scrollable set of records when building a Web application. Therefore, the `DataReader` is often used for Web applications, and is very similar to the forward-only cursor used by many ADO developers today.

Although much has been made about ADO.NET's disconnected architecture, the `DataReader` uses a connected model. You are connected as you loop through the records, and the `Connection` object cannot be used for any other purpose as long as a `DataReader` is open. Therefore, when using a `DataReader`, you want to make sure that you loop through the records as soon as possible and then close the `DataReader`, freeing up the `Connection` object to carry out other tasks.

Even though the `DataReader` uses a connected paradigm similar to what ADO uses, the `DataReader` tends to be the most efficient way to bring records from the server to the client. In this case, the client is the ASP.NET page, not the client browser. Bringing the data from the server to the client can be done in other ways, but the `DataReader` tends to be the most efficient because it does not have to create a scrollable cursor of any sort. However, the data is not stored in memory on the client, so each time the page is called, it requires a trip to the server. In contrast, ADO.NET's object for storing data in memory, the `DataSet`, caches data in memory, making subsequent accesses of the data faster as long as the object is still in memory. Because a Web page falls out of scope after processing, the DataSet would be lost, which means that the DataSet does not always make sense in a Web application.

Using the Web Forms Controls

Using the graphical controls included in Visual Studio .NET, you can create a Web page that displays data without writing much code. You'll still have to write some code, but the creation of the HTML table itself is handled by a server control, which frees you up to concentrate on working with the data, not formatting it for output.

Add a new Web Form to your VS .NET project, and just leave it named WebForm2.aspx. Now, from the Toolbar, click on the Data tab and drag over a SqlConnection control and drop it on the WebForm designer for WebForm2.aspx. A new control, SqlConnection1, is added to the component tray of WebForm2. In the Properties window, click on the drop-down arrow in the ConnectionString property. You might already see one or more connections showing up, but assume that you have to add a new one. Click on <New Connection...> and the Data Link Properties dialog will open.

Enter your server name, the username and password you want to use, and the database (Pubs) you want to use. Your screen should look something like the one in Figure 6.4. Click the OK button on the Data Link Properties dialog box and you will see the ConnectionString property has been filled in with the appropriate data.

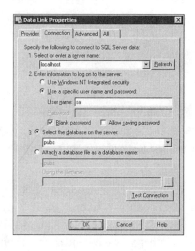

FIGURE 6.4
The Data Link Properties dialog box.

Next, drag a `SqlCommand` control from the Data tab of the Toolbox onto the designer. A new control, `SqlCommand1`, is added to the component tray. In the Properties window, expand the Existing node of the tree view to see the available connections, and set the `Connection` property to `SqlConnection1`. In the `CommandText` property, enter the following SQL statement:

```
Select * from Authors
```

After clicking OK, you will be prompted with a question asking if you want to regenerate the parameters collection. There are no parameters, so you can safely click No. On the other hand, you can also safely click Yes. This prompt is just asking you whether you want to automatically re-create a collection with all the parameters in the query. For example, you could add parameters that are passed in at runtime.

So far, you have done with controls what you did in code before. You have a graphical representation of an ADO.NET `SqlConnection` object; in this case, called `SqlConnection1`. It has a connection string to connect you to the Pubs database on a particular server. You also have a graphical representation of an ADO.NET `SqlCommand` object, named `SqlCommand1`. It uses the `SqlConnection1 Connection` object, and it issues the command to retrieve all the fields and all the records from the Authors table. This was all done with code in the previous example, but so far you haven't written any code.

Now, return to the Toolbox, but go to the Web Forms tab. Drag a `DataGrid` control from the Toolbox and drop it on the Web Form. If you prefer, you can click the Auto Format link in the Properties window and choose a format for the table, which adds colors and changes the font. When you are done, your form should look like the one shown in Figure 6.5, with the two controls in the component tray and the `DataGrid` on the form itself.

Before moving forward, you need to add some code. Think about what you've done: You've created a connection and a command, but you need something to actually retrieve the records. In keeping with the previous example, you need to create a `DataReader` and display the data on the Web page. However, it is easier when working with the controls, as you'll see when you write the code.

Go to the code view and find the `Page_Load` subroutine. You're going to add code to open the connection and then use the `ExecuteReader` method of the `SqlConnection1` object to create a `DataReader`. Then you will bind the `DataGrid` to the `DataReader`, and you can then close the `DataReader` and the `Connection`. You do not need to loop through the `DataReader`, nor do you need to format the data for output. Instead, the `DataGrid` will handle all of this for you.

Go to the code window and at the top, add your `Imports System.Data.SqlClient` command. In the `Page_Load` subroutine, enter the code in Listing 6.3.

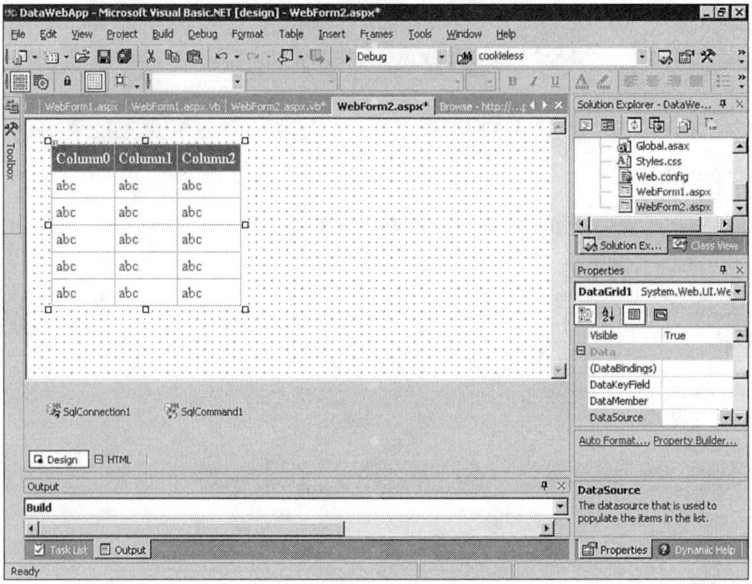

Figure 6.5

The Web Form with controls being used to create some of the data objects.

Listing 6.3 The Code Necessary to Bind a DataGrid Control to a DataReader Control Created Programmatically

```
Private Sub Page_Load(ByVal sender As System.Object, _
  ByVal e As System.EventArgs) Handles MyBase.Load
    SqlConnection1.Open()
    Dim dr As sqlDataReader
    dr = SqlCommand1.ExecuteReader()
    DataGrid1.DataSource = dr
    DataGrid1.DataBind()
    dr.Close()
    SqlConnection1.Close()
End Sub
```

The easiest way to view the page now is to save it, but then right-click on WebForm2.aspx in the Solution Explorer window and choose Build and Browse. This opens the page within the browser in VS .NET, as shown in Figure 6.6.

So far, you've seen two examples of using ADO.NET in a connected mode, similar to what you were likely doing with ADO. What about this ballyhooed disconnected model? That's where the DataSet comes into play.

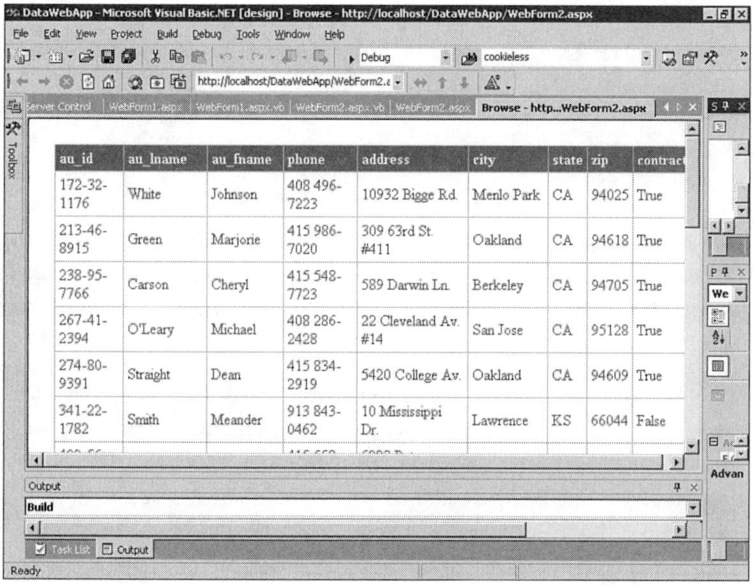

FIGURE 6.6
Data being displayed in a Web page, thanks to ASP.NET server controls and a little code.

Objects for Disconnected Data

As has already been discussed, ADO.NET leans heavily toward a disconnected model. This is because of scalability and performance, as discussed earlier. To this point, however, your data access has been in a strictly connected mode, in which you connect to the database, process the records one at a time, and disconnect. The disconnected model, of course, has you retrieving the records, but you cache them in memory, and you can (and should) close the connection before you begin working with the records. You should close the connection because doing so means that the entire time you're scrolling through the records, formatting them for output, and allowing people to sort or filter the data, you are not consuming expensive database connections.

To accomplish disconnected access in ADO, you used the Recordset object. However, that is the same object you used to access data in a forward-only manner, as you just did using the DataReader. This is one of the fundamental differences between ADO and ADO.NET: ADO used the same object (the Recordset) to perform connected and disconnected operations. ADO.NET separates connected and disconnected operations into separate components, the DataReader and DataSet, respectively.

Understanding the DataSet is critical to much of what you do with ADO.NET. It offers the ability to create much more scalable applications, and to share data more efficiently and more widely, than ever before. The DataSet makes working with XML easier, whether it acts as an XML consumer or producer. Therefore, it is important to understand a bit about the DataSet, and then see a quick example of the DataSet in action.

The DataSet and DataAdapter Objects

The DataSet object is a cache for storing disconnected data. ADO could cache data in a Recordset object, but that is one of the only similarities between the Recordset and the DataSet. The DataSet is designed to work like an in-memory database in some ways; it stores data in a schema, and this schema can include multiple tables, the relationships between the tables, and some constraints on those tables.

The DataSet needs this schema because it has no knowledge of the underlying data source (or sources, as the case may be). The DataSet is separated from the data source with another layer of indirection, much like ODBC acted as a layer of indirection between applications and the back-end database. Between the DataSet and its underlying data source sits the DataAdapter. The DataAdapter handles the messy details of actually retrieving data to fill the DataSet, and then taking changes to the data in the DataSet and synchronizing those changes with the underlying data source.

The DataSet schema is created with other objects, and the DataSet includes collections for holding these objects. The Tables collection holds one or more DataTable objects, and the Relations collection holds one or more DataRelation objects. Within the DataTable object, you have collections storing rows and columns, as well as collections storing parent and child relationships. These objects allow you to model a relational schema in memory, and this schema can be filled with data as you retrieve it from the database.

If you take any DataSet's schema, that schema can be defined as an XML Schema. As you will see in a moment, when you use VS .NET to generate a DataSet for you, an XML Schema file (XSD) is created for you. This XSD file describes the schema found in the DataSet. DataSets can also read and write XML Schemas natively, or they can look at data in XML format and infer a schema from the data if no XSD file is present.

Filling the DataSet

As you know, the DataSet is used to cache data in a disconnected mode from the underlying data source. In addition, the DataSet has no knowledge of the underlying data source. Therefore, how does the data get from the underlying data source into the DataSet? ADO.NET provides you with the DataAdapter, an object that acts as the intermediary between the DataSet and the underlying data source. The DataAdapter uses a Connection object, and then acts as one or more Command objects to actually perform selects, inserts, updates, and deletes.

Just as there are specific managed provider objects such as the SqlConnection and OleDbConnection objects for connections, and the SqlDataReader and OleDbDataReader objects, the `DataAdapter` comes in two flavors in VS .NET: the `SqlDataAdapter` and the `OleDbDataAdapter`. The `DataAdapter` is used to retrieve data from a data source and populate the `DataTables` in the `DataSet`. After the data is moved into the `DataSet`, the `DataSet` works with the data in memory as if it were the actual database, performing inserts, updates, and deletes. These changes are only occurring in memory, and when the changes need to be synchronized with the underlying data source, it is once again the job of the `DataAdapter` to take all the changes and modify the underlying source data appropriately.

Because of the ability to build a schema in the `DataSet`, you might actually have numerous `DataAdapters` filling the same `DataSet`. For example, imagine that you had to work with data in both SQL Server and Oracle. A change to a record in Oracle required an insert into a table in SQL Server. You could build one `DataSet` that contained tables representing the data from both SQL Server and Oracle. Now, your application works with one consistent schema. The `DataAdapters`, however, manage the difficult work of making the changes in the underlying data sources when you decide to commit the changes.

Using the `DataSet`

You have already seen an example of an application that uses the `DataReader`. In that example, you first did all the work programmatically, and then you used some of VS .NET's controls to help you along. Now, it is time to look at an example using a `DataSet`.

You will create a simple Windows application that displays the data in a grid. However, in this case, you will also be able to modify the data, which will be handled for you by the `DataAdapter`.

Create a new Windows Application project in VS .NET and name it DataWinApp, and again choose either VB .NET or C#. You will have a form designer showing. Click on the Toolbox and choose the Data tab. From the Data tab, drag a `SqlDataAdapter` object onto the form (or drag an `OleDbDataAdapter` if you are using a database other than SQL Server).

Dropping the control on the Windows form launches the Data Adapter Configuration Wizard (the "wizard" for the rest of this example). The first screen is just for informational purposes, so go ahead and click the Next button.

The first real screen of the wizard asks you to choose the data connection. This might already contain connections you have created, but assume for a moment it does not. Click on the New Connection button and the Data Link Properties dialog will open. Enter your server name, the username and password you want to use, and the database (Pubs) you want to use. Your screen should look something like the one in Figure 6.4. Click the OK button on the Data Link Properties dialog box and your wizard screen should now look similar to the one shown in Figure 6.7. Click the Next button to advance into the wizard.

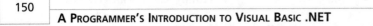

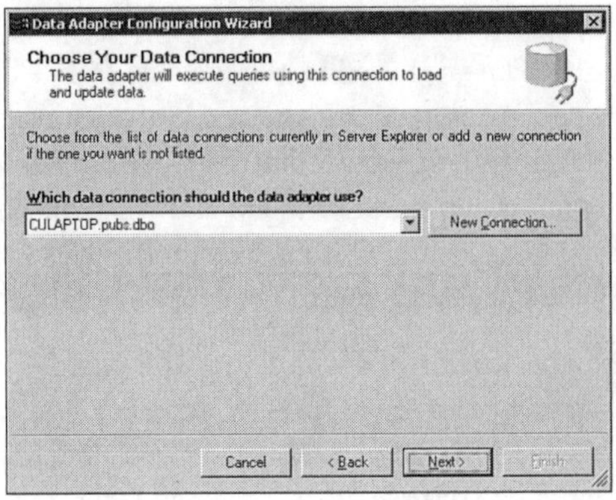

FIGURE 6.7
The Data Connection page of the Data Adapter Configuration Wizard.

The next screen in the wizard asks you what type of query you want to use. Stored procedures are almost always the best way to go, but in this example, you can get by with just typing in a SQL statement. Leave the first option chosen, as shown in Figure 6.8, and click the Next button.

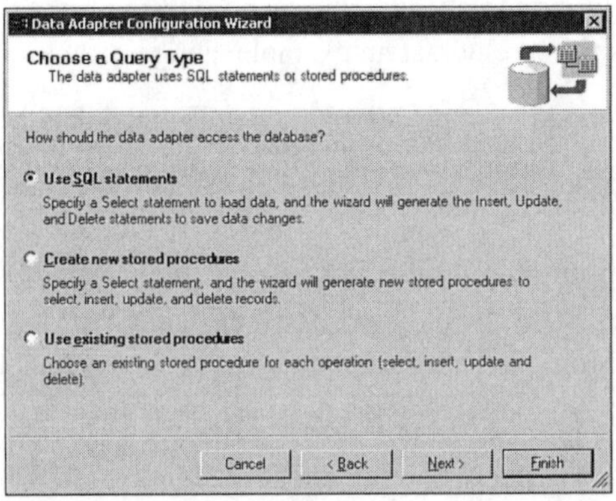

FIGURE 6.8
Choosing the type of query in the Data Adapter Configuration Wizard.

The next screen of the wizard asks you to enter the SQL statement. You do have the option of using the Query Builder, a tool for visually creating your queries. For now, just enter the same SQL statement you used before, which is

```
Select * from Authors
```

After you have typed the SQL statement, as shown in Figure 6.9, click the Next button. The final screen of the wizard shows you what the wizard has done for you, so just click the Finish button.

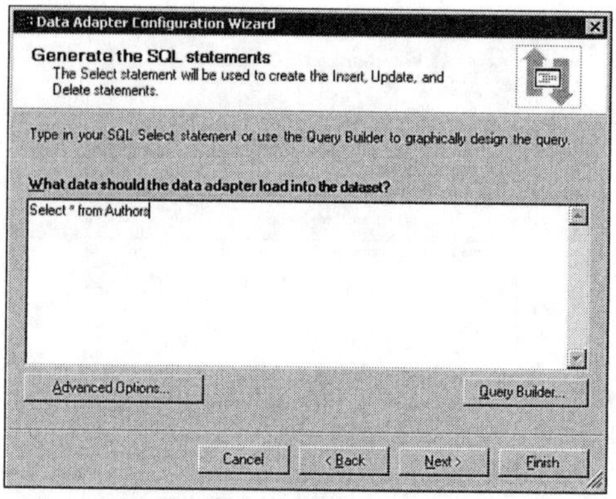

FIGURE 6.9

Entering the SQL statement in the Data Adapter Configuration Wizard.

You are now returned to VS .NET, and you can see that two controls have been added to your form. These controls, named SqlConnection1 and SqlAdapter1, appear in the component tray under the form. The SqlConnection1 control represents a SqlConnection object, just like the one you created in code in the last example. The SqlAdapter1 control represents an encapsulation of the data connection and one or more data commands.

Notice also that a new menu has been added to VS .NET: the Data menu. Click on the Data menu and choose Generate Dataset. A dialog box opens that asks you if you want to generate an existing or new dataset. Click on the New radio button and name the dataset dsAuthors. Make sure that the Authors table is checked, and also make sure that the option to add the dataset to the designer is checked. These options are visible in Figure 6.10. Click the OK button when you are finished.

A couple of things happen when you close the Generate Dataset dialog box. First, a DsAuthors1 control is added to the component tray. This is a graphical representation of the dataset, which will be used to cache data in memory. Second, a dsAuthors.xsd file is added to the project, and is visible in the Solution Explorer window. This file is an XML Schema of the dataset you will be creating.

You now have your data objects created and ready to go. However, you need something to display them on the form, so you can use a Windows Forms control to do this. Click on the Toolbox and choose the Windows Forms tab. Drag a DataGrid control onto the Windows form designer, and resize it as you desire. This DataGrid can automatically bind to a DataSet, as you will see in a moment.

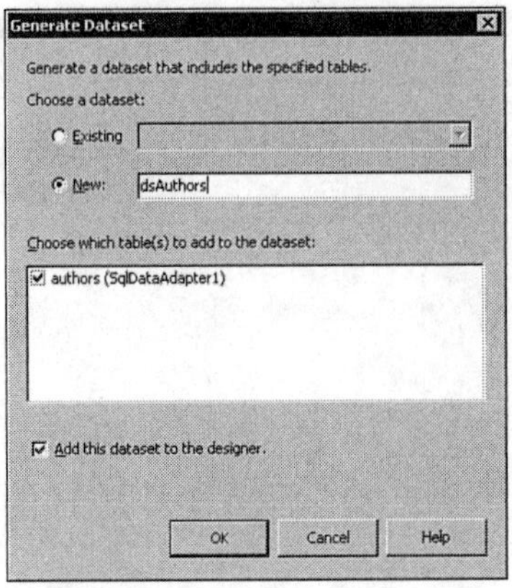

FIGURE 6.10

The Generate Dataset dialog box being used to generate a dataset based on the Authors table.

In the Properties window, find the DataSource property for the DataGrid and set it to DsAuthors1. Next, set the DataMember property to authors. This is necessary because a DataSet could contain multiple tables (called *DataTables*), so you must specify to which table this DataGrid will bind. By default, the DataGrid will set up a column for each field in the DataTable to which you bind it.

Finally, add two buttons to your form, under the grid. Label one of the buttons Load, and name it cmdLoadData. Label the other button Update, and name it cmdUpdateData. Your project should now look similar to the project in Figure 6.11.

In Figure 6.11, you'll notice the three data controls in the component tray under the form designer, the DataGrid and two buttons on the form designer, and the dsAuthors.xsd file in the Solution Explorer window. You have all pieces in place, except for the code.

The step at this point is to double-click on the Load button, and add the code to actually fill the DataSet so that it can be bound to the DataGrid. Make the code for the procedure look like this:

```
Private Sub cmdLoadData_Click(ByVal sender As System.Object, _
  ByVal e As System.EventArgs) Handles cmdLoadData.Click
    SqlDataAdapter1.Fill(DsAuthors1)
End Sub
```

If you look at this, you've only added one line of code. Nowhere in this code do you see an explicit opening or closing of the connection. Nor do you see any sort of execute statement being issued. This is because the DataAdapter encapsulates both the connection and the command, and the Fill method automatically connects you to the server, issues the command, and places the returning data into the DataSet. Go ahead and run the application. After clicking the Load button, you should have the data loaded into the grid, as shown in Figure 6.12.

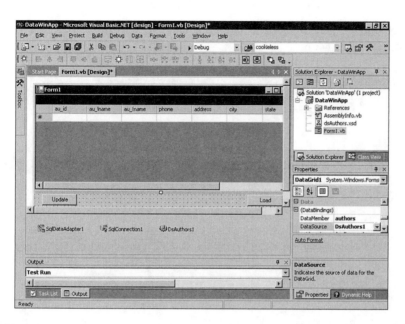

FIGURE 6.11

Your new form, with all the controls added and properties set.

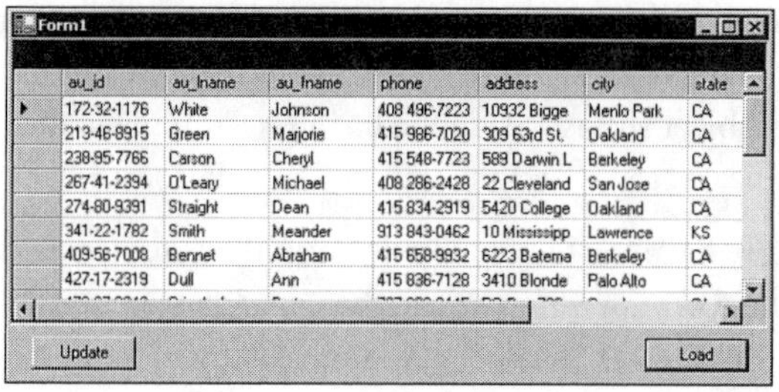

FIGURE 6.12

The data in a DataSet *being displayed in a grid in a Windows form.*

While viewing the data in the grid, you can make some changes to the data. For example, the first author listed is Johnson White. Change his last name to Whitehall. As you begin typing, the symbol on the left margin of that row becomes a pencil, meaning that the record is being edited. When you are done, move to another row, and you will notice the change has been made.

Now, however, open the SQL Query Analyzer (or the SQL tool of your choice) and query the data in the Authors table. As you can see in Figure 6.13, Johnson White's last name is still

White. You changed the data in the grid, and it seemed to accept the change, but the data in the table in SQL Server has not been updated.

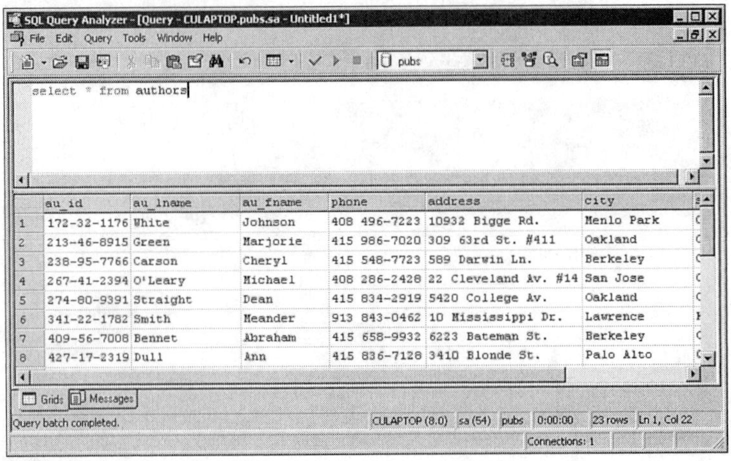

FIGURE 6.13

Despite the changes you made in the grid, the data has been updated only in the DataSet, *not in the underlying data source.*

Remember that the DataSet has no knowledge of the underlying data source. When you changed Johnson White's last name to Whitehall, you did update the value in a table. However, that table is a DataTable object sitting inside the DataSet. You made the change to the disconnected data you have in the DataSet, and the underlying data source has never been touched.

To get changes made in the DataSet to actually occur in the source data, you need to call upon the DataAdapter to do the work for you. Having the DataAdapter update the underlying data source with your changes in the DataSet is easy, until you start running into concurrency conflicts. For now, you'll see it the easy way, by adding the following code:

```
Private Sub cmdUpdateData_Click(ByVal sender As System.Object, _
  ByVal e As System.EventArgs) Handles cmdUpdateData.Click
    SqlDataAdapter1.Update(DsAuthors1)
End Sub
```

Again, one line of code is all it takes. The Update method takes the changes (inserts, updates, and deletes) in the DataSet and attempts to apply those changes to the underlying data source. Rerun the application, click the Load button, and then change Johnson White's last name to Whitehall. This time, however, click the Update button when you have changed his name. Now, check the data in SQL Query Analyzer again, and notice that, as shown in Figure 6.14, the data has been updated to reflect the value you changed in the DataGrid.

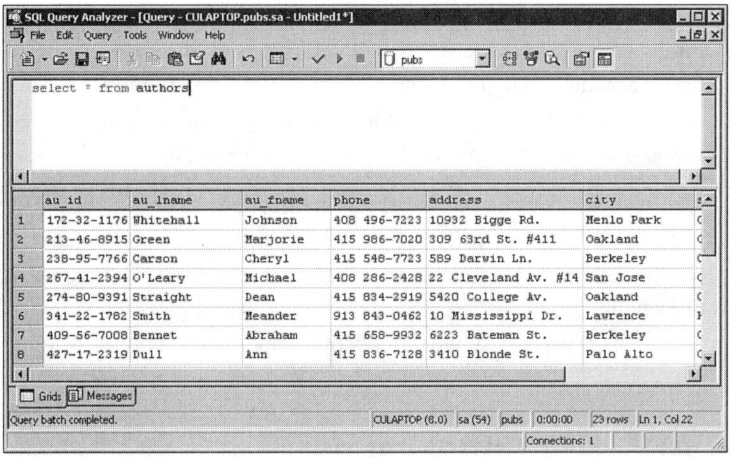

FIGURE 6.14
Using the DataAdapter*'s Update method, changes in the* DataSet *can flow back to the underlying data source.*

You have now built an application that uses the DataSet to populate a DataGrid, and you have allowed for changes in the data to be synchronized with the underlying data source. It only took some dragging and dropping and two lines of code for these simple examples.

Comparing ADO and ADO.NET

Most people reading this book will have some level of familiarity with ADO. For those people, it is useful to provide a discussion comparing ADO.NET to the familiar ground of ADO. If you have not had ADO experience, this section might still provide you with meaningful information, or you can skip to the end of the chapter.

Much has been written, and much more will be written, about ADO.NET's disconnected methodology. ADO operated in a connected mode, although it did contain some support for disconnected recordsets. ADO provided a consistent set of objects to access relational and non-relational data, allowing the developer great flexibility in using a consistent interface to a wide variety of data. However, the reliance on a connection in ADO limited the scalability of applications. In addition, the way ADO accessed and cached data led many developers to unwittingly use methods that were far less efficient than they could have been. This meant that applications could run much slower and consume far more overhead than should have been required.

ADO.NET seeks to streamline the objects, properties, and methods to ensure that the developer is making better choices. For example, ADO let you create a recordset in three ways: You could use the Execute method of the Connection object; you could use the Execute method of the Command object; or you could use the Open method of the Recordset object. Each method had its own strengths and weaknesses, but few developers took the time to determine when to use one method over another. ADO.NET, on the other hand, greatly reduces the options you have for retrieving data and storing it in memory, providing a much more focused approach when it comes to maximizing performance and lowering overhead.

ADO.NET also seeks to support the new world of applications distributed over the Internet. Not only are components placed on different machines within the same organization, but also they may be placed on different machines located around the world. Tying these components to applications is one challenge, but efficiently passing data from one component to another becomes quite a challenge, especially when a client component might not be on the .NET Framework.

ADO and ADO.NET Connections

The connections in ADO and ADO.NET are fairly similar. Both are used to connect to an underlying data source. Both have a ConnectionString property that defines what server and database they will connect to, and what security to use to make the connection. This means that the connection strings look similar in both ADO and ADO.NET, so ADO developers will feel right at home.

In addition, to actually open a connection, both ADO and ADO.NET have an Open method on the Connection objects. Unlike ADO, however, each managed provider in ADO.NET uses its own Connection object. For example, VS .NET ships with both the OleDbConnection and SqlConnection objects, and there will be more as additional .NET managed providers come online.

ADO and ADO.NET Connection objects can both start transactions. Transaction handling can be done in ADO or ADO.NET, or it can be handled by COM+ Component Services (called Microsoft Transaction Server, or MTS, in NT 4.0). In ADO, the Connection object had methods to start, commit, and roll back transactions. In ADO.NET, the Connection object starts a transaction, but it actually creates a transaction object that contains the commit and rollback methods.

One of the biggest changes from the ADO to ADO.NET Connection objects is that the ADO.NET Connection objects no longer contain an Execute method. In ADO, it became quite common to create a Connection object and then use that connection to issue a SQL statement, completely bypassing the need for a Command object. However, the Connection object did not always give you the most efficient way to execute commands, so ADO.NET has removed that capability, requiring you to use the Command objects (or the DataAdapter objects) to execute commands. This is one area where ADO.NET should improve application performance by removing a potentially inefficient shortcut and requiring developers to use the right objects for the job.

ADO and ADO.NET Commands and the `DataAdapter`

ADO had a powerful `Command` object that was often underutilized, especially by novice developers. The `Command` object was incredibly powerful when working with stored procedures, and that was its forte. When simply issuing SQL text, however, most developers opted for the ADO `Connection` object's `Execute` method. This is a shame because the vast majority of the time, code should be in stored procedures if at all possible because stored procedures are precompiled and their query plans (which indexes to use, and so forth) are already determined. Performance of stored procedures is usually vastly superior to passing a string to the parser and having it optimize the query with each call.

ADO.NET forces you to use the `Command` object more often, because the `Execute` method is no longer found on `Connection` objects. Now, you will use the `Command` object to call stored procedures or to execute SQL statements as text. This actually adds a level of consistency to ADO.NET that should lead to better applications as a whole.

ADO.NET's `Connection` objects actually include four types of `Execute` statements, each one of which is designed for a specific purpose. These Execute methods are finely tuned to return certain types of data, which should lead to more efficient database access. For example, the `ExecuteNonQuery` method is used to issue statements that do not return records, such as inserts, updates, deletes, dropping or creating of database objects, and so forth. By using `ExecuteNonQuery`, you prevent ADO.NET from having to create a `DataReader` object in memory, which requires overhead you want to avoid if possible. To achieve this sort of thing with ADO, you used the `Execute` method of the `Command` or `Connection` objects, but you had to add the magic `adExecuteNoRecords` constant to the end of the `Execute`. In ADO, executing a command meant calling the `Execute` method, and it was up to the developer to remember to put the `adExecuteNoRecords` constant in the method call. With ADO.NET, the developer has to decide which `Execute` method to use in each situation.

The `DataAdapter` does not have a correlation to a single ADO object. Instead, the `DataAdapter` represents a data connection and one or more commands. The `Command` object mentioned earlier exists to work in ADO.NET's connected mode, whereas the `DataAdapter` is used for the disconnected mode. The `DataAdapter` takes the data from the underlying data source and puts that data in the `DataSet`, ADO.NET's disconnected data caching object. The `DataAdapter` encapsulates all the connection and schema details about the data source, freeing the `DataSet` to manage the data, not how to access the data. The `DataAdapter` also steps in and fills the role when it comes time to update the underlying data sources. The `DataSet`, having no knowledge of the underlying data sources, must call on the `DataAdapter`, which handles making the changes back in the source data.

Recordsets, DataSets, and the DataReader

In ADO, the `Recordset` object held data in memory. In most cases, the `Recordset` utilized a client-side or server-side cursor to access data. Cursors are quite expensive for any database to handle, and minimizing cursors is one of the goals of most application developers. One way to avoid opening an expensive cursor in ADO was to use the ADO `Recordset` object's `Open` method. Using the `Open` method, you could specify the type of cursor to use, and one of those was the `adForwardOnly` cursor, which did not actually create a cursor. This was often called the *firehose cursor* and was the fastest way to stream data down.

ADO.NET provides a `DataReader` object, which is an object built for retrieving data in a forward-only, or firehose, method. The `DataReader` is roughly equivalent to the `Recordset` in ADO when the `Recordset` was opened with the `adForwardOnly` cursor type chosen. By forcing this into a new type of object, the developer is removed from having to remember to specify the `adForwardOnly` cursor type.

> **NOTE**
>
> The default cursor type in ADO is supposed to be the `adForwardOnly` cursor. However, it is always good to specify the value to ensure that you are getting the firehose when you want it.

Perhaps one of the most dramatic changes from ADO to ADO.NET is when you want to have data in something other than a firehose cursor. With the firehose, you can only scroll through the records one at a time in a forward direction. If you need a fully scrollable cursor, you use the `DataSet`. The `DataSet` acts somewhat like an ADO `Recordset` that used a Static cursor: It contains a copy of the data in memory, it is fully scrollable, and it is disconnected from the data source (the ADO `Recordset` with a static cursor could operate just fine, even if the connection was closed).

Where the `DataSet` is different from the ADO `Recordset` is in how it actually stores the data. In ADO, if you wanted data from multiple tables, you had to use the Join syntax in SQL to join the tables. The data you brought back, however, looked like a single table. With the `DataSet`, however, you could retrieve the data from each table independently and store the data in separate `DataTable` objects within the `DataSet`. You could then define `DataRelation` objects between the tables, building an entire schema in memory. The issue, of course, becomes just how much of your database you actually store in memory. Some developers will want to copy the entire database into memory, but the sheer volume of data could make this a losing proposition. Instead, you'll want to cache only necessary data locally, and if any of the data could be modified by others, you'll want to move your changes back to the underlying database often.

By being disconnected, the DataSet can be much more scalable than the Recordset. Although the Recordset could operate in a disconnected fashion, it could also operate in a connected fashion using keyset or dynamic cursors. These modes could be terribly expensive for the server, requiring a live connection, frequent base table reads, and cursor sets stored in memory. The DataSet avoids cursors by operating only in a disconnected state.

Finally, the data in a Recordset was not always easily passed from one process to another. Passing even a disconnected Recordset required COM marshalling, a process that was limited to only COM-standard data types. Any nonstandard data types had to be converted, which further slowed down the process. DataSets, meanwhile, simply transmit data as XML. No conversion or marshalling is required. XML also flows freely through firewalls, which was often not the case with the binary format of COM marshalling.

Summary

As you can see, ADO.NET represents a major change in the way of thinking about accessing and working with data. ADO.NET can operate in either a connected or disconnected mode, just as ADO could. However, ADO.NET uses separate objects for working with connected and disconnected data.

ADO.NET uses managed providers to access data. Each managed provider provides its own set of objects. The SQL Server managed provider, for example, provides objects such as the SqlConnection and SqlDataReader objects. The OLE DB managed provider provides OleDbConnection and OleDbDataReader objects.

For connected data access, ADO.NET uses a Connection object to connect to the database, a Command object to issue SQL statements or call stored procedures, and a DataReader object to retrieve data in a highly efficient, forward-only method. The records are not cached in memory, but instead are brought down for immediate access. This is the most common technique for making a simple pass through the data.

For working in the disconnected mode, ADO.NET provides a DataAdapter, which encapsulates a Connection and one or more Commands. The DataAdapter retrieves the records, but it doesn't actually store them; instead, the data is stored in a DataSet object, which stores data in an in-memory schema. Data in a DataSet can be accessed as if it were a regular database, and it can be modified. Data modifications made in the DataSet can be synchronized with the underlying data sources using the DataAdapter object.

ADO.NET uses a disconnected model in order to increase scalability, and it speaks XML to allow for efficient data passing. The DataSet's schema information can be written as an XML Schema (an XSD) and the DataSet can write its data out in XML format. The DataSet can also directly read XML as a data source.

Upgrading VB6 Projects to VB .NET

IN THIS CHAPTER

So far, this book has focused on learning Visual Basic .NET, and how it differs from VB6. However, most readers have many projects written in VB6, and want to port those applications to VB .NET. Recoding every VB6 application into VB .NET is not something most people want to do, so it is helpful to see how VB .NET handles upgrading your applications.

Upgrading applications is a two-part process: First, you will use the Visual Basic Upgrade Wizard (sometimes called the *Migration Wizard*) to convert your VB6 application to a VB .NET application. Second, you will probably need to make some modifications to complete the upgrade process.

You can improve the conversion and minimize the number of changes you need to make by making a few modifications to your VB6 code. For example, avoiding the use of late-bound variables in your VB6 code is helpful to the wizard when it comes time to migrate. Other suggestions will be examined later.

Upgrading Your First VB6 Application

To get a feel for what the Migration Wizard does for you and what modifications you'll need to make, you will create a new, simple VB6 application and then run it through the Migration Wizard.

Start VB6 and create a new Standard EXE project. Put a text box, a list box, and two buttons on the form. Using the Properties window, change the Sorted property of the list box to True.

Double-click on the first button to open the code window. Enter the following code in the Command1_Click event procedure:

```
Private Sub Command1_Click()
    List1.AddItem Text1
    List1.ListIndex = List1.NewIndex
End Sub
```

Press F5 to run the application. Notice that each time you click the command button, the contents of the text box are added to the list box. The list box displays the text in alphabetical order, and selects each line of text as it is added. Now, stop the application and return to VB6. Add a second form to your application. Add a label to the form and resize it to make it larger than normal. Double-click on the form and add the following code in the Form_Load event handler:

```
Private Sub Form_Load()
    Label1 = "The text entered on Form1 is: " & Form1.Text1
End Sub
```

Go back to `Form1`, and add the following code to the `Command2_Click` event procedure:

```
Private Sub Command2_Click()
    Form2.Show
End Sub
```

You now have an application with two forms. One button adds the values entered in the text box to a list box on `Form1`. The second button opens the second form, which has a reference back to the first form. You can run the application to make sure that it works. Save the project as `VB6upgrade.vbp` and save the forms with any name you choose; this example will assume that you left them named `Form1.frm` and `Form2.frm`.

Save the application with the name VB6upgrade. Close VB6 and open VB .NET. Choose to open an existing project and open the `VB6upgrade.vbp` file you just created. Opening a VB6 project in VB .NET automatically starts the Visual Basic Upgrade Wizard.

The Visual Basic Upgrade Wizard

The Visual Basic Upgrade Wizard starts automatically because you opened a VB6 project in VB .NET. The first screen just displays some general information, so click the Next button to move into the wizard.

Step 2 of the wizard is shown in Figure 7.1. In most cases, you will leave the options at their default settings, but we will examine the options here for completeness. First, the wizard asks you what type of project you are upgrading. In this case, your only choice is EXE, and that is correct. (If you were upgrading an ActiveX EXE server, you would have the choice to upgrade it to an EXE or DLL.) Below that is one check box; this option tells the wizard to generate default interfaces for any public classes you created. This is useful if the project is a DLL that exposes base classes that are implemented by other applications. Because you do not have any public classes, you can ignore this option. Leave the page as you see it in Figure 7.1 and click the Next button.

Step 3 of the wizard asks for the location of the resulting .NET project. By default, the wizard places the VB .NET project in a new directory inside the VB6 project directory called `<projectname>.NET`. If you want, you can change the path to another name and click the Next button.

Step 4 of the wizard says that you are now ready to upgrade. So, if you click the Next button, the upgrade will start, and at the conclusion of the upgrade, the upgraded project will open in Visual Basic .NET. The wizard always creates a new project; the old VB6 project is left unchanged.

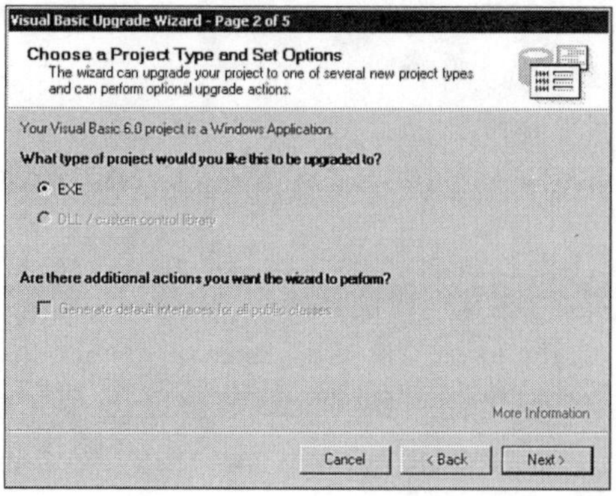

FIGURE 7.1

Step 2 of the Visual Basic Upgrade Wizard.

Remember from before that you will have to make some modifications to your project after it is upgraded? Well, the Upgrade Wizard creates an upgrade report in HTML format that lists those modifications. This report shows up in the Solution Explorer as _UpgradeReport.htm, so you'll need to double-click on it to open it. Even though this was a very simple application, one error is reported. Figure 7.2 shows the upgrade report, with the section for Form1 expanded to show the details of the error that was generated.

Examining the Upgraded Forms and Code

Now, double-click on Form1.vb to open it in the designer. Notice first that a ToolTip1 control shows up in the component tray at the bottom of the form. By default, controls in VB .NET do not have a ToolTip property. Therefore, you must add a ToolTip control to a form for your controls on that form to have a ToolTip property.

Double-click on Command1 to get to the code view. Notice that the line of code in the event handler has changed. The old line was:

```
List1.AddItem Text1
```

The wizard has upgraded that code to the following line:

```
List1.Items.Add(Text1.Text)
```

First, you now have parentheses around the argument. You saw this in Chapter 2, "Your First VB .NET Application." Also, in VB6, you referred to Text1, but in VB .NET, this has changed to Text1.Text. This should not be surprising because you have learned that VB .NET does not support default properties unless they accept parameters. You'll also notice that the method has changed from List1.AddItem to List1.Items.Add.

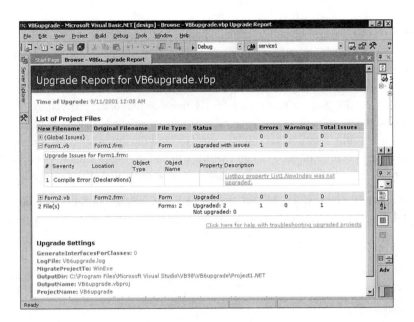

FIGURE 7.2
The upgrade report is created by the Upgrade Wizard as it upgrades your VB6 projects to VB .NET.

Also notice that an upgrade issue was added that alerts you to a problem with the following line:

```
'UPGRADE_ISSUE: ListBox property List1.NewIndex was not upgraded.
Click for more: ms-help://MS.MSDNVS/vbcon/html/vbup2059.htm
List1.SelectedIndex = List1.NewIndex
```

If you click on the Click for more hyperlink, you will be taken to a help topic that explains the issue. In VB6, the `ListBox.NewIndex` property returned the index of the most recently added item. In VB .NET, the property doesn't exist; the index of the newly added item is returned from the `Items.Add` method.

To fix the problem, change the body of the event to this:

```
Private Sub Command1_Click(ByVal eventSender As System.Object, _
 ByVal eventArgs As System.EventArgs) Handles Command1.Click
   Dim NewIndex As Integer
   NewIndex = List1.Items.Add(Text1.Text)
   List1.SelectedIndex = NewIndex
End Sub
```

Running this project reveals that all the code runs fine, and the project works as it did before. Not all projects will transition as smoothly, of course.

Modifications

Why do you need to make modifications yourself? Why can't the upgrade tool do the entire upgrade for you? The answer to this is twofold. In some cases (as in the preceding example), there is not an exact one-to-one correlation between the way code is written in VB6 and the equivalent in VB .NET. So, the best option for the upgrade tool is to alert you to the difference and tell you what you should change yourself. The second reason is that VB6 code that uses late binding is not fully interpreted until it is run. Because the upgrade tool examines the design-time representation of code, it can't perform default property resolutions or name changes for late-bound objects. To see this, take a look at the following examples.

In VB6, the default property of a label control is `Caption`. In VB .NET, the default property is `Text`, and the property has to be fully qualified. The upgrade tool knows this, so the following VB6 code

```
Dim l As Label
Set l = Me.Label1
l = "Hello World"
```

upgrades perfectly to

```
Dim l As System.Windows.Forms.Label
l = Me.Label1
l.Text = "Hello World"
```

However, if you wrote the code using late binding, the upgrade tool could not perfectly upgrade the code because o is late-bound, so it cannot be resolved at design time:

```
Dim o As Object
Set o = Me.Label1
o = "Hello World"
```

upgrades to

```
Dim o As Object
Set o = Me.Label1
'UPGRADE_WARNING: Cannot resolve default property of object o
o = "Hello World"
```

In this case, you would need to resolve the default property yourself or change the code in VB6 and upgrade it again.

The upgrade tool alerts you to the changes you need to make by listing them in the upgrade report, and by putting to-do comments in code. There are four types of to-do comments:

- `UPGRADE_ISSUE`—Compile errors; these are things that must be fixed before the code compiles

- UPGRADE_WARNING—Differences in behavior; these are things that might cause a problem, and you certainly should look at before running your application

- UPGRADE_TODO—Code that was partially upgraded, but that you need to complete yourself

- UPGRADE_NOTE—Code that was significantly changed; you do not have to anything here—the message is purely informational

Differences in Form Code

If you examine the code in the Command2_Click event handler in Form1, you'll notice that the call has changed to this:

```
Private Sub Command2_Click(ByVal eventSender As System.Object, _
 ByVal eventArgs As System.EventArgs) Handles Command2.Click
   Form2.DefInstance.Show()
End Sub
```

This points out one of the biggest differences between VB and VB .NET: Forms are not automatically created and ready for you to call. In other words, you couldn't use the following line in your code on Form1:

```
Form2.Show
```

Instead, forms are just another type of class, so you have to create the class first and then call a Show method. The Upgrade Wizard's approach to this is to create a new public property called DefInstance, and this property returns an instance of Form2. Therefore, you call this property, and then the Show method on the form that is exposed through the property. There is an alternative way to do this.

NOTE

The DefInstance property is created for you in the Upgrade Support section that is automatically added to the code of each form.

Instead of the code generated for you by the wizard, you could have shown Form2 using this code:

```
Dim frm2 as New Form2()
frm2.Show()
```

As you add new forms to your project, the best way to show forms is to use code like the following:

```
Dim MyNewForm as New NewForm()
MyNewForm.Show()
```

Another thing the tool changes: At the top of the form file, the following two lines are added:

```
Option Strict Off
Option Explicit On
```

`Option Explicit` is turned on, even though you didn't explicitly turn it on in the VB6 project you just created. `Option Strict` is turned off here, which means you can do some implicit conversions.

In the middle of your code is a collapsed block labeled `Windows Form Designer generated code`. If you expand this, you will see quite a bit of code that creates the form and the controls on the form, and sets up the size, location, and other properties of the form and controls. Similar code was always created for you in previous versions of VB, but it was not revealed to you. Now, you can see it and you can even modify it. Modifications, however, should be left to the designer, which means you go to the designer and make changes and the code is generated for you.

An interesting effect of upgrading is that code is always upgraded to `Option Explicit On`—so if you have variables that are implicitly created, they will be explicitly created in the upgraded code.

The Visual Basic Compatibility Library

If you look in the Solution Explorer window and expand the References node, you'll see a reference to the `Microsoft.VisualBasic.Compatibility` library. This library is provided to make it easier to move from VB6 to VB .NET. In a normal VB .NET project, you would have to add a reference to the library yourself. Any project that is upgraded, however, has the library added automatically.

The compatibility library contains classes and helper methods that allow the upgrade tool to upgrade your application more smoothly. For example, it includes `TwipsPerPixelX` and `TwipsToPixelsX` functions for working with screen resolutions, and control array extenders that give control array functionality to Windows forms.

As a rule of thumb, although it's fine to use the compatibility library functions, you'll find the new .NET Framework classes and methods offer richer and more powerful functionality. Where possible, the upgrade tool upgrades applications to use these objects instead of those in the compatibility library.

Perhaps one of the most important reasons to avoid the compatibility layer is performance. Although the actual speed hit is impossible to determine at this time, estimates of the penalty paid for using the compatibility layer range from ten to fifty percent over the equivalent .NET code.

Upgrading a More Complex Example

In the previous example, you might have noticed that you placed intrinsic VB6 controls on the form, such as the button, the text box, and the list box. VB .NET changes these controls to their VB .NET equivalents. For example, if you clicked on the button in the upgraded application and looked at the Properties window, you would see that it is listed as an object of type `System.Windows.Forms.Button`. VB .NET attempts to update your VB6 controls to the new WinForms controls in .NET, but you know this is not always possible. For example, as you learned in Chapter 3, "Major VB. NET Changes," the line and shape controls are gone. In addition, what if you wanted to use some ActiveX controls that did not have corresponding .NET WinForms controls?

ActiveX Controls and WinForms

Most ActiveX controls work just fine in WinForms. *Most*, of course, does not mean *all*. Windowless controls do not work, which is why the line and shape controls are not in VB .NET. Other controls, such as the `ssTab` and the `Coolbar`, do not work in .NET because they break certain rules. The `ssTab`, for example, cannot contain ActiveX or WinForm controls when it is placed on a WinForm. Despite the fact that not all ActiveX controls work in .NET, don't worry; most of these controls have replacements in .NET, such as the `TabControl`.

Close VB .NET and reopen VB6. Open your `VB6upgrade` project in VB6 and add a third form. Add a `Line` control to the form (the location and orientation don't matter). Next, add a `Shape` control. Change the `Shape` property to 3-Circle. Now, right-click on the Toolbar and choose Components. In the components dialog, scroll down and choose the `Microsoft Rich Textbox Control 6.0`, as shown in Figure 7.3.

Because the `Rich Textbox` is not one of the control types in .NET, .NET will not be able to switch the `Rich Textbox` with a .NET equivalent. Therefore, .NET will leave the control as ActiveX, as you will see in a moment. Go ahead and add a `Rich Textbox` control to `Form3`.

`Form3` also has a `Line` and a `Shape`, neither of which exist in .NET. As Chapter 3 pointed out, you might want to mimic a line using a label with a height of one. Shapes are most often created using the GDI+ library. If you're curious as to whether .NET will upgrade the circle to GDI+ code, your question will be answered in a moment.

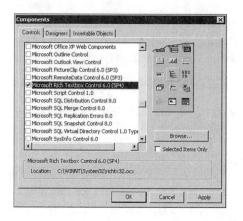

FIGURE 7.3
The ActiveX Rich Textbox control is being added to your VB6 application.

Exactly what your form looks like isn't critical. Figure 7.4 shows one example of how your form might appear. Save the application and exit VB6 (there's really no need to run it first because you don't have any way to show Form3 anyway).

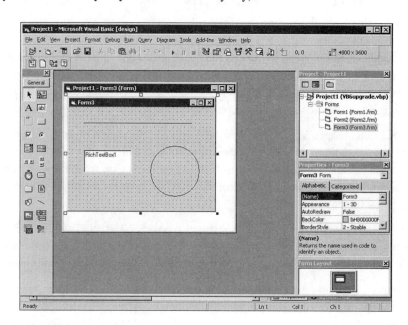

FIGURE 7.4
A VB6 Form containing Line, Shape, and Rich Textbox controls.

Now, open VS .NET again but don't open the VB6upgrade project that shows up in the list! This is the project you've already converted, and it's in a different folder from your VB6 project. Instead, click the Open Project button and navigate to the directory containing your VB6 project.

When you open the project, the Upgrade Wizard will launch again. Perform the same steps you did earlier. You will get a message that the destination folder is not empty, but feel free to continue, which will delete all files in the destination folder. After the conversion is complete, open the Form3 in the designer.

Figure 7.5 shows you what you will see in VB .NET. First of all, the Line and Rich Textbox look unchanged. However, click on the Line control, and look in the Properties window. You'll notice that, although the name is still Line1, the type of the control is System.Windows.Forms.Label.

Click on the Rich Textbox. If you look in the Properties window, you'll notice the name is still RichTextBox1, but the type is AxRichTextLib.AxRichTextBox. VB .NET automatically adds the Ax prefix to ActiveX controls it upgrades.

Also notice the two links toward the bottom of the Properties window. The first, ActiveX-Properties, opens any custom property pages for this ActiveX control. The second link, ActiveX-About, opens the About box for the control. Not all ActiveX controls will have both, or even one, of these links.

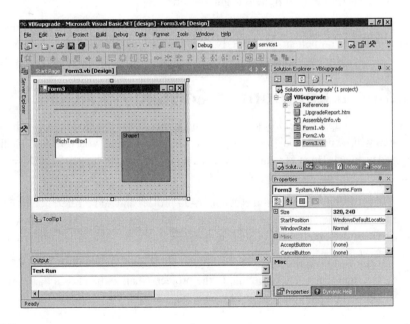

FIGURE 7.5

The upgraded VB6 form as it appears in VB .NET.

Notice also that the ActiveX Rich Textbox control has some new properties, such as Anchor and Dock. These properties are available to ActiveX controls because they are provided by the .NET Framework. Properties available to standard .NET controls are added to ActiveX controls because .NET adds a wrapper around ActiveX controls that provides these additional properties.

Perhaps the biggest thing you will notice right away, though, is that your circle is now a square. If you click on it and look at the properties, you will see it is a System.Windows.Forms.Label. That's right: The Shape control was converted to a Label, and *not* the corresponding GDI+ code. To make it a circle again, you'll have to use the GDI+ code yourself, using the System.Drawing namespace.

A Key Issue to Upgrading Projects with ActiveX Controls

There is one very important point to remember if you are upgrading a project that contains ActiveX controls, and this is good advice for any project you are upgrading: Perform the upgrades from a computer that has both VB6 and VB .NET installed, and make sure that the project compiles under VB6 before you perform the upgrade.

If you simply copy the source code for a VB6 project to another machine in order to do the upgrade, that machine might not have necessary ActiveX controls or DLLs needed to properly build the project. Therefore, the upgrade is guaranteed to fail.

You should first verify that the project builds correctly using VB6. This will ensure that you have all the necessary components to properly compile the application. After you have been able to build successfully the project using VB6, you can perform the upgrade to VB .NET.

Upgrading a Component Containing ADO

So far, you have been upgrading projects containing visual elements. However, much of what will be updated will be non-visual components. To keep this simple, you'll just add a class to the VB6upgrade project. However, this class will also include some simplistic ADO code to see how this affects the upgrade process.

Close VS .NET and open VB6. Open the VB6upgrade project and add a reference to ADO. Click on the Project menu and choose References. Scroll down and find Microsoft ActiveX Data Objects. There will likely be a variety of versions listed, as you can see in Figure 7.6. Choose the highest number, which in the first release of .NET is likely to be version 2.7.

After clicking OK, add a new Class module to the project. Change the class's Name property to Customer. Add the following code to the Customer class:

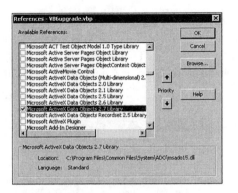

FIGURE 7.6

The References dialog box being used to add ADO to your VB6 project.

```
Dim msFirstName As String
Dim msLastName As String

Public Property Get Name() As String
    Name = msFirstName & " " & msLastName
End Property

Public Sub GetCustomer(piCustID As Integer)
    Dim cn As ADODB.Connection
    Dim rs As ADODB.Recordset
    Set cn = New ADODB.Connection
    cn.Open ("Provider=SQLOLEDB;User ID=sa;" & _
      "Initial Catalog=northwind;Data Source=(local);PASSWORD=;")
    Set rs = cn.Execute("Select * from Employees where " & _
      "EmployeeID=" & piCustID)
    msFirstName = rs("FirstName")
    msLastName = rs("LastName")
End Sub
```

You are creating a single property, Name, and a single method, GetCustomer. Name concatenates the first and last name variables together and returns a single string.

The GetCustomer method uses ADO to connect to the Northwind database on the local computer. You might need to change the Data Source value to match the name of the server on which you have SQL Server. Of course, you might also need to modify the User ID and Password properties as well.

After connecting to the database, you execute a SQL statement to retrieve a customer that matches the Customer ID that is passed into the GetCustomer method. You then assign the FirstName and LastName fields to the msFirstName and msLastName variables, respectively.

Finally, to finish the Customer class, click on the Tools menu and choose Procedure Attributes. This opens the Procedure Attributes dialog box. Choose Name (the Name property) in the Name drop-down list box. Click on the Advanced button, and in the Procedure ID box, choose (Default). This sets the Name property as the default property for this class. You can see these options in Figure 7.7.

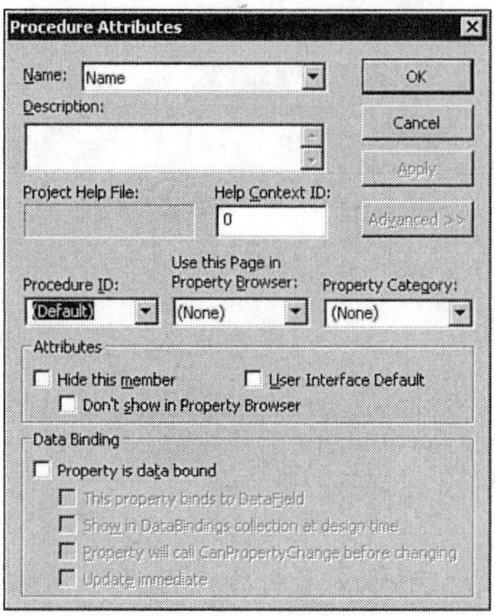

FIGURE 7.7
The Procedure Attributes dialog box.

To test this, go back to Form1 and add a third button. In the code for the third button, enter the following code:

```
Private Sub Command3_Click()
    Dim Cust As New Customer
    Cust.GetCustomer (1)
    MsgBox Cust
End Sub
```

Run the application to verify that it is working. When you click Button3, you should see a message box displayed with the name Nancy Davolio.

Save the project and close VB6. Open VB .NET, and open the VB6upgrade project (again, open the files in the VB6 directory, not the VB .NET directory). The Upgrade Wizard will start, so run through the upgrade process. Don't hesitate to delete any existing files in the destination directory.

Examine the code in the upgraded class. Notice that the class module in VB .NET is named Class1.vb. Within that class, however, you see the definition for Class Customer. The first thing you might notice is that the word ReadOnly has been added to the Name property. This has been added because you did not have a Public Property Let statement in VB6.

You might notice the lack of the word Default for the Name property. Recall that default properties are not supported in .NET unless the property has parameters. This property is not a parameterized property, so the Name property cannot be the default property in this project.

The big news is the lack of change in the GetCustomer method. The ADO is untouched. This is a key point: The Upgrade Wizard does not update ADO code to ADO.NET. The differences between ADO and ADO.NET are significant enough that the Upgrade Wizard does not attempt to update ADO code. Therefore, if you want to move to ADO.NET, you'll have to code that yourself.

The code you added in Button3 on Form1, however, does upgrade properly. In VB6, you did not specify the property when you wanted to print the name; VB .NET automatically adds the Name property to the code.

The Upgrade Process

When upgrading your applications, there is a process you should consider following. It is

1. Learn VB .NET
2. Pick a small project and make sure that it works
3. Upgrade the project and examine the upgrade report
4. Fix any outstanding items in VB .NET

Learn VB .NET

One reason this chapter is after all the chapters on the changes from VB to VB .NET is because you have to learn VB .NET before you can successfully upgrade a project. The reason for this is that the Upgrade Wizard can't do it all. There are too many programming styles and too many ambiguities in VB6 (especially with late-bound objects), and the Upgrade Wizard can't handle every situation. Therefore, you have to make sure that you can look at your upgraded code and not only fix any outstanding problems, but see where inefficiencies might lie and fix them also.

Learning VB .NET is as much learning the .NET Framework and what it offers as it is learning the new features of VB .NET. Make sure that you become familiar with the System namespaces and what they can do for you.

Pick a Small Project and Make Sure That It Works

In this chapter, you created a very small project and upgraded it. You'll want to start with your smaller projects, too. This way, you might just have one or two errors to fix and the task will not seem difficult. If you try to upgrade an application with 100 forms, 200 class modules, and API calls spread throughout, the task might be daunting if you see a large number of errors.

You should have both VB6 and VB .NET installed on the same machine on which you perform your upgrades. Why? You want to make sure that the project compiles and runs on that machine. For example, if you have dependencies on particular objects or controls and you do not have those installed on the machine performing the upgrades, there is no way for the Upgrade Wizard to verify the code, and your upgrade will fail. Therefore, make sure that the VB6 project compiles and runs on the machine performing the upgrade before you try to upgrade that project.

In addition, if you start with small projects, you might find the Upgrade Wizard repeatedly tripping over something you do often in your code. This would allow you to fix the repetitious problem in the VB6 project before you upgrade, allowing for a smoother conversion.

Upgrade the Project and Examine the Upgrade Report

Perform the upgrade on your project and then examine the upgrade report. The upgrade report shows you warnings and errors, and documents where they occurred. You can use this report to begin examining the code and making changes. In addition, the Upgrade Wizard adds comments into your code to identify any problems it had while converting, or to point out things you must do to ensure a smooth transition.

Fix Any Outstanding Items in VB .NET

Now that you have performed the upgrade and examined the upgrade report, it is time to fix any outstanding issues. This is when you have to use your knowledge of VB .NET to correct any problems that the Upgrade Wizard could not. You now see why the Upgrade Wizard is not a solution unto itself, but the first step in the process.

Helping Your VB6 Applications Upgrade

There are a number of things you can do in your VB6 application to make the upgrade easier. This is not a comprehensive list, but it covers some of the most important aspects.

Note that this chapter refers to upgrading VB6 projects—what about VB3, VB4, and VB5 projects? Although the upgrade tool recognizes the format of VB5 and VB6 project types, some VB5 ActiveX references have problems after they are upgraded. For this reason, it's better to upgrade your VB5 applications to VB6—and upgrade the controls to VB6 controls—before upgrading the application to VB .NET. The upgrade tool cannot upgrade projects saved in VB4 and earlier.

Do Not Use Late Binding

As you saw earlier in the chapter, late binding can present some problems because properties and methods cannot be verified during the upgrade process. Avoid late binding whenever possible.

Specify Default Properties

In the previous example, imagine if you had typed the last line of code this way:

```
oLbl="Hello World"
```

The Upgrade Wizard has no idea how to handle this. In fact, if you try to upgrade this code, the Upgrade Wizard will include a comment that says it cannot resolve the default property of oLbl.

You should specify the default properties on all your objects. If you don't, the Upgrade Wizard attempts to determine default properties wherever it can. However, default properties on late-bound objects are impossible for the wizard to resolve. You should avoid late binding and also specify any default properties.

Use Zero-Bound Arrays

In VB6, you could create an array with a lower boundary (LBound) of any number you wanted, using this syntax:

```
Dim MyArray(1 to 5) As Long
```

VB .NET does not support an LBound of anything but 0, so your code here will end up looking like this in an upgraded project:

```
'UPGRADE_WARNING: LBound was changed from 1 to 0
Dim MyArray( 5 ) As Integer
```

The real interesting point here is that the array is not larger by one element; MyArray now has six elements, from zero to five. This could cause problems if you are used to iterating through an array using LBound and UBound, but recall that LBound is not supported in VB .NET.

Examine API Calls

Most API calls work just fine from VB .NET. After all, the underlying operating system is still there and available. Some data types need to be changed because the Long data type in VB .NET is different from the Long data type in VB6. However, the Upgrade Wizard handles most of these for you.

There are some cases in which the Upgrade Wizard can't make the change, however. VB .NET doesn't natively support fixed-length strings, but some APIs expect a structure with a fixed-length string as one of the members. You can use the compatibility layer to get fixed-length strings, but you might have to add a MarshalAs attribute to the fixed-length string.

Also, any API calls that perform thread creation, Windows subclassing, or similar functions can cause errors in VB .NET. Most of these now have VB .NET equivalents, such as .NET's native inheritance and its threading classes.

Form and Control Changes

The OLE Container control is gone. If you have used it, you'll have to code a different way. The Line and Shape controls are gone as well, so lines, squares, and rectangles are replaced by labels. Ovals and circles cannot be upgraded by the wizard, so you'll have to recode those using the GDI+ library.

The Timer control must be disabled to stop it; the interval cannot be set to 0.

The Drag and Drop properties have changed so much from VB6 to VB .NET that they are simply not upgraded by the wizard. You'll have to rewrite that code.

These are not the only changes, of course, but they are some of the most common ones you will see as you upgrade your applications.

Summary

Microsoft has attempted to give you a good upgrade path for your Visual Basic 6 projects. The Upgrade Wizard is just one step, albeit an important one, in that process. You must first learn VB .NET and understand the underlying .NET Framework before you can hope to successfully port your applications to VB .NET.

Even before you move your applications, however, there are modifications you can make to your VB6 applications to ease the migration path. Keep these modifications in mind as you develop new VB6 applications between now and the final release of Visual Studio .NET.

There are several things to remember. Don't forget to check the _UpgradeReport.htm file. This will indicate areas that could not be upgraded, and will help you locate the areas that need your attention.

ActiveX controls typically upgrade without issues, but make sure that you can compile the application in VB6 on the same machine on which you will be upgrading.

Finally, don't forget that ADO code is not upgraded to ADO.NET for you. If you want to take advantage of ADO.NET, you'll have to rewrite the database access sections yourself.

Building Web Applications
with VB .NET and ASP.NET

IN THIS CHAPTER

Most developers today are building Web applications in one form or another. For the past three and a half years or so, Microsoft developers have been building Web applications using Active Server Pages, or ASP. ASP is a technology in which the pages are a mix of HTML and a scripting language, such as VBScript or JavaScript. The HTML was basically static, and was rendered on the client just as you typed it in the page. The script was interpreted on-the-fly, and generated additional HTML. This generated HTML was mixed in with the static HTML, and the page was sent to the browser.

Web applications, including Active Server Pages applications, follow a simple request/response metaphor because that is all that is allowed by HTTP. The user requests a page, and the page is sent to the browser to be rendered. The person can fill out data fields, and when he clicks a button, he is making a new request to the server, and the response is generated on the server and returned.

ASP.NET has to use request/response, of course, because you're still using HTTP. However, ASP.NET seeks to simplify the coding model, by making it appear as an event-driven programming model. ASP.NET has the following advantages over ASP:

- Spaghetti code can be virtually eliminated. Script does not need to be intermixed with HTML any more. This makes the user interface code much smaller, cleaner, and easier to maintain. This is made possible by the event-driven page processing.

- New controls have been introduced that promote user interface encapsulation. These controls give browser-independent rendering, which means that you write code only once for multiple clients.

- Page services have been introduced that reduce the grunt work involved in creating form pages that post back to themselves: `ViewState` and `PostBack` data processing.

- New application services make applications faster and more scalable. These include caching, farmable session state, and security, to name a few.

Before going into the full details of how ASP.NET works, and how it differs from ASP, it might be helpful to build a quick ASP.NET application and examine the resultant code.

Your First ASP.NET Application

Start Visual Studio .NET and choose to create a new Visual Basic project using the ASP.NET Web Application project type and name the project WebAppTest. Notice, as shown in Figure 8.1, that the location of the project is an HTTP address, not a directory on the machine. The server to which you connect must have Internet Information Server (IIS) 4.0 or higher. Windows 2000 ships with IIS 5.0, so if your Web server is running Windows 2000, you are fine. Don't forget, however, that IIS does not install, by default, on Windows 2000 Professional. The server must also have the .NET Framework loaded, so you might want to use your local machine as the Web server.

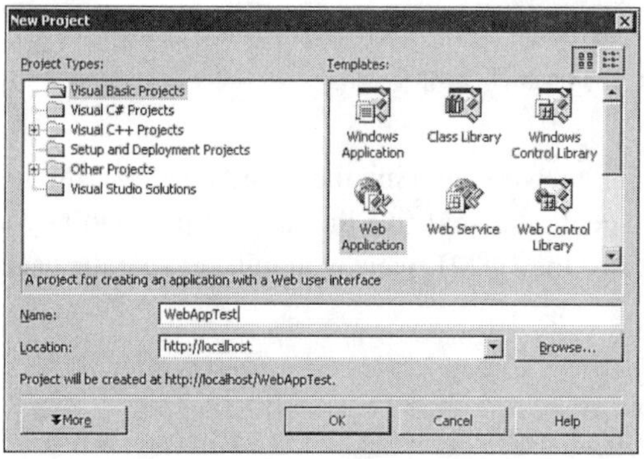

FIGURE 8.1
Creating a Web Application project requires a server running IIS and Visual Studio .NET (or at least the .NET Framework).

After you click the OK button, VS .NET attempts to communicate with the Web server. Provided this communication is successful, the project is created on the Web server, and you are ready to begin working with the project.

The page will open as a blank form in the designer, with a little descriptive text in the middle. If you look in the Solution Explorer, you will see that this page is named WebForm1.aspx. ASP uses the .asp extension, whereas ASP.NET files use the .aspx extension. ASP and ASP.NET can coexist in the same directory if desired.

If you look at the designer, it is just a blank form right now. The default starting point is for the form to be in GridLayout mode, which means that you can drag and drop controls onto the form and easily position them by using the standard snap-to-grid feature of the designer. There is also a FlowLayout mode that allows you to get absolute positioning by placing the controls exactly where you want. To switch between FlowLayout and GridLayout modes, change the pageLayout property in the Properties window.

Go ahead and switch the pageLayout property to FlowLayout. This mode works like a word processor in some ways. If you click once on the form, you have a cursor blinking in the upper-left corner. Type Welcome to my first ASP.NET page and then press the Enter key. As you can see, the text is placed on the form, just as you would expect in a word processor. Highlight the text and look at the toolbar. There is a drop-down box that says Normal. Drop down this list and choose Heading1. The text enlarges significantly.

8

BUILDING WEB
APPLICATIONS
WITH VB .NET

Along the bottom of this window are two buttons: Design and HTML. If you click the HTML button, you will be shown the HTML making up the page. Right now, the line that creates the Heading1 is as follows:

```
<H1>
    Welcome to my first ASP.NET page
</H1>
```

Now, go back to the Design view by clicking the Design button. Highlight the text again, and click the Center button to center the text (it's the same Center button you're used to seeing in Word). If you switch back to the HTML view, you will see that the earlier Heading1 line has changed to this:

```
<H1 align="center">
    Welcome to my first ASP.NET page
</H1>
```

At this point, you might think you have a high-powered HTML editor, not much different from FrontPage or a hundred other HTML editors. Now, however, it is time to see an example of some ASP.NET.

Go back to the Design view and move to the line below the Heading1 line you added. Click on the Toolbox and notice that there is a tab for Web Forms. Click and drag a Label from the Web Forms tab to your form. Next, click and drag a button from the Web Forms tab to the form. You should now have a label and a button next to each other. Both the label and the button have a small green triangle in the upper-left corner.

Double-click on the button and you will open the code window. Notice that this code window creates a file with the same name as the ASPX, but the file has a .vb extension. As you will see, this is called a *code-behind page*. One of ASP.NET's design goals is to separate the code and the user interface.

In the code window, you will be in the Button1_Click event procedure. Type the following code:

```
Private Sub Button1_Click(ByVal sender As System.Object, _
 ByVal e As System.EventArgs) Handles Button1.Click
    Label1.Text = "Hello, World!"
End Sub
```

Notice that you are programming this just as you would a standard Windows application. Go ahead and click the Start button. The page renders in Internet Explorer (hereafter referred to as IE), as shown in Figure 8.2. What is interesting is not what you see in the browser, but the code behind it. On IE's menu bar, select View, Source and you will see the HTML that is making up the page. Examine this HTML (which has some lines shown as two lines so that they fit in this book).

FIGURE 8.2

Your first ASP.NET page being rendered in the browser.

```
<!DOCTYPE HTML PUBLIC "-//W3C//DTD HTML 4.0 Transitional//EN">
<HTML>
    <HEAD>
        <title></title>
        <meta name="GENERATOR" _
            content="Microsoft Visual Studio.NET 7.0">
        <meta name="CODE_LANGUAGE" content="Visual Basic 7.0">
        <meta name="vs_defaultClientScript" content="JavaScript">
        <meta name="vs_targetSchema" _
            content="http://schemas.microsoft.com/intellisense/ie5">
    </HEAD>
    <body>
        <form name="Form1" method="post" _
            action="WebForm1.aspx" id="Form1">
<input type="hidden" name="__VIEWSTATE" value="dDw2NjY0NzU40Tc70z4=" />

        <H1 align="center">
            Welcome to my first ASP.NET page
        </H1>
        <P>
            <span id="Label1">Label</span>
            <input type="submit" name="Button1" _
                value="Button" id="Button1" />
        </P>
        </form>
    </body>
</HTML>
```

For now, just notice that there is no VB .NET code here. You created a procedure for the Button1_Click event and typed a line of code. However, none of that has made it to the client.

This is because ASP.NET just sends HTML to the client, whereas the code is compiled and lives on the server. That means this page can be used by anyone, using any browser and operating system.

Test the page by clicking the button. You will notice the text `Hello, World!` now appears in the label. If you select View, Source again, you will notice that the `Label1` tag has changed from this:

```
<span id="Label1">Label</span>
```

to this:

```
<span id="Label1">Hello, World!</span>
```

How did this change? How was the click event handled? The next section covers how ASP.NET processes pages.

How ASP.NET Works

Basically, ASP.NET works by using server-based components to generate HTML. The HTML is sent to the client and rendered in a browser. ASP.NET determines the capabilities of the client browser and generates HTML appropriate for that browser.

ASP.NET works by using server-based components to generate markup, such as HTML, and script. The HTML and script are sent to the client and rendered in a browser. ASP.NET determines the capabilities of the client browser and renders HTML appropriate for that browser. The type of markup sent to the client is determined by the controls. This markup code doesn't have to be HTML; for example, the mobile controls send WML to wireless devices.

ASP.NET user code (for example, the code that set the label text in your first project) is precompiled. This is in contrast to ASP, which interprets the script code that is intermingled with static HTML. Even if you were using compiled COM components with ASP, the calls to the components were late-bound. Using ASP.NET allows you to benefit from all the services of the .NET Framework, such as inheritance, security, and garbage collection.

ASP.NET also provides some of the functionality that has been coded by hand in the past. Like ASP, ASP.NET can provide automatic state management. Because HTTP is a stateless protocol, maintaining state in Web applications has always been a problem. ASP.NET provides state management that, unlike ASP, is scalable across Web farms, survives IIS crashes, and can be used without relying on cookies.

Web Pages and Code

The pages you create are divided into two parts: the user interface and the code. You can see this in the WebAppTest project because you have `WebForm1.aspx` and a `WebForm1.vb`. The `.vb` file is a class file, called a *page class*, and it segregates your logic code from the HTML. When you create the page in VS .NET, you see the ASPX and the VB files as two views of the same page. When you compile the page through VS .NET, ASP.NET generates a new class and compiles it. This new class has the static HTML, ASP.NET server controls, and code from your form compiled in. Unlike ASP, all the HTML sent to the client is generated from the class on-the-fly. This class is actually an executable program, and whenever the page is called, the executable generates the HTML that is sent to the browser.

In the case of the page you created earlier, a compiled class was created from these two files. When someone browses the ASPX page, the class is executed and generates the HTML to send to the browser. If you look at the HTML sent to the browser, you'll notice that all the controls you added (the label and the button) are inside an HTML <FORM>...</FORM> block. This is because an HTML form is the only way for standard HTML to get data from an HTML page back to the server.

The code you wrote for the click event runs only on the server. When someone clicks the button, it acts as a submit button, which you can also see in the code. So, the user clicks the button, and the form is submitted to the server. In effect, you take the click event and send it to the server for processing. The generated class is instantiated, and the click event code is processed. A new HTML stream is generated and sent back to the client browser. This new HTML stream contains a new string to be placed in the label; in this case, the string is the text Hello, World!. ASP.NET works this way because you added server controls to the page. Server controls are discussed in the next section.

Server Controls

One of the biggest shifts in the creation of Web applications in VB .NET is the idea of the server control. When teaching students about Visual InterDev over the past few months, I've explained that although the product Visual InterDev is going away, its functionality is being added to the .NET Framework. This means that any language that targets the Framework will have the capability to create Web applications. This might give some of you nightmares, but realize that this means you could write high-performance, dynamic Web applications in COBOL.NET. The server controls are a key component of the Framework, and they are one of the main tools that will be used by any .NET language in order to create Web applications.

If you open Visual Studio .NET, click on the form, and then open the Toolbox, you'll see several interesting tabs. One tab is labeled HTML, and it shows a series of HTML tags. These are just controls that you can drag and drop to your form to create a static HTML page; each element maps directly to an HTML tag. For example, if you were to drag and drop a Table from the HTML tab of the Toolbox and then look at the HTML, the following HTML would be generated (shortened for brevity):

```
<TABLE cellSpacing=1 cellPadding=1 width=300 border=1>
    <TR>
        <TD>
        </TD>
        <TD>
        </TD>
        <TD>
        </TD>
    </TR>
</TABLE>
```

Even though you can work with the table in the designer just as you can any other control, the designer is really just writing HTML in the background. That's HTML in the static sense. That means that you can't start writing VB .NET code against that table because it is just some HTML sitting in the page.

Because the elements in the HTML tab map to standard HTML tags, they aren't as powerful as the controls you added earlier. Although the button and text box you added earlier are mapped to standard HTML tags, these are ASP.NET server controls. They act as controls against which you can program just as you would in a Windows form; you double-click on a button, for example, and you wind up in the code window with a Button1_Click event procedure.

Return to your WebAppTest application. In the designer for WebForm1.aspx, click down to the next blank line (you might need to press the Enter key to get to the line below the label and button you added). Drag over a button from the HTML tab of the Toolbox. Now, click on the Web Forms tab and drag over a button from the Toolbox. If you look in the designer, you'll have two buttons side by side, and they look identical except that the second one has the small green triangle in the upper-left corner, indicating that it is a server control.

If you look at the HTML, however, you will see a significant difference. Here are how the two buttons appear in the HTML view (slightly modified to fit the page):

```
<INPUT type="button" value="Button">
<asp:Button id="Button2" runat="server" Text="Button">
</asp:Button>
```

The first button is displayed with a standard HTML <INPUT> tag. The second button, however, is displayed with an <asp:Button> tag. This <asp:Button> tag is not standard HTML. Instead, when the .NET compiler sees this, it knows that the button is an ASP.NET server control, and you have basically the same functionality with this control that you would have with the same type of control in a Windows form.

In the Design view, double-click on the first button (the HTML button). When you do this, you'll see the dialog box shown in Figure 8.3. This message box informs you that this is an HTML element, which means you cannot write code for it. However, the box offers you an option: You can convert the button to an HTML *server control*. There is a distinction between what VS .NET calls an HTML server control and an ASP.NET server control.

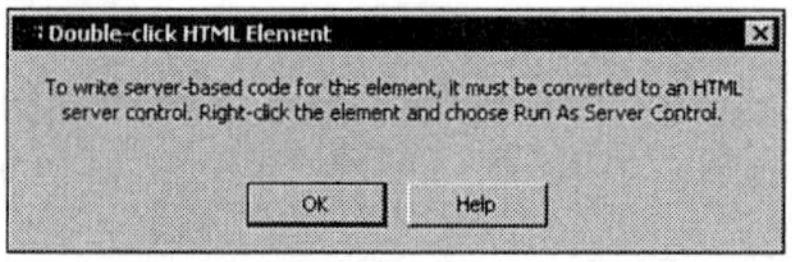

FIGURE 8.3
The message box explains that you cannot add code to an HTML element without first making it an HTML server control.

HTML server controls are standard HTML elements to which Microsoft has added server-side programming capabilities. When you add an HTML element, ASP.NET sees that as just text to be generated and passed to the client. HTML server controls, on the other hand, come with a programming model that exposes all the attributes of the HTML element on the server. Microsoft has made these controls quite powerful: They can maintain values between round-trips to the server, they can respond to events on the server (or, optionally, on the client), and the controls can be bound to a data source.

Don't confuse HTML server controls with the items listed on the HTML tab of the Toolbox. Those items are just HTML tags; they are *not* HTML server controls. All HTML and ASP.NET server controls will be found on the Web Forms tab of the Toolbox.

ASP.NET server controls are more abstract controls in that they do not necessarily have a single corresponding HTML tag. For example, if you look at the Web Forms tab of the Toolbox, you'll notice controls such as the `Calendar` and `Repeater`. Although these controls end up being generated as HTML, they are often composed of many HTML tags. For example, the calendar is a table, with many rows and columns. ASP.NET server controls have all the benefits you saw with the HTML server controls, and they can also determine the capabilities of the client browser and render more or less advanced HTML depending on the client. Some server controls have the ability to delay sending events to the server, instead caching them and sending them when the entire form is submitted.

You can take almost any element on a page and turn it into an HTML server control. For example, when you double-clicked the HTML button, the message box said that you had to convert it into an HTML server control to write code for it. The message box even said that you could right-click on the control and choose Run As Server Control. Behind the scenes, this would add `runat="server"` to the `<INPUT>` tag, and allow you to write server-side code based on that tag.

You can turn plain text into an HTML control. For example, you have a heading 1 at the top of the page that proudly proclaims, `Welcome to my first ASP.NET page`. Switch to the HTML view for a moment and you'll see that the code looks like this:

```
<H1 align="center">
   Welcome to my first ASP.NET page
</H1>
```

Now, switch back to the Design view and highlight the text. Right-click on the highlighted text and choose Run As Server Control. Now, switch back to the HTML view and you will see that the HTML has changed to this:

```
<H1 align="center" id="H11" runat="server">
   Welcome to my first ASP.NET page
</H1>
```

Although this doesn't immediately look like a big change, two attributes have been added to the tag: id="H11" and runat="server". The first attribute makes this tag an object against which you can write some code. This is a common practice when writing Dynamic HTML (DHTML). The second attribute, however, tells the ASP.NET engine that this object's code will run on the server side. So, the server will handle any properties or methods or events on this element.

Double-click on the second button you added (the HTML server control). In the code window, in the Button2_Click event handler, type the following code:

```
Private Sub Button2_Click(ByVal sender As System.Object, _
 ByVal e As System.EventArgs) Handles Button2.Click
   H11.InnerText = "It is now " & Now
End Sub
```

This code merely replaces the text inside the <H1> tag with the text It is now and then appends the current date and time. If you run the project and click the button, you will get results like those shown in Figure 8.4.

If your curiosity is getting the better of you, feel free to drag a Calendar ASP.NET server control from the Web Forms tab of the Toolbox and drop it on your form. If you view the code in the HTML view of the designer, you'll see that you have added an <asp:Calendar> tag to the HTML. However, if you run the page and then view the source code that actually reaches the browser, you'll see that the calendar is actually just generated as an HTML table, as the following code snippet shows:

```
...
Sun
</td><td align="Center">
Mon
</td><td align="Center">
Tue
</td><td align="Center">
Wed
...
```

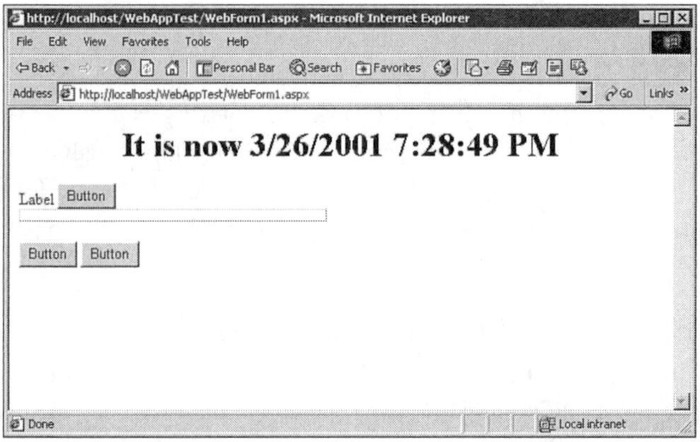

FIGURE 8.4
Almost any element can be turned into a server control, as this <H1> tag has been in this example.

Some client-side JavaScript is mixed in as well because the ASP.NET engine realized that the browser was capable of handling it, and sent the code to the browser. Remember, server controls work hard to determine the capabilities of the client browser, and to render HTML and/or JavaScript to give the users the most robust experience possible, given the capabilities of their browser.

Validation Controls

One of the most common requests for any Web application is the ability to perform client-side validation of input. It would have been nice if HTML were written with some sort of mask that could be applied to fields, but that isn't the case. In standard HTML, there is no way to perform validation of data on the client. To get around this problem, most browsers let you mix in some client-side script code, which is capable of performing validation, but the code for this can be tedious to write.

There are a number of reasons for performing validation on the client. First, you give the user a better experience. If you can immediately notify the user that she did not fill in a required field, you just saved her the time it would have taken to submit the form, have the server generate a message to inform her of the problem, and return the error message to her. In addition, using client-side validation lessens network traffic and server load by never sending invalid data to the server. This client-side code helps leverage the fact that, although browsers often act like dumb terminals, they are often running on computers capable of processing code.

Microsoft provides a series of validation controls in ASP.NET that automate client-side form validation. The validation controls in ASP.NET are smart; they will perform the validation at the client if possible. The controls will first determine whether the client can handle DHTML, and if so, they send the code down to the client. If the browser is less capable, the validation code will be executed on the server.

From a development standpoint, however, you code the controls exactly the same way. This means you don't have to dumb down your validation code for less-capable browsers. You can have robust validation code and be assured that the same code will be run for all browsers. It's just that the location of where the code is run changes depending on the capabilities of each browser.

Creating a Project with the Validation Controls

To try out some validation, it is useful to start from scratch. Add a new Web Form to your WebAppTest project and name it UserInfo.aspx. Change UserInfo's pageLayout property to FlowLayout. Click on the Toolbox and drag a text box from the Web Forms tab and drop it on your new Web form. For this new text box, change the (ID) property to txtSSN. Now, on the form, click to the right of the text box so that you can see the cursor. Press the Enter key to move to the next line. Click on the Toolbox, drag a button from the Web Forms tab, and drop it on the line below the text box. Now, from the Web Forms tab of the Toolbox, drag a RequiredFieldValidator control and drop it next to the text box.

The RequiredFieldValidator control checks whether a particular field has been filled in. You place the RequiredFieldValidator on the page, and then tie it to a particular input control, such as a TextBox, CheckBox, or DropDownList. In this case, you want to tie it to the text box. Click once on the RequiredFieldValidator if it is not already the current object. In the Properties window, you will see a property named ControlToValidate. Click here and drop down the list. The only input control that will appear is txtSSN; this is correct, so choose it.

You are ready for your first test. Before you run the page, however, you might be tempted to go to the project properties and choose to make UserInfo.aspx the startup object. However, Web Applications work differently: There is no startup object, per se. Instead, right-click on UserInfo.aspx in the Solution Explorer window and choose Set As Start Page. This notifies Visual Studio .NET which page to run when the user clicks the Start button. It does not change anything in the page itself. Now that you have set UserInfo.aspx as the start page, run the project. The page appears inside Internet Explorer.

After the page is running, click on the button without entering anything in the text box. Immediately, the text RequiredFieldValidator appears to the right of the text box. Now, enter anything into the text box and click the button. The RequiredFieldValidator text goes away, and the entered value stays in the text box. When the RequiredFieldValidator text disappears and the value you typed in the text box remains, it means that the submit action has taken place, which means you have made a round-trip to the server.

The fact that the text stayed in the text box even after a round-trip to the server is important. Before ASP.NET, you would have to have written server-side code to capture field values for you, and then write those values back into the text boxes. ASP.NET handles this automatically, meaning you get this advanced functionality without having to write the code.

If you use IE 4.0 or higher, the validation actually occurs on the client. This allows you to get immediate feedback that the field is blank, when in fact you specified that a value is required. After you fill in the value, you send the data to the server and perform a server round-trip. If you're using a less-capable browser, the code will run on the server.

If you feel that the error message `RequiredFieldValidator` is not particularly useful, you can modify the error message by changing the properties. You will see this shortly.

Types of Validators

If you look at the Web Forms tab of the Toolbox, you'll see a variety of validator controls. Briefly, they are as follows:

- `RequiredFieldValidator`—This validator requires that its `ControlToValidate` property have a value. In other words, the control to which this validator is tied cannot be left blank.

- `CompareValidator`—This validator compares the value the user entered with a value you specify. Your specified value could be a constant, a calculated value, or a value from a database.

- `RangeValidator`—This validator requires that entered data be within a particular range. The range can be numeric, dates, currency, or alphabetical.

- `RegularExpressionValidator`—Regular expressions are also known as *masks*. This validator can make sure that entered data matches a particular format, such as the format of phone numbers and Social Security numbers.

- `CustomValidator`—This validator uses code you write yourself to validate the data.

- `ValidationSummary`—This validator simply reports all the errors encountered by the other validators. You will see an example of this validator shortly.

Applying Multiple Validators to the Same Field

It is possible to apply more than one validator to the same field. For example, you might have a Social Security number field that is both required and must be in a particular format. Close IE, if you still have it running, in order to return to the design mode for the WebAppTest project. Drag a `RegularExpressionValidator` to the form, next to the `RequiredFieldValidator` you added earlier. On the `RegularExpressionValidator`, change the `ControlToValidate` property to `txtSSN`, and click on the ellipses on the `ValidateExpression` property. In the Regular Expression Editor dialog box that pops up, choose U.S. Social Security Number and then click OK.

Run the project, and try these three tests:

- Do not enter anything, and click the button. You will notice that the RequiredFieldValidator message appears.

- Enter Hello into the text box and press the button. The RequiredFieldValidator no longer appears because that condition is satisfied. However, the RegularExpressionValidator now appears because you are failing that condition.

- Enter 111-11-1111 into the text box and click the button. No validator text appears, and you will now see the form make a trip to the server because both validators are satisfied.

In some browsers, such as IE6, the validators run as soon as you tab out of the field, meaning that the user does not even have to wait to click the button to see the errors.

Modifying the Validators

Notice that the text in the validators is not the friendliest text that you could show your clients. If you return to design mode, click the RequiredFieldValidator in the Design pane, and look at the properties, you'll notice a property named ErrorMessage. Change this property to This field is required. Next, click on the RegularExpressionValidator and change its ErrorMessage property to SSN must be in ###-##-#### format.

Now, run the page again, and repeat the same three tests from the last section. You should get validator messages for the first two tests, but the text displayed should be the new values you entered in the ErrorMessage property of each validator.

You'll also notice that even when the RequiredFieldValidator is not displayed, the RegularExpressionValidator appears far enough to the right that you can tell where the RequiredFieldValidator appears. That is because the validators have a Display property, and its default value is Static. If you change this property to Dynamic for the RequiredFieldValidator and run the page again, you'll see that the RegularExpression Validator now appears next to the text box when it is displayed. The Dynamic value says that the field will not take up any space unless it is displayed. This is supported by IE 4.0 and higher, but support on other browsers might not exist. In those cases, the validator fields will work as they did when you had the property set to Static.

Providing a Validation Summary

It is possible simply to mark the fields that failed their validations with a symbol and provide a summary of all the validations at the top or bottom of the page. The ValidationSummary control allows you to build just such a list of all the errors that occurred.

To see this work, you will want to modify the UserInfo.aspx quite a bit. Add text before the first box identifying it as the Social Security Number field. Drop down to the next line and add the text First Name and then add a TextBox ASP.NET server control. After you add the text box, change its `ID` property to something meaningful, such as `txtFName`. Now, go to the next line, type `Last Name`, add a `TextBox` ASP.NET server control, and give it a meaningful name. Add the following additional labels and controls, and give the text boxes meaningful names by setting the (`ID`) properties:

- `Address 1`
- `Address 2`
- `City`
- `State`
- `Zip`
- `Phone`

Now, add a `RequiredFieldValidator` next to `First Name`, `Last Name`, `Address 1`, `City`, `State`, and `Zip`. That means the `Address 2` and `Phone` fields are optional. Make sure that you bind the `RequiredFieldValidators` to the correct text boxes.

Next to the `Phone` text box, add a `RegularExpressionValidator` and set the `ValidationExpression` property to `U.S. Phone Number`, and bind this to the `Phone Number` text box. At this point, your form will look something like what you see in Figure 8.5.

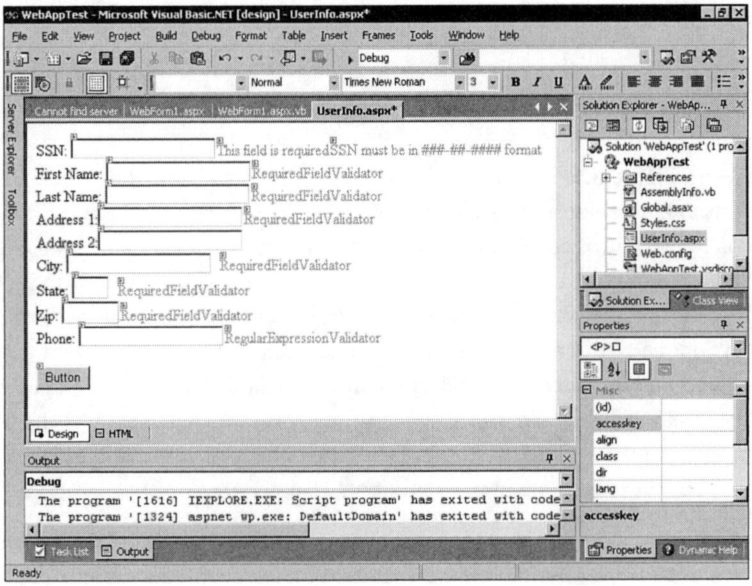

FIGURE 8.5

A more complex data entry screen with validator server controls.

Now, change the text on the validators so that they make sense. For example, on the `RequiredFieldValidator` for the `First Name` text box, set the `ErrorMessage` property to `The First Name field is required`. Change all the validators this way, including the `RequiredFieldValidator` for the Social Security Number field you added a while ago. When you are done, run the project. After it is running, press the button without entering anything. You should get a page like the one shown in Figure 8.6.

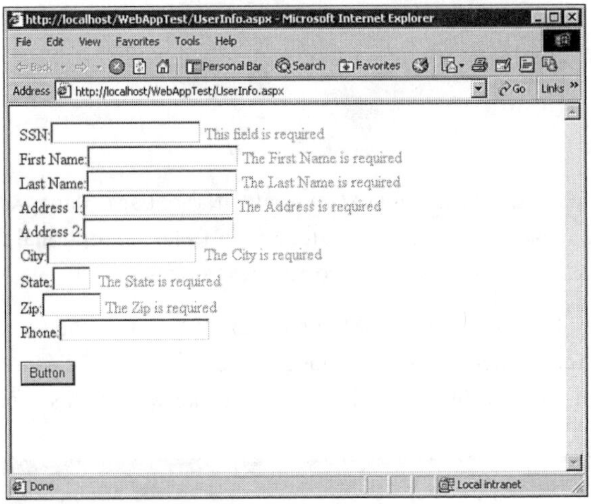

FIGURE 8.6

The data entry form is now being run, showing most of the validator messages.

As you can see in Figure 8.6, this can be a cumbersome way to show the errors. Instead, you might want to have a listing of all the errors in one place. That's where the `ValidationSummary` control comes into play. Add an extra line between the `Phone` text box and the button. Drag a `ValidationSummary` control onto the form and drop it above the button but after the `Phone` text box and validator. Highlight the control on the form, change the `HeaderText` property to `The following errors occurred:`, and then run the form. Click the button without entering anything, and you will see that the validator messages appear next to each text box, and the same messages appear in the `ValidationSummary` at the bottom of the page. Having this validation summary at the bottom can be handy, but do you need the same message beside each text box and in the summary? Usually not.

Return to the designer and on each validator tied to a field, change the `Text` property to an asterisk (*). Do not change anything in the `ValidationSummary`. Now, run the page again. If you press the button without filling in any fields, you will get an asterisk next to the required fields, but the `ErrorMessage` text you entered for each validator still appears in the `ValidationSummary` control.

In Figure 8.7, some fields have been entered, but some have not. In addition, the `Phone` field has been entered incorrectly. Notice the results in the `ValidationSummary` field.

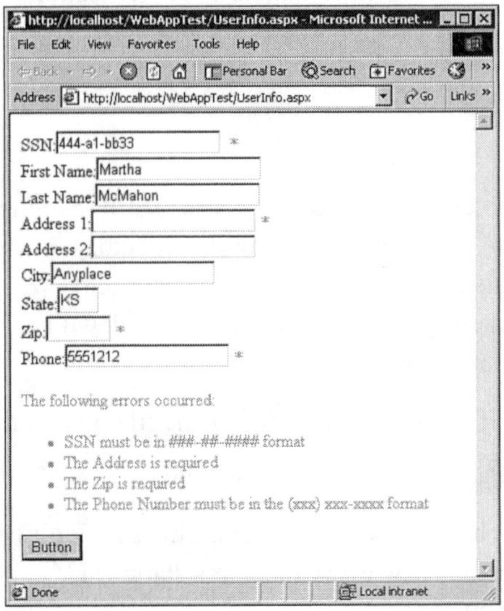

FIGURE 8.7

The `ValidationSummary` *control allows you to show all the validation errors in one place and, optionally, to mark each field.*

You can see that the fields that have been entered properly do not have any indicator next to them. Those that are incorrect have an asterisk by them, and the error messages are listed in the validation summary at the bottom of the page. This provides a very easy, powerful mechanism for handling form validation. In the past, the alternative was client-side code that examined each field and then displayed error messages to the user. Here, you have gained the same functionality without writing any code.

Creating ASP.NET Pages Without Visual Studio .NET

So far, you have been creating ASP.NET pages with Visual Studio .NET. This was certainly not the case for traditional ASP developers. While Microsoft did have Visual InterDev, many ASP developers continued to use Notepad as their editor of choice.

Given the richness of the VS .NET environment, and the support for full programming languages in ASP.NET, many developers are expected to create their ASP.NET applications in VS .NET. However, you do not have to create your pages in VS .NET. You can still create them using Notepad, as these examples will show you.

Creating a Simple ASP.NET Page with Notepad

Open Notepad (or any other text editor of your choice) and enter the following code. Don't worry that this HTML doesn't have all the standard HTML sections; it is still valid HTML as far as Internet Explorer is concerned.

```
<html>
   <h1>Hello, world!</h1>
</html>
```

You'll also notice there is no code here. However, you'll still save the file with an .aspx extension. Choose File, Save, and place the file in the directory in which you have created WebAppTest. By default, this is c:\Inetpub\wwwroot\WinAppTest, but this could vary. Before saving the file, make sure to change the Save as type drop-down list box to All Files. Then, name the file NotepadTest.aspx and save it.

After saving the file, open IE and enter the URL for the file, in this format:

```
http://<servername>/WebAppTest/NotepadTest.aspx
```

The page should load in the browser without errors. This shouldn't be too surprising because .NET just compiled the page and saw everything was static HTML, so that is all that was generated in response to the client request.

Now, edit the page in Notepad. Your new code should look like this:

```
<html>
   <h1 id="myHeader" runat="server">Hello, world!</h1>
   <script language="vb" runat="server">
      Sub Page_Load(Source As Object, e As EventArgs)
         myHeader.InnerText="Changed in Code"
      End Sub
   </script>
</html>
```

In this code, you have first changed the header into a scriptable element, by adding an ID attribute and telling ASP.NET to run it at the server. Then, you added a script block and threw in some VB .NET code. When the page is loading, you change the InnerText property of myHeader. To verify that this is happening, run this page, and you will see that everything works fine.

Adding Controls

You just created a simple example, and made an element of the page scriptable by giving it an ID attribute. You can continue to do this, or you can use the richer server controls. As you saw in the previous section, the tags are somewhat different for a server control. Modify your code to look like this:

```
<html>

<form id="Form1" method="post" runat="server">
   <h1 id="myHeader" runat="server">Hello, world!</h1>
   <asp:Label id="lblDateTime" runat="server">Hello</asp:Label>
   <p>
   <asp:Button id="btnDateTime" runat="server"
               text="Click Me" Onclick="btnDateTime_Click" />


   <script language="vb" runat="server">
      Sub Page_Load(Source As Object, e As EventArgs)
         myHeader.InnerText="Changed in Code"
      End Sub

      Sub btnDateTime_Click(Source As Object, e As EventArgs)
         lblDateTime.Text = Now
      End Sub
   </script>
</form>
</html>
```

What you have done is add two server controls: a label and a button. You've set some properties of these controls, and then you've added code to handle the click event of the button. Run the page and verify that when you click the button, the label shows the current date and time.

This is just a quick example of how you can create your ASPX pages using a simple text editor. For the rest of the chapter, you will return to using VS .NET.

Data Binding

One of the most common feats you will want to perform with your Web applications is presenting data from a database. Not surprisingly, Microsoft has added some ASP.NET controls specifically for displaying data. In addition, most of the regular ASP.NET server controls, such as the TextBox, can be bound to a data source.

Chapter 6, "Getting Started with ADO.NET," contains much more about data binding. However, it is useful to repeat some of that information here, in case you skipped Chapter 6.

The good news about data binding is that you use many of the same data controls you used in Chapter 6, which discussed the data controls and a little bit about ADO.NET. There is a wrinkle with Web forms, however, and it is that you work with the controls in a slightly different way. In addition, the process that is outlined in this section might change slightly between Beta 2 and the final release of VS .NET. Still, the concepts should be the same.

Create a new Web Form in the project and name it `DataTest1.aspx`. This will open the form in the designer, and it is initially blank. To add some data-bound controls to this page, you must provide it with a datasource. Click on the Toolbox and from the Data tab, drag a `SqlDataAdapter` to the page. This starts the DataAdapter Configuration Wizard, as you saw in Chapter 6. Click the Next button and you will have a choice of what data connection to use. Use the one you created in Chapter 6 that points to the Northwind database (if you skipped Chapter 6, you'll find the instructions on adding a new data connection in the section "Using the Web Forms Controls"). Click the Next button.

On the next page, choose Use SQL Statement and click the Next button. In the text box, type in this SQL statement: `Select * from Products`. Click the Finish button.

> **NOTE**
>
> If all this seems like a lot of work, it is. There is a simpler way to achieve the same results. Using the Server Explorer, you can drag the Products table over from the appropriate server and drop it on your form. You're done.

Two controls are added to your form: a `SqlDbConnection` and a `SqlDbDataAdapter`. From the Data menu, choose Generate DataSet. A dialog box will open. Choose to create a new DataSet named `dsProduct`, and leave checked the box asking whether you'd like to add an instance of the class to the designer.

Visual Studio now adds a `dsProduct` object, named `dsProduct1`, to your designer. At this point, you have a DataSet that can be filled with data.

In the Toolbox, change to the Web Forms tab. Drag a `DataGrid` control to the designer. The `DataGrid` is a control that automatically displays the data in a grid format, using HTML tables.

After the `DataGrid` is displayed on the form, right-click on it and choose Property Builder. This opens a Properties dialog box. On the General page, drop down the DataSource combo box and choose the `dsProducts1` DataSet. In the DataMember combo box, choose the Products table. In the Data Key Field combo box, drop down the list and choose the primary key of the `Products` table, `ProductID`. At this point, click the OK button.

Back in the designer, you will see that the grid has grown, and now has a column for each field in the database. You might be tempted to run this page now, but you aren't quite done.

Double-click on the form (but not the `DataTable`) to get to the code window. You should see a `DataTest1_Load` event procedure. There is already some code in there as well. You need to add two lines of code, so you end up with this:

```
Protected Sub Page_Load _
 (ByVal Sender As System.Object, ByVal e As System.EventArgs)
   If Not IsPostback Then    ' Evals true first time browser hits the page
       Me.SqlConnection1.Open()
       Me.SqlDataAdapter1.Fill(dsProducts)
       Me.SqlConnection1.Close()
       DataGrid1.DataBind()
   End If
End Sub
```

The first line of code you added, Me.sqlDbConnection1.Open(), opens the actual connection
to the database. The next line, FillDataSet(dsProduct1), calls a routine that was created for
you when you chose to generate the methods. This goes to the database, executes the statement
in the SqlDbDataAdapter, and stores the resulting records in the DataSet you pass in as a parameter (in this case, dsProduct1). The fourth line of code, DataGrid1.DataBind(), binds the
grid to the DataView control, which is in turn bound to the DataSet.

Make sure that your DataTest1 form is set as the startup form and run the project. You should
see the records from the Products table appear in a grid format on the page in IE, as shown in
Figure 8.8. If you select View, Source in the browser, you will see a tremendous amount of
state information at the top, but if you scroll past it, you will see that the data is displayed in a
simple HTML table.

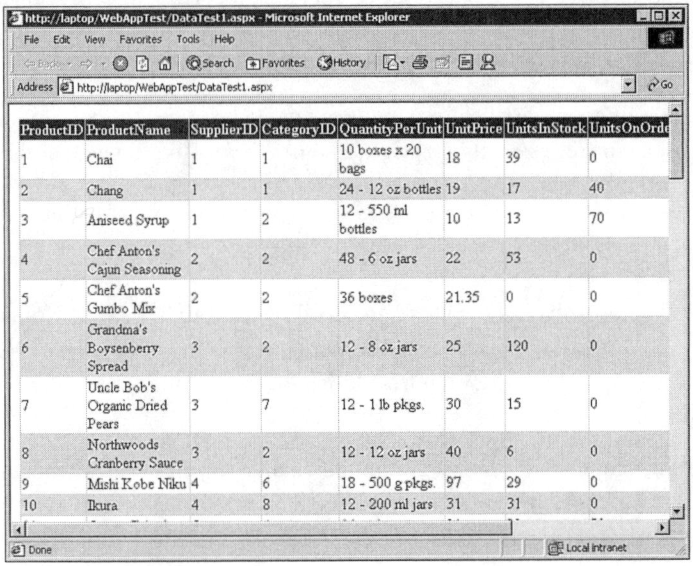

FIGURE 8.8

*The DataGrid displays the contents of the Products table. You have opened a database connection, executed a SQL
statement, and filled a grid with data, with only two lines of code.*

8

BUILDING WEB
APPLICATIONS
WITH VB .NET

This just scratches the surface of what you can do with data binding in your ASP.NET applications. However, the discussion will stop here because you have seen the basic functionality provided, and future changes to Visual Studio .NET might require changes in how data binding is done.

Handling Re-entrant Pages

You might have noticed some code in the `DataTest1_Load` event handler. That code was

```
If Not IsPostback Then    ' Evals true first time browser hits the page
```

The `IsPostback` check is used to determine whether the user has called this form before. Think about the stateless nature of HTTP: Any time someone calls a form, it looks like a brand-new user to the Web server. ASP.NET, however, writes some `ViewState` information into the page when it is rendered and sent to the client. That way, when the client submits the page back to the server, ASP.NET can see that the page has been sent back to the user before. Therefore, the code inside this `If` statement runs only once for each user who requests this page. This can be important. For example, if you want to know which users visit which pages, you can record that information just once instead of each time that an event is passed back to the server.

ASP.NET server controls work on a re-entrant page model. In other words, when a control's events cause the form in the page to be submitted, the page calls itself. In an HTML sense, the `Action` attribute in the `<Form>` tag points to the same page you are already viewing. This means that many forms call themselves over and over, and the `IsPostback` is important to improve the scalability and performance of the application.

Therefore, unlike a Windows application, the `Load` and `Unload` events can fire many times while using the same page. `IsPostback` provides an easy way to see whether this is truly the first load for a particular user.

Summary

As you can see, Microsoft has added some powerful features to VB .NET. No longer do you have to go into another tool to create your Web applications. In Visual Studio .NET, you have a powerful HTML editor and a host of controls to handle everything from static HTML to form validation to data binding.

Microsoft has removed much of the programming challenge you faced when handling events over the Web. By and large, you code your applications just as you would any Windows application, and they will work fine.

However, there are some issues that are clearly different when building Web applications. For example, state issues still require some planning and forethought. Many of the controls you use are still not as powerful as the native Windows controls. And accessing resources on the user's machine, such as reading or writing to files, is not always permitted.

Still, Visual Studio .NET represents a huge leap forward in the ability to easily create event-driven Web applications. The next chapter carries that improvement a step further.

8

BUILDING WEB APPLICATIONS WITH VB .NET

Building Web Services with VB .NET

IN THIS CHAPTER

Microsoft likes to point out that part of the goal of .NET is to act like a huge operating system. In effect, the entire Internet becomes your operating system, or at least your network. This means that pieces of your applications can be distributed over the Internet, but your applications run as if the pieces were all on your local machine.

Imagine if you had told someone back in the early days of Visual Basic that someday they'd be writing their applications in a number of separate components and putting those parts on different machines. The application sitting on the user's desktop would call these components on other machines, and those components would access the data on still other machines. The data would be returned to these components and finally flow back to the client application.

Of course, this sounds quite normal today, but to a developer back in the days of Visual Basic 1.0, it would sound quite strange. However, now consider taking those components, and even the database, and removing them from your internal network. Spread them out all over the Internet, so that the only way with which you can communicate with them is HTTP. This is precisely what a Web service is all about.

The idea behind a Web service is to create a reusable component that can be called over standard HTTP. .NET allows you to create Web services that have the full power of a .NET application, including access to all the .NET Framework namespaces. These components are *discoverable*, which means that you can locate and call available components on other machines. The format for calling particular methods is exposed as well, so anyone can determine what methods are available and how to call them.

Web services, like COM components, can be called by any front-end application. Therefore, both Windows forms and Web forms can call the same Web services. Web services are free to call other Web services. Your .NET Web services are also callable by any non-Microsoft application as well because Web services are, by nature, callable by any client on any platform using just HTTP.

To learn more about Web services, you will dive in and create your first Web service. After that, you'll go back and learn more about how Web services work.

Creating Your First Web Service

Currency conversion is a common activity needed by Web applications. Because of the global nature of the Web, you can browse stores anywhere in the world. Normally, of course, those stores show prices in their local currency. You might need to convert these values into your local currency. In this section, you'll build the basis for a currency conversion Web service.

Open Visual Studio .NET. Create a new Visual Basic project of the type ASP.NET Web Service. Name the project CurrencyConverter and make sure that the server on which you create the project is a Web server running IIS 4.0 or higher and the .NET Framework.

After the project is loaded, you have a blank designer, much like you have seen before. If you look in the Solution Explorer window, you'll see that the current page is called `Service1.asmx`. `.ASMX` is the extension for a Web service. You'll also notice a file named `Currency Converter.vsdisco`. A `.VSDISCO` file is a discovery file, and the discovery process will be discussed later in this chapter.

Right-click on the `Service1.asmx` file in the Solution Explorer and choose Rename. Name the file `CurrConvert.asmx`. Notice that this just changes the filename; the service is still named `Service1`. Double-click on the designer of the `CurrConvert.asmx` file, and the code-behind file named `CurrConvert.asmx.vb` will open.

If you look at the code, you'll notice that a function is commented out. The function is a public function named `HelloWorld()`, but there is a strange element before the name of the function: `<WebMethod()>`. This marks the function as a method that is callable over the Web. Using the `HelloWorld()` example as a template, add the following code to the file:

```
<WebMethod()> Public Function ConvertCurrency(ByVal dAmount As Decimal, _
    ByVal sFrom As String, ByVal sTo As String) As Decimal
  Select Case sFrom
    Case "British Pounds"
       Return CDec(dAmount * 1.44333)
    Case "Japanese Yen"
       Return CDec(dAmount * 0.00859358)
  End Select
End Function
```

This code creates a method called `ConvertCurrency`. The method accepts three parameters: the amount of the currency to convert, the type of currency to convert from, and the type of currency to convert to. Inside the procedure is a simple `Select Case` statement that determines whether you are converting from British pounds or Japanese yen. Inside each case, you convert the amount into United States dollars.

In the real world, of course, the money could be converted to one of many countries. More importantly, you could query a database or some other resource to determine the current exchange rate, instead of hard-coding it as is done here. Again, the purpose of this exercise is merely to show you how Web services work.

Now, click on the Build menu and choose Build. This will build the Web service on the Web server. The service is now ready for testing.

Testing the Web Service

Visual Studio .NET provides a very simple way to test a Web service. Right-click on `CurrConvert.asmx` in the Solution Explorer window and choose View in Browser.

.NET creates a default page that allows you to work with methods in your service whose parameters can be input via HTTP POST or GET. The only option on the page is the one method you created: ConvertCurrency. Click on the ConvertCurrency link, and a new page appears. The new page allows you to enter values for any parameters in the method you created, and also contains a button to submit those values. Figure 9.1 shows what this form looks like.

> **NOTE**
>
> Although the page that is generated for you does have the ConvertCurrency method listed, there is also a discussion on the fact that your Web service is using http://tempuri.org as the default namespace. You will want to change this before distributing it. This will be discussed in more detail in Chapter 13, "Configuration and Deployment."

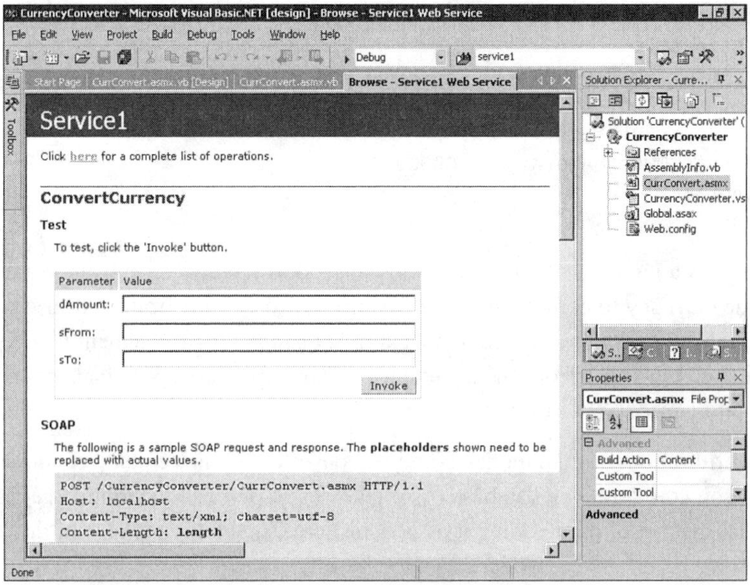

FIGURE 9.1
Visual Studio .NET automatically generates a page that allows you to test your Web services.

You can see three text boxes in the middle of the page that allow you to enter values and then test them by using the Invoke button. Enter 100 in the dAmount box, British Pounds in the sFrom box, and US Dollars in the sTo box. Technically, in this example, it doesn't matter what you enter in the sTo box because your code never checks it. However, you can't leave the sTo box blank because the parameter is not optional. It helps to go ahead and put in an actual value for the "convert to" field.

When you click the Invoke button, the page passes the data to the Web service. The method runs and the data is returned in an XML stream that looks like this:

```
<?xml version="1.0" encoding="utf-8" ?>
<decimal xmlns="http://tempuri.org/">144.333</decimal>
```

You can see that the return is a value, of the decimal data type, of 144.333. This means that 100 British pounds buys 144.333 U.S. dollars. If you run the form again but put Japanese Yen in the sFrom field, you will see that 100 yen buys approximately .86 U.S. dollars.

Immediately, you can see that the return from the Web service is an XML stream. What you can't see is that the call to the service is formatted as an XML stream as well. You'll learn more about this later.

Creating a Web Service Client

Now that you have created and tested the Web service, it is time to create a client that can access it. The client can be almost any kind of application, including a Windows application, Web application, or Web service. For this example, you'll create an ASP.NET Web Application project to test the service.

Create a new ASP.NET Web Application in Visual Studio .NET and name it ConversionClient. Make sure that you have it set to close the existing solution because you do not want this project to be added to the Web service solution.

You will wind up with a blank designer. Add the following Web Forms controls to the designer: four labels, one text box, two drop-down list boxes, and one button. Lay them out so that they look something like Figure 9.2.

> **NOTE**
>
> The instructions had you drag four labels from the Web Forms tab of the Toolbox. Unless you're going to change them via code, you're actually much better off using the labels from the HTML tab. This HTML label just inserts a lightweight <DIV> tag, instead of creating a server control. In this case, as you'll see in a moment, the first three labels could have been HTML labels.

Now, modify the Text properties of the first three labels to Amount:, From:, and To:. Change the text on the button to Convert. Clear out the Text property in the last label. Change the name of the last label to lblResult by changing its ID property.

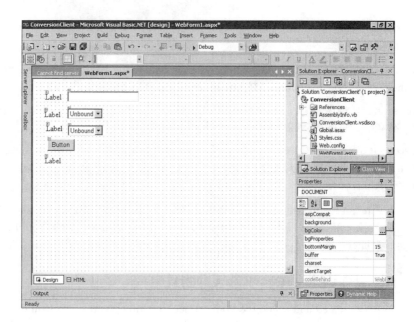

Figure 9.2

The construction begins on a client that will use your Web service.

Click on the drop-down list box next to the From: label and name it cboFrom. Now, locate the Items property under the Misc section and click the ellipses. This opens the ListItem Collection Editor, as shown in Figure 9.3. Click the Add button, and in the ListItem Properties panel, set the text to Japanese Yen and change the Selected attribute to True, as shown in Figure 9.4. Click the Add button again, but this time, enter British Pounds into the Text attribute. Do not set Selected to True for this one. Click the OK button.

Now, click the drop-down list box next to the To: label. Change its name to cboTo. Click the ellipses in the Items property box. Add one item, US Dollars, and mark it as Selected. Your final form should look like the one in Figure 9.5.

Next, double-click on the Convert button to get to the code window. Before you write the code for the click event, however, you need to add a reference to the Web service you created in the last section. Adding a reference is critical; doing so allows you to program against the Web service as if it were a local component.

In the Solution Explorer, right-click on the ConversionClient project name and choose Add Web Reference. This is different from the Add Reference option, so make sure that you choose the correct one. The Add Web Reference dialog box will appear. In the Address field, you need to type the address of your Web service. This takes on the following format:

```
http://<servername>/<projectname>/<disco file>
```

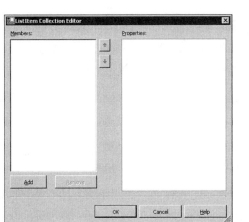

FIGURE 9.3

The ListItem Collection Editor.

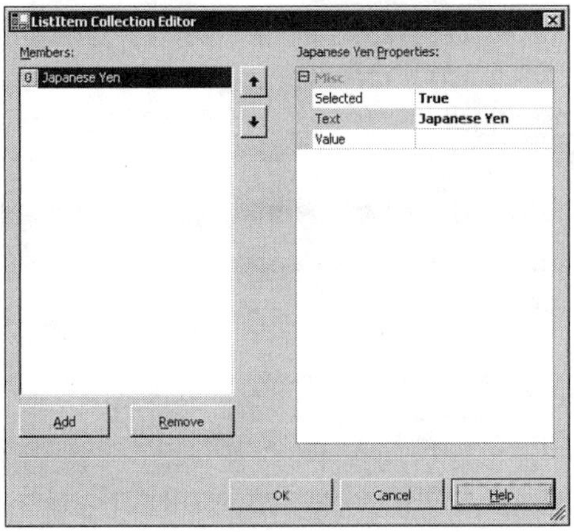

FIGURE 9.4

Adding items to the drop-down list box.

Your server name might be different, but in my case, the address looks like the following (you could just use `localhost` as the server name if it is on the same machine):

```
http://laptop/CurrencyConverter/CurrencyConverter.vsdisco
```

After you have entered the URL, click the go arrow. The dialog box will make contact with the discovery file and retrieve the necessary information from the Web service. Your Add Web Reference dialog box will look like the one in Figure 9.6. Click the Add Reference button to complete this process.

9

BUILDING WEB
SERVICES WITH
VB .NET

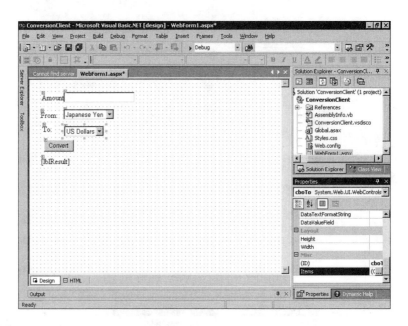

FIGURE 9.5

The final user interface for the form, showing the drop-down list boxes containing default values.

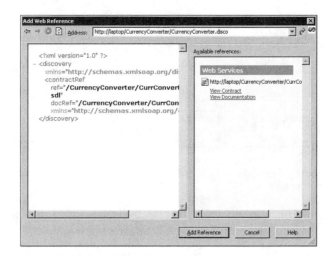

FIGURE 9.6

The Add Web Reference dialog box has retrieved information about your Web service.

NOTE

On some machines, it can take several minutes for the right-side pane of the Add Web Reference dialog box to be filled in. Be patient if it doesn't happen immediately.

After you add the reference, you'll see a Web References node appear in the Solution Explorer. If you expand the node, you'll see an item with the name of the server holding the component to which you just connected. You can rename this if you want, so right-click on the server name and change the name to ConversionService. Figure 9.7 shows what this should look like when you are done.

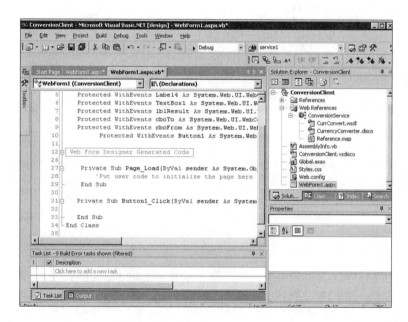

FIGURE 9.7
The Add Web Reference dialog box has retrieved information about your Web service.

Now, in the WebForm1.aspx.vb code window, you need to import the namespace for the Web service. The namespace is the name of your current application and the name of the server on which the Web service resides. However, you just changed the name to ConversionService, so add the following code before the Public Class WebForm1 line:

```
Imports ConversionClient.ConversionService
```

ConversionClient is the name of the client application in which you are currently working, and ConversionService is the name you gave to your reference to the Web service. Actually, ConversionClient is both the name of your client application, and also the default namespace. Recall that the default namespace for an application is the application name unless you change it.

In the Button1_Click procedure, you need to write the code to call the Web service, pass in the proper parameters, and then display the output. Type the following code:

```
Public Sub Button1_Click(ByVal sender As Object, _
   ByVal e As System.EventArgs)
     Dim cService As New Service1

     Dim dAmount As Decimal
     Dim sFrom, sTo As String
     Dim dAnswer As Decimal

     dAmount = CType(TextBox1().Text, Decimal)
     sFrom = cboFrom().SelectedItem.ToString
     sTo = cboTo().SelectedItem.ToString
     dAnswer = cService.ConvertCurrency(dAmount, sFrom, sTo)
     lblResult.Text = dAnswer.ToString
End Sub
```

This code first creates an object of type Service1, which is the name of the service you created in the last section. You can call it this way because it resides inside the ConversionService namespace you imported at the top of the code window. Next, some variables are created and filled with values from the controls on the form. The code calls the ConvertCurrency method and passes in the parameters. The result is returned into a variable, which is then used to set the lblResult.Text property.

Go ahead and run the project. You'll see the Web form start up in IE. Put 100 in the Amount: box, and choose Japanese Yen for the From: box. Click the Convert button, and you should see the value 0.859358 appear below the button after the page makes a round trip to the server. The resulting page should appear like the one shown in Figure 9.8.

One of the important things to understand about this process is that you never had to get your hands dirty handling the underlying XML. Instead, you programmed using the service just like a Class Library application, with properties and methods. Your client application calls the service just like any other component, except that you are now calling components that could be anywhere on the Internet.

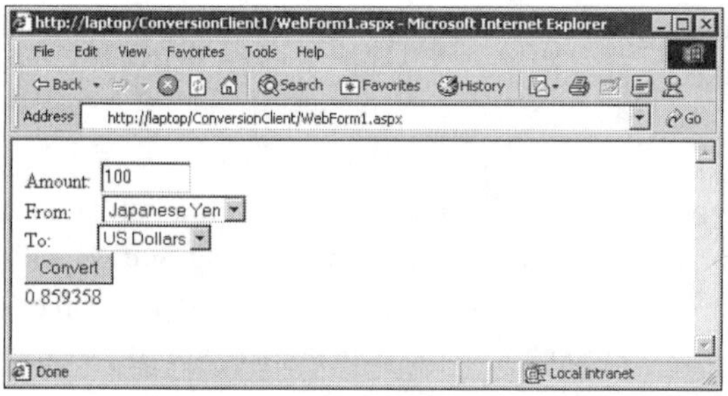

FIGURE 9.8
Your Web Application project has just received a result from your Web service.

Another thing to realize is that you have basically supplanted DCOM, which is specific to the Microsoft platform, and replaced it with the ubiquitous HTTP and XML. This means that the client does not have to be running the Windows operating system. Because the communication is all text, it flows freely through firewalls. The actual call you made to the service was simple text flowing over HTTP, but this was hidden from you by .NET, which allowed you to treat the Web service as a component.

Building Data-Driven Web Services

One of the greatest strengths of Web services is their capability to return data from a database. This allows you to share data from your server without having to open up the database for direct access. SQL Server allows you to grant direct access to the database via HTTP, but the user is free to enter any kind of statement, including inserts, updates, deletes, and DDL statements. Giving this kind of open access to your database is almost always undesirable. Web services are one way in which you can restrict the access to the database while still making the necessary data available.

By creating methods, you control what data can be accessed. For example, a `GetOrders` method might be used to return one or more orders from the database. An `AddOrder` method might be used to add new orders to the system. The consumers of this service are merely calling methods and passing parameters; they don't have to know anything about the underlying database.

Creating the `OrderInfo` Service

In VS .NET, start a new ASP.NET Web Service project named `OrderInfo`. The designer will appear for Service1.asmx. In the Solution Explorer, rename the file from Service1.asmx to

`OrderInfo.asmx`. Go to the code for the service and change the class name from `Service1` to `Orders`. Your class definition should now look like this:

```
Public Class Orders
```

Now, return to the designer. From the Toolbox, go to the Data tab and drag over a `SqlDataAdapter` control. As you saw in Chapter 6, "Getting Started with ADO.NET," this will launch the Data Adapter Configuration Wizard. Click Next to move past the informational screen to the screen asking you to choose the data connection. If you have already performed the examples in Chapter 6, you should already have a data connection that points you to the Northwind database on some computer. If you do not, perform the following steps:

1. Click on the New Connection button.
2. On the Connection tab Data Link Properties dialog box, enter the server name, user ID, password, and database (in this case, Northwind).
3. Click OK.

After you have chosen the connection, click the Next button to choose a query type. Choose the first option, Use SQL Statements, and click the Next button.

On the next page of the wizard, you can type in the SQL statement. The SQL statement is somewhat lengthy, so you can instead click on the Query Builder button. This launches the Query Builder, a tool that lets you graphically design your queries. When you first start the tool, the Add Table dialog box will be shown. Add the following tables to the query:

- Customers
- Order Details
- Orders
- Products
- Shippers

The Query Builder will determine the relationships between the tables. Your Query Builder should now look something like that shown in Figure 9.9.

Now, choose the following fields by clicking the check box next to them in the tables:

- `OrderID` in the Orders table
- `CompanyName` in the Customers table
- `ProductName` in the Products table
- `Quantity` in the Order Details table
- `CompanyName` in the Shippers table
- `ShippedDate` in the Orders table

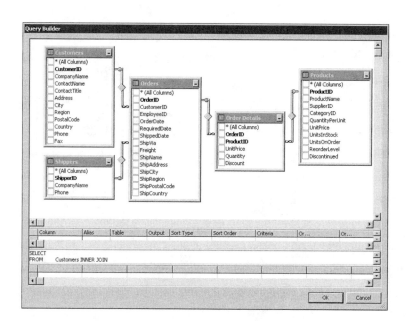

FIGURE 9.9
The Query Builder showing the tables in the query.

As you click these fields, you might notice that you have two fields named CompanyName. Obviously, SQL isn't going to like this, so if you look in the grid of the Query Builder, you'll see that it gives the second CompanyName field an alias of Expr1. Go to the grid; in the Alias field for CompanyName from the Customers table, type **Customer**; in the Alias field for the CompanyName from the Shippers table, type **Shipper**. Your grid should look like the one in Figure 9.10.

Verify your SQL statement against this one, and then click the OK button to close the Query Builder:

```
SELECT
    Orders.OrderID, Customers.CompanyName AS Customer,
    Products.ProductName, [Order Details].Quantity,
    Shippers.CompanyName AS Shipper, Orders.ShippedDate
FROM
    Customers INNER JOIN Orders ON
    Customers.CustomerID = Orders.CustomerID
    INNER JOIN [Order Details] ON
    Orders.OrderID = [Order Details].OrderID INNER JOIN
    Products ON [Order Details].ProductID = Products.ProductID
    INNER JOIN Shippers ON Orders.ShipVia = Shippers.ShipperID
```

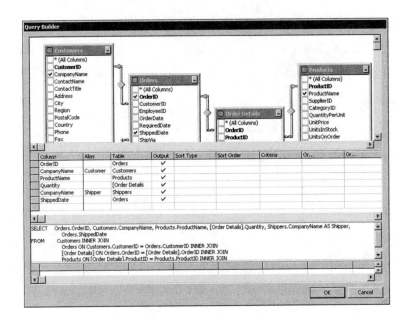

FIGURE 9.10

The grid of the Query Builder with your more complex query.

Back in the wizard, you will see the SQL statement generated by the Query Builder. Click the Next button to move to the next page of the wizard. You'll just see more textual information, so click the Finish button.

Just as you saw in Chapter 6, two controls are added to the designer: SqlConnection1 and SqlDataAdapter1. A Data menu is also added to the VS .NET IDE. Click on Data and then Generate Dataset. The Generate Dataset dialog box appears. Choose to add a new dataset, and name it dsOrders. In the Choose which table(s) to add to the dataset box, only one table will be shown. Make sure that this table is chosen, and *remember which table you see here*. Finally, click the check box to add a copy of the dataset to the designer and then click the OK button. A new DataSet control, named dsOrders1, is added to the designer.

Return to the code view for the service. Create the following method:

```
<WebMethod()> Public Function GetOrders() As DataSet
    SqlDataAdapter1.Fill(dsOrders1)
    GetOrders = dsOrders1
End Function
```

This method, called GetOrders, simply calls the Fill method of the SqlDataAdapter you added to the Web service. It fills the dataset you created, dsOrders1. Then, dsOrders1 is returned from the method.

Recall from Chapter 6 that this is legal. The dataset was created to be passed across process boundaries, using XML as the default transport mechanism. Here, you are taking a dataset and returning it to a client. In this case, your client will be a .NET client also using ADO.NET, so you will be able to work with the result as you would any other ADO.NET dataset.

Go ahead and build the Web service. You will now create a client to call the Web service and display the data. However, before you create a client, you can test it in your browser. Open IE, and then type in the appropriate URL, which will look something like this:

```
http://server/OrderInfo/OrderInfo.asmx
```

The default page appears, generated for you by .NET. You will see that the only method available is GetOrders, as you can see in Figure 9.11. Go ahead and click on GetOrders.

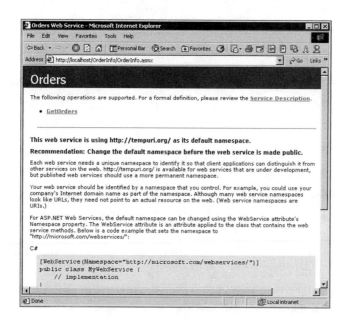

FIGURE 9.11

The default test page for the Orders Web service.

On the next page, go ahead and click the Invoke button. Remember, your GetOrders method is designed to return an ADO.NET DataSet object, something that typically wouldn't have any meaning on platforms other than .NET. However, after you click on the Invoke button, you'll be able to verify that ADO.NET does indeed pass the data across the wire as XML. In fact, Figure 9.12 shows some of the XML that is returned from the GetOrders method of the Orders Web service.

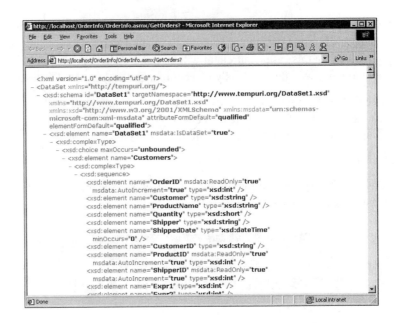

FIGURE 9.12

The XML output of the GetOrders *method.*

Building the Client

Now that you have created the Web service and are returning data from it, it is time to create a client application. In this example, you'll create a regular Windows application that will consume the data. Create a new VB .NET Windows Application project named OrderTracker.

The first step will be to add a reference to your Web service. You are free to add the reference in the same way you did in the previous example. However, the tool used in VS .NET to add Web references sometimes has some challenges. There are two console applications, however, that will give you the same functionality, although they require more work.

Adding Web References Using disco.exe and wsdl.exe

To use the console applications to add your Web reference, make sure that disco.exe and wsdl.exe are in the path, or at least be sure that you know where they are so that you can type in the complete path. In these examples, both executables have been copied to the root of the C: drive to minimize typing.

Open a console window and go to the directory containing the OrderTracker application. Actually, you don't have to go to this directory, but it's probably the best place to put the files you are about to generate. In Windows 2000, the default directory for the OrderTracker application is c:\documents and settings\<user>\my documents\visual studio projects\OrderTracker. From here, you'll want to execute `disco.exe` first, which examines the Web services and generates some files, including the `.discomap` file you'll use in a moment. In the console window, you'll want to type the following command, but first note that the disco.exe application is probably not in the path. This means you'll have to locate it and put in a directory that is in the path, or you'll have to type the full path to the executable.

```
disco http://server/OrderInfo/OrderInfo.vsdisco
```

After `disco.exe` finishes, you will have three files created for you: `OrderInfo.wsdl`, `OrderInfo.disco`, and `results.discomap`.

Next, you'll use the `wsdl.exe` application, which generates a class module that you can use in your application. It contains all the necessary code to call the Web service. At the console prompt, type the following command:

```
wsdl /language:VB results.discomap
```

If you fail to specify the language, you will get a C# class file. After running this code, you will be informed that a new file, named `Orders.vb`, has been created for you. You can see this file if you examine the directory.

You can see the commands that were typed, and the resulting messages, in Figure 9.13.

FIGURE 9.13

The disco.exe *and* wsdl.exe *applications and their output.*

9

BUILDING WEB
SERVICES WITH
VB .NET

You are not quite done. Back in VS .NET, you need to add the class file that you just created. In the Solution Explorer window, right-click on the project and choose Add, and then choose Add Existing Item. Choose `Orders.vb` and click the Open button.

Double-click on the `Orders.vb` file to open the code. If you look at the Imports statements, you'll notice that the two that start with `System.Web` are underlined. This is because your program does not currently have a reference to the `System.Web` namespace. In the Solution

Explorer, right-click on the References node and choose Add Reference. The Add Reference dialog box will appear. On the .NET tab, scroll down and highlight `System.Web.dll` and `System.Web.Services.dll`, and then click the Select button. Your Add Reference dialog box should look like the one in Figure 9.14. Click the OK button to close the dialog box, and you'll notice that the two `Imports` statements starting with `System.Web` are no longer underlined.

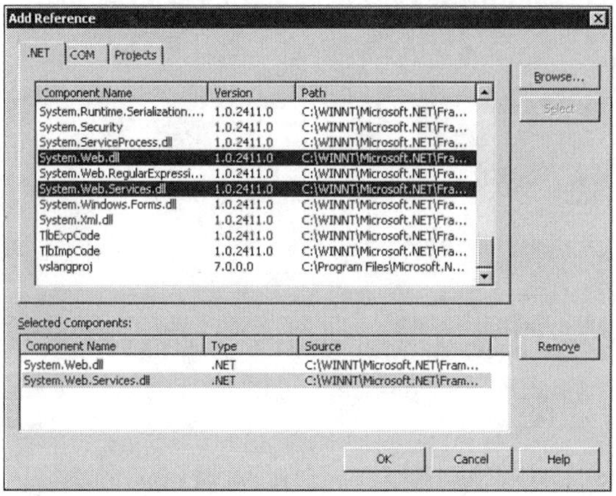

FIGURE 9.14
The Add Reference dialog box being used to add a reference so that you can call Web services.

Go back to Form1 and add two controls: a button and a DataGrid. Enlarge the form and stretch the grid to make it wider. Now, double-click on the button and add the following code to your application:

```
Private Sub Button1_Click(ByVal sender As System.Object, _
 ByVal e As System.EventArgs) Handles Button1.Click
    Dim myOrders As New Orders()
    Dim myDS As New System.Data.DataSet()
    myDS = myOrders.GetOrders
    DataGrid1.DataSource = myDS
    'the DataMember will be whatever table you saw
    'when you created the dataset
    DataGrid1.DataMember = "Customers"
End Sub
```

You might have to change the `DataMember` property; earlier, you were told to remember the table that showed up when you created the dataset.

Go ahead and run your application. When you click on the button, you create a new `Orders` object, called `myOrders`. This is an instance of the `Orders` class you added in `Orders.vb`. However, this class acts as a reference to the Web service, and provides all the plumbing necessary to call the Web service for you. You then call the GetOrders method and return the value into a DataSet object named myDS. This allows you to easily code against the data on both ends using the ADO.NET objects, but as you saw, the data is sent across the wire as XML.

When the data is back, you bind the DataGrid control to the dataset, and the table in the dataset. Recall that a dataset can have multiple tables, but in this case it looks like one flat table. The dataset simply grabbed the table name of the first table you added to the query.

When the binding is complete, you are done. Figure 9.15 shows what the application looks like after clicking the button. Enough records do come across that it can take a number of seconds for the grid to add them all. Be patient.

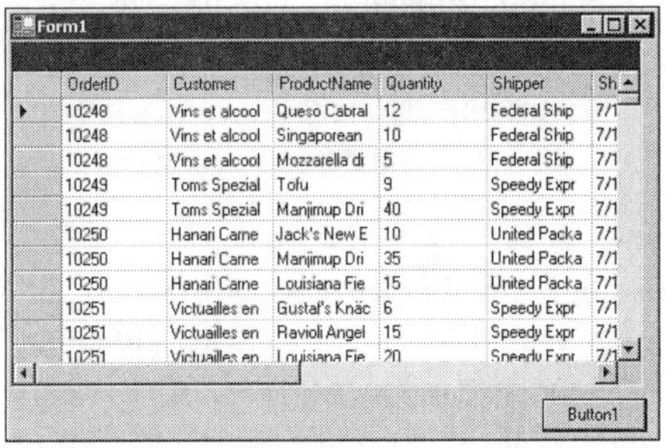

FIGURE 9.15
Your Windows application pulling data from a Web service, and then binding that data to a grid.

How Web Services Work

As you saw in the code, any method that you want to publicly expose is made available by adding the <WebMethod()> attribute to the method declaration. This makes the method automatically discoverable by anyone accessing the project's URL. Any class that has one or more methods marked with <WebMethod()> becomes a Web service. The Framework handles the task of setting up all the necessary hooks for the component to be callable via HTTP.

Most Web services will import the System.Web.Services namespace. This isn't necessary, but if you don't, you'll have to use the full System.Web.Services.<class> syntax to use any of the classes, such as the WebMethod you placed in front of your ConvertCurrency method. Many services also inherit from the System.Web.Services.WebService base class because doing so gives them access to the intrinsic ASP objects, such as the Application and Session objects. This class contains the underlying methods to enable the Web service functionality. Web services also have a discovery file (the VSDISCO file, sometimes called just the DISCO file) that later helps generate a WSDL (Service Description Language) file. You will see more on this later.

You saw earlier that you could test a Web service by choosing the View in Browser option from the ASMX file. .NET builds a page on-the-fly that contains text boxes that map to each parameter in the various methods in the service. This page also contains some descriptive text and a link to view the SDL for the service. The SDL is quite lengthy even for the small, single method service you created earlier, but it is this file that allows any client, using any operating system, to call the Web service.

And You Thought Disco Was Dead

After you have created the service, it is time to deploy it to the Web server. Earlier in the chapter, deployment was easy because you just had to choose to build the project. However, if you now want to copy the service to another machine, you have to make sure that you place the proper discovery document on that machine. The DISCO file allows a user to determine what services are available on your server, and what methods these services support. When users point their browsers to your VSDISCO file, they can discover the Web services you have to offer.

However, what if a user does not know the path to—or the name of—the discovery document? Any development machine with VS .NET installed has the dynamic discovery document, `default.vsdisco`. In general, ASP.NET servers rely on `default.vsdisco` files for static discovery. Therefore, the Web service developer needs to think carefully about which services should be available to the outside world on the deployment machine, and must author the static disco file properly.

How you actually deploy the Web service depends on whether you are using Visual Studio .NET or performing a manual copy. Furthermore, it changes depending on whether you are distributing a binary file or the text-based ASMX file. This deployment discussion will be covered in Chapter 13.

Speaking of discovery, you should be aware of UDDI. UDDI stands for Universal Discovery, Description, and Integration. The UDDI Project is an attempt to form a registration service for Web services. This means that you could search for Web services within a particular industry or even a particular company. This vendor-independent initiative represents a real attempt to create a central repository for Web components, which means you could easily create Web applications using components that already exist and are accessible over the Web. You can learn more about the UDDI Project by visiting its site at `http://www.uddi.org`.

Accessing Web Services

ASP.NET currently supports three methods for accessing a Web service: HTTP-GET, HTTP-POST, and SOAP. SOAP, which stands for Simple Object Access Protocol, defines an XML format for calling methods and passing in parameters, all surrounded by the schema definition. In addition, the result comes back in an XML format. HTTP-GET and HTTP-POST can call

Web services, but SOAP adds the ability to pass more complex data types, such as classes, structures, and datasets. Despite these advanced features, SOAP is still all text, which has the advantage of being portable and able to traverse firewalls, unlike other methods for calling distributed components, such as DCOM and CORBA.

The Web services you create with VB .NET automatically support all three mechanisms. In fact, because your services support SOAP, they can be called not only with HTTP, but with other protocols as well, such as SMTP.

If you know the URL for your Web service, you can enter it in the browser and you will get the same type of page that was generated for you when you tested the service inside the IDE. For example, the following is a line that points to the service you built in this chapter. Don't forget to change the name of the server as necessary:

```
http://localhost/currencyconverter/currconvert.asmx
```

This creates a page that allows you to test the service. This is important because by knowing this address, anyone can connect to your Web service using any tool. There is also a link to the WSDL contract, which is used by your client application. This contract contains more detailed information about the service. More importantly, it is the file used to generate a Web service proxy on the client. You don't have to worry about doing this if your client is built in Visual Studio .NET and you add a Web reference, as you did in this chapter. VS .NET creates the proxy for you, which is just a VB .NET class file (or C#, depending on your language preference). If you want to create it manually, you merely save the SDL to your machine and run the Webserviceutil.exe program that comes with VS .NET.

Security is a topic that often comes up when discussing Web services. You do have control over the security on these services, and you might not want everyone in the world to be able to access the service freely. Let's face it: Some companies actually want to *charge* people for the use of certain services, in a display of what our capitalist system is all about. Because you are building your Web services for .NET, you can take full advantage of the security features it offers. Because these services are being offered via HTTP, Internet Information Server is another possible point for adding security. As with deployment, security will be discussed later in this book; specifically, security is discussed in Chapter 12, "Performance and Security."

Summary

Although this chapter is short, it shows you the basic building blocks for creating Web services. Web services are one of the most exciting technologies in the .NET Framework because they allow you to use the architecture of the Internet as a way to extend the distributed nature of applications. No longer are you tied to accessing components only within your organization. Now you can access components anywhere, via HTTP. And you can do it without worrying about firewalls, or what operating systems exist on the host or the client.

Building Windows Services and Console Applications with VB .NET

IN THIS CHAPTER

Visual Basic .NET lets you build Windows Services natively in VB for the first time. Windows Services, formerly called NT Services, are potentially long-running executables that can start without a user logging in, can be paused and restarted, and can be configured to run under different security contexts. Windows Services had been the domain of C++ developers until now, when the .NET Framework opens the ability for any .NET language to create services.

Windows Services should not be confused with XML Web Services, which are implemented as a different project type. Services are supported on only Windows NT, Windows 2000, and Windows XP.

Services work a little differently from just about any other project type. You cannot start a project within the Visual Studio .NET environment and step through it for debugging purposes. You must install your application as a service with the operating system in order for it to run. Then, after it is running, you can attach a debugger to it. Because Windows Services do not have a user interface, they typically use the event log to communicate problems or messages to the user or administrator.

Services are useful in certain circumstances. For example, I worked on an application in which files could arrive at any time, via FTP. A service ran that monitored a directory, and received an event when a file was added to the directory. The service then went about processing the file as necessary. This was a perfect use for a service: It needed to run all the time, regardless of whether anyone was logged in. The files could arrive at any time, so the service had to be running constantly. Finally, no user interface was necessary.

Once again, you will dive into a project and get it working, and then examine its various pieces. The service you will write checks the processor usage on a regular basis and logs the information to a file. This service introduces something new: capturing performance counters. This will be woven into your first service.

Creating Your First Windows Services Project

Open Visual Studio .NET and create a Windows Services project. Name the project LearningVBservice. You'll see that all you have in the Solution Explorer is a .VB file named Service1, along with the AssemblyInfo.vb file.

Click once on the designer to access the properties for the service. Change the ServiceName property from Service1 to UsageMonitor. Also change the (Name) property from Service1 to UsageMonitor. Now, double-click on the designer to access the code. You'll notice that the first line after the Imports statement is this:

```
Public Class UsageMonitor
```

If you expand the code the IDE generated for you, you'll notice that you have a Sub New, which is not surprising. However, you also have a Shared Sub Main, which is not something you have seen in most of your other applications. As you might suspect, the Shared Sub Main is the first procedure that will run by default. Therefore, there is already some code in this routine to initialize the service. One line of code in Shared Sub Main references Service1, but you've changed that name. Therefore, find the following line of code:

```
ServicesToRun = New System.ServiceProcess.ServiceBase() {New Service1()}
```

Change the code to this:

```
ServicesToRun = New System.ServiceProcess.ServiceBase() {New UsageMonitor()}
```

Now, go back to the designer page. Open the Toolbox and in the Components tab, drag a Timer over and drop it on the designer. The entire Windows service is a component, which as you have seen, has a form-like designer. Because this designer is not a form, the Timer does not end up in the component tray; instead, VS .NET shows the control on the designer surface.

If you select the Timer1 component and look at its properties, you'll see that by default it is enabled, and its Interval property is set to 100. The Interval property is in milliseconds, and is of type Double. Therefore, to wait one second, you put in a value of 1000. For this example, you want to capture statistics once every five seconds, so enter 5000 in the Interval property. In a real application, you might want to grab values only every minute or every five minutes, but you probably don't want to sit and wait ten minutes just to make sure that this first Windows Services project works properly.

> **NOTE**
>
> The Enabled property of the Timer has switched from being True or False numerous times throughout the beta process. Therefore, it is entirely possible that timers will be disabled by default in the final release of VS .NET.

Next, drag over a PerformanceCounter control from the Components tab of the Toolbox. This allows you to access the same performance information you can get with the Performance tool (often called Performance Monitor, or PerfMon). Highlight the PerformanceCounter1 control and modify the following properties:

- Set CategoryName to "Processor"
- Set CounterName to "% Processor Time"
- Set InstanceName to "_Total"
- Leave MachineName set to a period, which is a shortcut for the local machine name

10

> **NOTE**
>
> An alternative approach is to drag over a `PerfCounter` object from the Server Explorer, and then tweak the properties. Don't forget about the Server Explorer when working with services.

Double-click on the `Timer1` component to open the code window. By default, the IDE puts you in the `Timer1_Elapsed` event procedure. This isn't what you want, because you want to respond to an event every time the timer fires. Therefore, you want to work with the `Timer1_Tick` event procedure. Before entering anything for the `Timer1_Tick` procedure, go to the very top of the code window and add the following line of code:

```
Imports System.IO
```

Now, create the `Timer1_Tick` event procedure and make it look like the following code:

```
Protected Sub Timer1_Tick(ByVal sender As Object, _
  ByVal e As System.EventArgs)
  Dim file As TextWriter = New StreamWriter("c:\output.txt", True)
  file.WriteLine("CPU Usage: " & _
    PerformanceCounter1.NextValue.ToString & " - " & Now)
  file.Close()
End Sub
```

This is the code that runs every five seconds. It opens a text file called `output.txt` in the root of the C: drive. The `True` argument of the `WriteLine` method appends to the existing file. The code writes a string that contains the CPU usage from the performance counter, and then appends the current date and time. Finally, it closes the file. Notice that to use the shortcut name `StreamWriter`, you had to add the `System.IO` namespace, which has classes that handle many different types of I/O operations. This keeps you from having to type `System.IO.StreamWriter` to reference the class.

If you look further down in the code, you should see stubs for the `OnStart` and `OnStop` routines. Modify the stubs—and add an `OnContinue` routine—as shown in the following:

```
Protected Overrides Sub OnStart(ByVal args() As String)
    timer1.Enabled = False
    Dim file As TextWriter = New StreamWriter("c:\output.txt", True)
    file.WriteLine("Service Started")
    file.Close()
    timer1.Interval = 5000
    timer1.Enabled = True
End Sub
```

```
Protected Overrides Sub OnStop()
    Timer1.Enabled = False
    Dim file As TextWriter = New StreamWriter("c:\output.txt", True)
    file.WriteLine("Service Stopped")
    file.Close()
End Sub

Protected Overrides Sub OnContinue()
    Dim file As TextWriter = New StreamWriter("c:\output.txt", True)
    file.WriteLine("Service Restarted")
    file.Close()
End Sub
```

As you can see in the OnStart procedure, when the service starts, the code writes to the text file that the service is starting. Then the timer's interval is set and the timer is enabled, just to make sure that the settings are correct. In the OnStop procedure, you record the fact that the service is stopped if someone does stop the service. If someone pauses the service and later resumes it, the fact that the service was restarted is written in the text file in the OnContinue procedure.

This is all that needs to be written in the service. However, you have to do more to make the service usable: You have to add installers to your application.

Adding Installers to Your Service

You need to return to the designer for your service. Right-click on the designer and choose Add Installer. A new window is added to the designer area, labeled ProjectInstaller.vb [Design]. Two components will be added to the project. One, the ServiceInstaller1, is for installing your service, whereas the other, ServiceProcessInstaller1, is for installing the process that hosts your service while it is running. All services run in their own process so that they can run independently of any particular user. Both the ServiceInstaller and the ServiceProcessInstaller are used by an installation utility to properly register and configure the service.

Before building the project, you need to perform a couple of tasks because you changed the name of the class from UserService1 to UsageMonitor. On the ProjectInstaller.vb designer, click on the ServiceInstaller1 control and verify that the ServiceName property is set to UsageMonitor, changing it if necessary. Then, in the Solution Explorer window, right-click on the LearningVBservice project and choose Properties. In the property pages, change the Startup Object combo box to UsageMonitor and click OK.

Next, click on the ServiceProcessInstaller1 and look at the Account property. The Account property determines the type of account under which this service will run. The default is User,

10

but the Username and Password properties are blank by default. If you leave the Username and Password properties blank, the installation (not the build) will fail. In certain interim builds of VS .NET, installing a service without the Username and Password defined causes a box to prompt you for the necessary information. This is no longer the case, although it is still documented, so you will have to either enter a Username and Password, or change the type of account under which you want the service to run.

In this example, simply change the Account property to LocalSystem. This will allow the service to run under the local system account and will obviate the need for you to enter a hard-coded Username and Password.

You are now ready to build the service. Choose Build from the Build menu. Your service will now be built.

Configuring Your Service

Your service is compiled, but the system doesn't know anything about it yet. You have to install this service before it will be available for starting and stopping in the Service Control Manager. Open a command or console window (that's a DOS prompt), and go to the directory where the service was compiled. For most of you, this will be C:\Documents and Settings\ *<your username>*\My Documents\Visual Studio Projects\LearningVBservice\bin. When you're there, type in the following command:

```
installutil LearningVBservice.exe
```

> **NOTE**
>
> InstallUtil.exe must be in the path in order to work in this example. If it is not in the path, you'll have to type the full pathname.

This will take a moment. After the installation is done, you are ready to start your service and set its startup options.

Open the Services management tool, which can be found in the Computer Management application in Windows 2000. Your service, UsageMonitor, will appear in the list, as you see in Figure 10.1. Double-click the UsageMonitor service to open the Properties dialog box. You can change the startup type from Manual to Automatic if you want the service to start every time Windows boots up, and it will launch and begin operations even if no one logs on. At this point, you can just click the Start button and let the service run for a while. After it runs for a time, stop it. Now you can examine the log that it produced.

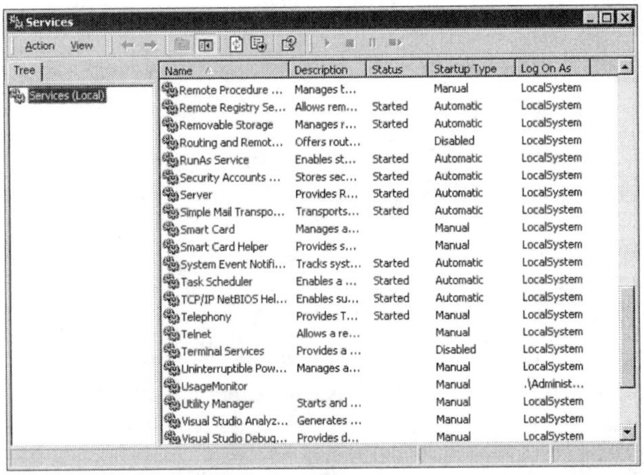

FIGURE 10.1
Your first Web service showing up in the Windows Services Control Manager.

The log file that is produced shows the CPU utilization every five seconds. The service can only be stopped and started. It cannot be paused because the CanPauseAndContinue property is set to False by default, and you did not change that before you built the service. Here is a sample of the file that was produced:

```
Service Started
CPU Usage: 0 - 2/24/2001 4:21:55 PM
CPU Usage: 9.504132 - 2/24/2001 4:21:57 PM
CPU Usage: 9.8 - 2/24/2001 4:22:02 PM
...
CPU Usage: 23 - 2/24/2001 4:24:07 PM
CPU Usage: 1.19760478 - 2/24/2001 4:24:12 PM
CPU Usage: 5.61122227 - 2/24/2001 4:24:17 PM
CPU Usage: 4.2 - 2/24/2001 4:24:22 PM
Service Stopped
```

The first value for the CPU usage is often a throwaway value. After that, all the numbers look legitimate.

Understanding Windows Services

As you know, Windows Services can run when Windows starts, even if no one logs in. These applications have no user interface and run in the background, independent of any user. They "log in" as the *service* account or as a specific user, which means they can run under the security context of a specific user, regardless of who is logged in.

Windows Services are unique in several ways. You cannot debug a service by starting it within the IDE because you must install it first so that Windows can manage it. You will see how to debug it later.

You had to add installers to this project, something you have not had to do in any other project. This, again, is because the service must be installed so that Windows can handle starting and stopping it.

Because a service does not have a user interface, you should plan to write any messages from the service into the Windows event log. This is the key to a long-running service; nothing blocks execution, such as waiting for a user to click the OK button to clear a message box. You want to have exemplary error handling in your service, capturing errors so that they can be written to the event log instead of causing a message to be displayed to the user, indicating that an error was encountered. If you try to pop up a message box, it will not be visible to the user, and the program might hang, waiting for the dialog box to be cleared.

Service Lifetime and Events

A service has a number of events to which it can respond, and these mirror the stages of a service's lifetime. For example, you've already seen the OnStart event handler. Here are the events to which the service can respond:

- OnStart—OnStart fires when the service starts. As you saw in the code in your service, this event writes to the log file the fact that the service is starting, and the date and time that the start occurred.

- OnPause—If the CanPauseAndContinue property is set to True for your service, the service can be paused from the Service Control Manager. If the service is paused, this event fires and can perform actions before the processing is actually paused.

- OnContinue—If the CanPauseAndContinue property is set to True for your service, this event fires when the service is continued after being paused.

- OnStop—When the service is stopped, this event is fired before the service stops. There is a CanStop property that is set to True by default. If the property is set to False, the service does not receive the stop event (but it is still stopped).

- OnShutdown—If the service is running and the machine is shut down, this event is fired. This is different from an OnStop in that this fires only when Windows is shutting down. There is a CanShutdown property that is set to False by default; this property must be set to True for your service to receive this event.

Your projects also have an AutoLog property, which is set to True by default. This allows your service to log certain events automatically. For example, if you run the service you created earlier, you can check the Event Viewer and, in the application log, you will see information messages about your service starting and stopping. These are created for you, but if you choose to turn them off, simply set AutoLog to False.

Earlier, you saw that you could set the Account property to User, which allows you to specify a particular user under whose account the service will run. However, after you have installed the service and the Service Control Manager is handling the service, you can change the security context for the service by modifying the properties of the service in the Service Control Manager.

Debugging Your Service

Your service cannot be debugged in the usual sense because it has to be installed into the Service Control Manager first. Because this is a Windows Service, the IDE cannot start it for you; you need the Service Control Manager to start it for you. Therefore, to debug your Windows Services application, you'll have to build it, install it, and start it. This means that you actually are debugging a running application, which had to be installed before you started debugging. Although the IDE cannot start a service for you, it can debug one for you.

Place a breakpoint on one of the lines inside the Timer1_Tick event handler. Next, choose Processes from the Debug menu. After the Processes dialog box is open, check the Show system processes box. In the list, your service will be listed as the name of the EXE, not the name of the service. Choose LearningVBservice.exe as shown in Figure 10.2. Click the Attach button, and you will see the screen shown in Figure 10.3. Choose Common Language Runtime and click the OK button. Now, click Close on the Processes dialog box.

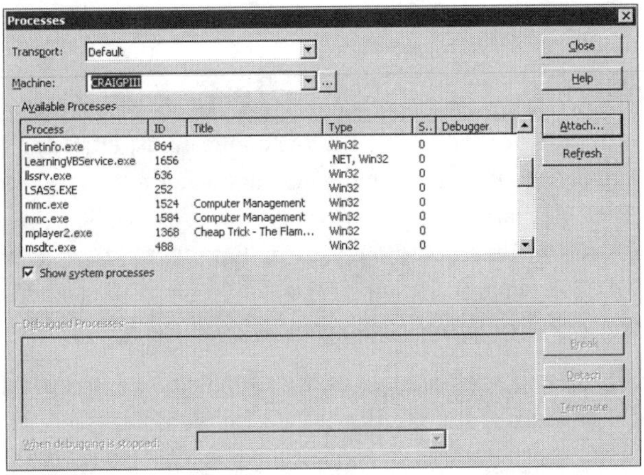

FIGURE 10.2
Attaching the Visual Studio .NET debugger to a running process.

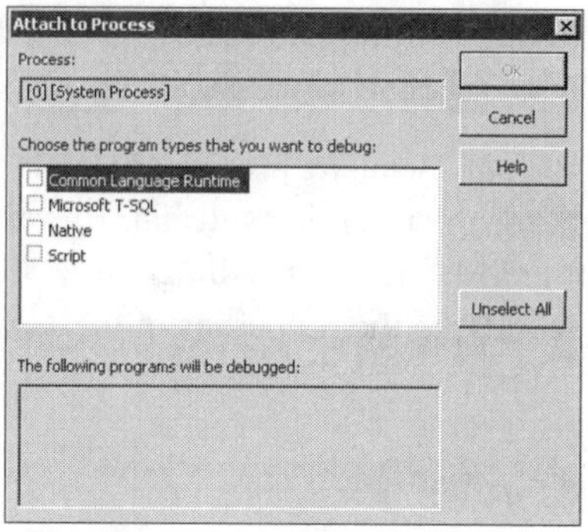

FIGURE 10.3

The form that allows you to choose what types of applications you want to debug.

Because the service is running, the breakpoint in your code will be hit within five seconds, and you can now interactively walk through the program as you would any other. Your running service is now in debug mode, so it is no longer running in the normal fashion; instead, it is responding only to your debugging commands. To stop the debugging process, just choose Stop Debugging from the Debug menu. Note that when you stop debugging, the service returns to running normally.

Before leaving this chapter, you might want to remove your service. To do this, go back to a command prompt, go to the directory holding the EXE for your service, and type the following line:

```
installutil /u LearningVBservice.exe
```

Building Console Applications

Console applications are often called command-line applications, DOS applications, and so on. They are non-GUI applications that run in the command window, and are often used for administrative tasks such as changing settings. Many Microsoft applications are still console applications. For example, in Windows 2000, you can type IPCONFIG at a command prompt to get information regarding the current IP settings on a machine. You can add command-line switches to obtain more detail or to release and renew your IP address.

Building console applications would seem to be very simple to do, and in fact, this section will be brief, because building them is simple. However, VB6 did not natively create console applications. You could do it, but it wasn't easy without the help of third-party utilities.

When you create a console application, you start without a designer, similar to what you see when you start a new class library. You also start with a Sub Main, which is what runs when the application starts. Control is basically top to bottom through the Sub Main routine, meaning that console applications tend to be written as top-down, traditional applications. These console applications are not event driven, as are other VB .NET applications.

Building a Console Application

You can build your first console application by starting a new project. Choose the Console Application project type, and name it LearningConsole. The project opens, and the only files you have are the AssemblyInfo.vb and a file named Module1.vb. Module1 is where you will be creating your console application.

In your code window, you create a module, not a class, called Module1. In all the other projects you've created so far, you have had a class created for you. This is not the case with a console application. Inside the module is a Sub Main.

To work with the console, you will accept user input and output data to the console. Outputting information to the console is relatively simple. Make your Sub Main code look like this:

```
Sub Main()
    Console.WriteLine("Hello, World!")
End Sub
```

Build this application, and then open a console window. You'll have to navigate to the default directory, which can be rather deep. The default will be c:\documents and settings\ <username>\my documents\visual studio projects\learningconsole\bin. When you're there, simply type LearningConsole (your application was compiled into LearningConsole.exe) and you should see the output Hello, World! appear in the window. You can see this in Figure 10.4.

As you can see, this is a very simple example. It is also possible for a console application to read data from the console so that it can operate on it. For example, you might want to create a simple calculator to add two numbers. Modify your code in Sub Main to look like this:

```
Sub Main()
    Dim firstNum As Double
    Dim secondNum As Double
    Console.Write("Enter the first number: ")
    firstNum = Console.ReadLine
    Console.Write("Enter the second number: ")
    secondNum = Console.ReadLine
    Console.WriteLine("The sum is: " & firstNum + secondNum)
End Sub
```

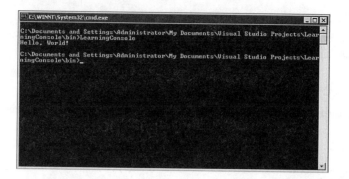

FIGURE 10.4

Your first console application outputting information to the console.

In this application, you are creating two variables of type `Double`. Then, you use the `Write` method of the `Console` object. `Write` outputs data but does not go to the next line, so the cursor remains on the line of the output. Then, the user can type in the first number. After the user presses the Enter key, the `Console.ReadLine` reads everything the user typed in, and assigns it to the `firstNum` variable. Note that there is no error checking here, so it would be easy to cause an error by entering text data here.

After getting the second value, `WriteLine` is called and used to output a string and the sum of the numbers. Then, the `End Sub` is encountered, and the application ends. You can see an example of this application in Figure 10.5.

Handling Command-Line Arguments

Most console applications accept command-line arguments or command-line parameters. To handle command-line arguments, you use the same basic mechanism as you did in earlier versions of Visual Basic: You use the `Command()` command. `Command` reads all the arguments on the command line. You can then parse the arguments using the `Split` method of the `String` class in .NET.

For example, make your code look like the following:

```
Sub Main()
   Dim args As String = Command()
   Dim argsArray() As String = args.Split
```

```
    Dim loopCounter As Integer
    For loopCounter = 0 To UBound(argsArray)
        Console.WriteLine(argsArray(loopCounter))
    Next
End Sub
```

FIGURE 10.5

A console application accepting user input in the console window.

In this code, you first read the arguments added after the application name using the Command function. You then split the values into a one-dimensional array using the string's Split method.

You then enter a loop that goes from zero (remember, in VB .NET, all arrays are zero-based) up to the UBound of the array. For each element, you write the value out to the console line. Figure 10.6 shows you an example of adding a couple of command-line arguments to the application, and having the console application parse those arguments and output them to the console.

Is this all you can do with console applications? Of course not. However, most of the functionality you will need can be handled by Read, ReadLine, Write, and WriteLine. It is possible to change the input and output streams, but you have to be running in unmanaged mode to do this, something Microsoft warns you against.

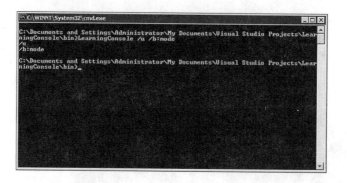

FIGURE 10.6

A console application accepting command-line arguments and parsing them into an array, which is then echoed back to the console window one element at a time.

Summary

This chapter introduced you to Windows Services and console applications. These are powerful classes of applications that can be written natively by VB developers for the first time. The examples in this chapter were rather simplistic; in the Windows service, you might want the data logged to a database instead of a flat file, for example.

The programming models for services and console applications are quite simple. However, when working with Windows services, there are a number of caveats. Debugging is one of the major differences between these services and most other projects, of course. In addition, don't forget to avoid any kind of UI, and have very thorough error handling.

Console applications are very simple, but useful for very quick applications that do not need the overhead of a GUI. For example, you could build very fast, high-performance parsing applications, such as SQL Server's bcp utility for loading data from a text file into SQL Server.

Creating Multithreaded Visual Basic .NET Applications

IN THIS CHAPTER

You were first introduced to Visual Basic .NET's multithreading capabilities in Chapter 3, "Major VB .NET Changes." Chapter 3 had you create an application and place a procedure on a separate thread to keep you from blocking the execution in the calling procedure. This chapter starts with a similar example, and then proceeds to more advanced topics with the multithreading process.

In computer terms, a *thread* is something on which some execution occurs. On a single-processor system, the processor can actually execute only one thread at a time. However, multiple threads are executing all the time, and the CPU uses a scheduling mechanism to give each thread a time slice on the processor. In Visual Basic, all the functionality in an application ran on the same thread by default. If you called a procedure that ran for a long period of time, nothing else in the application ran until that procedure was finished. To have a long-running process yield to other input, VB had a DoEvents function that allowed the application to check for other input, such as mouse clicks or keystrokes. Although a new DoEvents method has been added to VB .NET, multithreading is one way that you can push processing off to other threads so that the rest of your application remains active.

DoEvents is not meant to run various pieces of code at the same time. Instead, it can just handle events that are raised, but it has to interrupt the processing of the current task in order to handle the event. The processing in the running task is halted while the event is handled. With multiple threads, you could have two pieces of code executing at the same time, each getting time slices on the CPU so that both continue operating.

Creating a Multithreaded Application

In most of this book, the examples have been as simplistic as possible to focus on the new technology. In Chapter 3, you saw a very simple example of a multithreaded application that allowed you to place a long-running process on a separate thread so that the user interface continued to respond to users. Now, however, you will see a more complex example, and it will build on the XML Web services example from Chapter 9, "Building Web Services with VB .NET." If you have not gone through Chapter 9, you will want to build the service mentioned in the "Building Data-Driven Web Services" section. The XML Web service you built in that section of Chapter 9 works just fine, but it can be slow. Your client application is frozen during the time it takes to retrieve the data and fill the grid. Now, you will work on rewriting that application to make it multithreaded. This example will attempt to keep the code at a minimum, while showing you as much about handling multithreaded applications as possible.

Open the OrderTracker application you created in Chapter 9. This is the client application that calls the OrderInfo Web service. The GetOrders method returns orders from the Northwind database in an ADO.NET dataset. You then bind this dataset to the DataGrid control and display the data.

Creating Multithreaded Visual Basic .NET Applications

CHAPTER 11

241

11

CREATING
MULTITHREADED
APPLICATIONS

After the application is open, you will want to make a number of modifications. Add two additional buttons to the form. In Chapter 9, you left the first button named Button1, but now you will modify the Name and Text properties for the three buttons. Make the following modifications to the buttons:

- Button1: Change the Name property to cmdGetData and the Text property to Load Data.

- Button2: Change the Name property to cmdBeep and the Text property to Beep.

- Button3: Change the Name property to cmdLoadGrid and the Text property to Load Grid.

Now, you will make major modifications to the code. Go into the code window, and replace any existing code with the following code, except you want to leave the "Windows Form Designer generated code" section as it exists:

```
Public Class Form1
    Inherits System.Windows.Forms.Form
    Dim myDS As New System.Data.DataSet()

#Region " Windows Form Designer generated code "

    Private Sub cmdGetData_Click(ByVal sender As System.Object, _
     ByVal e As System.EventArgs) Handles cmdGetData.Click
        GetData()
    End Sub

    Private Sub cmdBeep_Click(ByVal sender As System.Object, _
     ByVal e As System.EventArgs) Handles cmdBeep.Click
        Beep()
    End Sub

    Private Sub GetData()
        Dim myOrders As New Orders()
        myDS = myOrders.GetOrders
        Beep()
    End Sub

    Private Sub cmdLoadGrid_Click(ByVal sender As System.Object, _
     ByVal e As System.EventArgs) Handles cmdLoadGrid.Click
        If myDS.Tables.Count > 0 Then
            DataGrid1.DataSource = myDS
            'the DataMember will be whatever table you saw
            'when you created the dataset
            DataGrid1.DataMember = "Customers"
        End If
    End Sub
End Class
```

If you look at the code, you'll notice that one of the first things you do is define an ADO.NET DataSet named myDS. The reason for defining this at the module level will become obvious in the next section, when you will read about returning data from the procedures on another thread.

Inside the code for the cmdGetData button, you simply call the GetData sub that you create, and the GetData sub instantiates an instance of the Orders XML Web service. You then call the GetOrders method on Orders, and put the result in the module-level myDS that you created earlier.

The code inside the cmdBeep event handler is very simple—it just issues a beep. You'll use this to test when the main thread of the form is blocked and when it is not.

The code inside cmdLoadGrid first checks whether myDS has any DataTables in it. This keeps you from getting an error if you click the button before you have clicked the GetData button. Next, the code binds the DataGrid to the myDS DataSet, and then the table within the DataSet. As you were warned in Chapter 9, make sure that you use the table name displayed to you when you created the DataAdapter. Even though the query is returning records from five tables in SQL Server, you are returning them all into one flat, table-like structure, and not multiple DataTable objects.

Go ahead and run the project. After the form loads, click the Beep button to make sure you hear the beep. Now, click the Get Data button and immediately click the Beep button again; you will not hear a beep from the Beep button this time. This is, of course, because the long-running (in computer terms) GetData process blocks the execution of the main thread. When the data is returned, you will hear a beep because there is one in the GetData sub. You can then click the Load Grid button to load the data into the grid. Your application should look something like Figure 11.1.

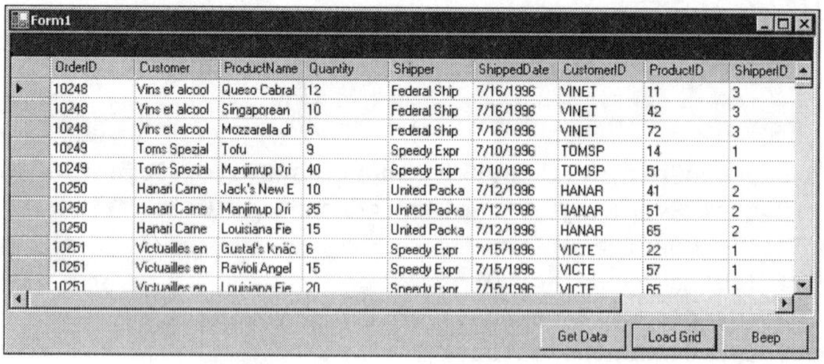

FIGURE 11.1

Your new client application calling an XML Web service and loading data into a grid.

So far, you might be thinking this isn't anything great, and wondering just where all the multi-threading is supposed to happen. In fact, the next step will be to spawn the GetData sub on its own thread, so that your user interface is no longer blocked while the data is being retrieved.

Making the OrderTracker Application Multithreaded

In your application, pressing the Beep button while the XML Web service is being called doesn't work because the action is blocking the thread. You might want to place that function-ality on another thread so that the user interface continues to respond while the data is being retrieved. To accomplish this, you need to use the System.Threading.Thread class. The Thread class can be used to create a new thread, on which you can launch some processing.

The GetData sub that you created on the client is used to instantiate a variable of type Orders, where Orders is the XML Web service. You then call the GetOrders method of the Orders object to retrieve the data. The process of instantiating the Orders object and calling the GetOrders method can be time-consuming, and is therefore a good candidate to place on its own thread.

One of the nice things about multithreading is that, in its simplest form, your changes are made in the calling routine, not the called routine. This means that the called routine doesn't actually know it's running on a separate thread from the client that called it. Instead, it just operates normally.

The calling routine, on the other hand, requires some changes in order to process the called routine on a separate thread. The change requires you to instantiate a Thread object, using the Thread class in the System.Threading namespace. When you instantiate a thread, a required parameter must be passed into the constructor of the Thread class. That parameter is a pointer to the function (or sub) that will run on the thread you are creating.

Before you worry about VB .NET not supporting pointers, remember that VB .NET includes support for delegates, which are, in essence, function pointers. A delegate can represent the memory address for a function, so it acts as a pointer in this case. There is an easy way to cre-ate a delegate in VB .NET: use the AddressOf operator. AddressOf creates a function delegate that the Thread class then uses to run that function on the new thread. Your syntax looks some-thing like this:

```
Imports System.Threading
...
Dim myThread As New Thread(AddressOf CalledFunction)
```

You now have created a new thread, called myThread, which points to the CalledFunction routine. However, creating the thread does not automatically call the CalledFunction routine;

instead, you now need to initiate the call to CalledFunction using the thread. You do this by starting the thread, using the Thread.Start method, as shown here:

```
myThread.Start()
```

Starting the thread makes the call to this new thread. To test all this, you will make some changes to your code. First, you will change your call from the cmdGetData_Click sub to create a new thread, similar to what was shown earlier. Second, you will change the called routine, GetData, to display a message box instead of beeping when it is finished. The reason is that you will now be able to click the Beep button while the GetData routine is running, so you want something other than a beep to indicate that you are finished retrieving the data.

Change your cmdGetData_Click sub to look like this:

```
Private Sub cmdGetData_Click(ByVal sender As System.Object, _
 ByVal e As System.EventArgs) Handles cmdGetData.Click
    Dim threadGetData As New System.Threading.Thread(AddressOf GetData)
    threadGetData.Start()
End Sub
```

Notice that you could have added Imports System.Threading to the top to simplify reference to the Thread class.

Now, modify your GetData sub to look like this:

```
Private Sub GetData()
    Dim myOrders As New Orders()
    myDS = myOrders.GetOrders
    MsgBox("Done")
End Sub
```

Now, run the application again. After it starts, click on the Get Data button. Then click on the Beep button. You will hear the beep immediately because the data is being retrieved on a separate thread. The CPU is giving time slices to both threads, so your user interface is still able to respond to events.

When the GetData sub is done, you will get a message box indicating that it is finished. However, unlike what you are most likely used to in Windows applications, you can click on the Beep button without clearing the message box! This is because the message box is running on a different thread, so it is not blocking the execution of the user interface.

Go ahead and click the OK button on the message box to close it. The Load Data button still works as it did before, and loads the ADO.NET dataset into the grid. This example demonstrates that you can take some of the long-running parts of your application and move them to other threads so that people can continue to use your application while those processes are running. In this example, there wasn't actually anything else for the person to do, but you might

Creating Multithreaded Visual Basic .NET Applications

CHAPTER 11

245

11

CREATING
MULTITHREADED
APPLICATIONS

well have applications that need to parse or search through large files, and that can be done in the background while the person does other things.

Returning Values from Other Threads

In the previous example, you most likely thought it odd, or at least inefficient, to have to notify the user when the thread is done, and then to have the user click a button that loads the data into the grid. A seemingly obvious answer would be to have the GetData sub return an ADO.NET dataset when it is done, and then have the calling procedure fill the grid.

There are two problems with this approach, however. First, because you are running the GetData sub on a separate thread, the calling routine continues executing immediately after starting the new thread. That means any code you had to fill the grid after calling GetData would execute immediately, even though GetData would most likely not be finished. Obviously, this is not a good approach.

The second problem with adding a return value to the GetData sub is that you can't return a value from a different thread. When you are calling procedures or methods on another thread, those procedures or methods cannot return a value.

Given these two issues—the second of which is an intentional limitation—how would your client application know that the GetData method has finished and then be able to fill in the grid automatically? There are two approaches: You can set a global variable, or you can fire an event from the method on the thread.

Returning Data Using Global Variables

The current example uses global variables, in the sense that the DataSet is a module-level variable, and the GetData sub assigns the return value of the XML Web service to it, even though GetData is running on a separate thread. However, your program doesn't know when the value is actually created, so you'll have to add some code to the client to figure this out.

When you use global variables, you can use either of two ways to determine when the thread has finished. First, you could check from the client application to see whether the thread still exists. Second, you could have the application running on a separate thread fire an event, which you could handle in the client. You'll read more about handling the event in the next section, because an event can be used to pass data back to the calling program, which can eliminate the need for having to use global variables.

To see how to use global variables and check the status of the thread, you will use the IsAlive property of the Thread class. IsAlive returns a Boolean indicating the status of the thread. IsAlive returns True as long as the thread is started and running; after the thread dies, IsAlive returns False.

To check the IsAlive property and wait for the thread to die, you need to have either a loop that constantly checks to see whether IsAlive is False, or you need to have a timer check periodically. Neither of these approaches is really ideal because both continuously run code to check for conditions, when an event would serve the same purpose without chewing up processor cycles to check a status.

To see how you could check the IsAlive property, modify your cmdGetData_Click sub to contain the following code:

```
Private Sub cmdGetData_Click(ByVal sender As System.Object, _
 ByVal e As System.EventArgs) Handles cmdGetData.Click
    Dim threadGetData As New System.Threading.Thread(AddressOf GetData)
    threadGetData.Start()
    Do While threadGetData.IsAlive
       Application.DoEvents()
    Loop
    DataGrid1.DataSource = myDS
    'the DataMember will be whatever table you saw
    'when you created the dataset
    DataGrid1.DataMember = "Customers"
End Sub
```

In this code, you start the thread, and then enter a loop that runs as long as IsAlive is True. Notice that inside the loop, however, is an Application.DoEvents(). This is necessary to free up the resources for the main thread to actually see the change in the status of threadGetData's IsAlive property. Without this DoEvents, your code will never see IsAlive change to False.

Before you run the example, you'll want to remove the message box from the GetData procedure because its presence would require you to clear the box in order for the thread to die. Reduce your GetData procedure to just the following code:

```
Private Sub GetData()
    Dim myOrders As New Orders()
    myDS = myOrders.GetOrders
End Sub
```

Run the application. After the loop is finished, your code will set the DataSource and DataMember properties of the DataGrid, and the grid will be populated automatically when the thread is finished. This makes the application more intelligent, but it isn't the most efficient method. The first problem is that most programming purists frown upon the use of global or module-level variables. That argument aside, the fact that you have a Do...Loop means that you are consuming processor cycles the entire time the loop is running.

Creating Multithreaded Visual Basic .NET Applications

CHAPTER 11

247

11

CREATING
MULTITHREADED
APPLICATIONS

Using the Join Method

There is an alternative to checking the IsAlive property: The Join method of the Thread class waits until a thread dies. Actually, the Join method is overloaded. The first implementation waits until the thread dies. The second and third implementations wait either for the thread to die or for a specified time to lapse, with the only difference being how you specify the time.

You can see how the Join method works by modifying your code to look like this:

```
Private Sub cmdGetData_Click(ByVal sender As System.Object, _
  ByVal e As System.EventArgs) Handles cmdGetData.Click
    Dim threadGetData As New System.Threading.Thread(AddressOf GetData)
    threadGetData.Start()
    threadGetData.Join()
    DataGrid1.DataSource = myDS
    'the DataMember will be whatever table you saw
    'when you created the dataset
    DataGrid1.DataMember = "Customers"
End Sub
```

If you run this code, however, you'll notice one important facet of the Join method: It blocks other execution on the main thread while it waits for threadGetData to die. You can verify this by clicking the Get Data button and then clicking the Beep button: nothing happens. This means that as long as Join is monitoring the thread, nothing will happen on the thread handling the user interface. Obviously, this is not what is desired in this case.

Don't think that Join is not useful, however. Sometimes, you'll want one thread to wait for another thread to finish. For example, if one thread is getting the data, you might want a second thread to wait for the data to come back so that it can operate on that data. In this case, Join is much cleaner than looping constantly and checking the IsAlive property.

Returning Data Using Events

Many people prefer to raise events to return data from one thread to the parent thread. Unfortunately, this requires some changes to the current application. XML Web services are powerful, but they aren't really designed to raise events in the client program. Therefore, you need to create a simple class that raises the event for you. The good news is that this class can wrap around the call to the Orders Web service. So, you will still retrieve data with the Web service, but you'll notify the client that the thread is done by raising an event, and you'll pass the data back the same way.

In the project, add a new class and name it `ServiceWrapper.vb`. Inside the class, add the following code:

```
Public Class ServiceWrapper
    Public Event DataReturn(ByVal OrderDS As System.Data.DataSet)

    Public Sub GetData()
        Dim myDS As New System.Data.DataSet()
        Dim myOrders As New Orders()
        myDS = myOrders.GetOrders
        RaiseEvent DataReturn(myDS)
    End Sub
End Class
```

In `ServiceWrapper`, you define an event named `DataReturn`, which returns an ADO.NET `DataSet` object when it is raised. Then you define a method called `GetData`. `GetData` does in the wrapper class what had been doing in the client: It instantiates an instance of the `Orders` Web service and calls `GetOrders`. The return is an ADO.NET `DataSet`, which you then pass to the `DataReturn` when you call the `RaiseEvent` function.

Raising the event is great, but your client has to handle the event. In the client, you can get rid of the Load Grid button if you want. Make modifications to your code so that your final code looks like this (minus the "Windows Form Designer generated code" section, of course):

```
Public Class Form1
    Inherits System.Windows.Forms.Form

#Region " Windows Form Designer generated code "
    Dim WithEvents SW As New ServiceWrapper()

    Private Sub cmdGetData_Click(ByVal sender As System.Object, _
     ByVal e As System.EventArgs) Handles cmdGetData.Click
        AddHandler SW.DataReturn, AddressOf DataReturnedEH
        Dim threadGetData As New System.Threading.Thread(AddressOf SW.GetData)
        threadGetData.Start()
    End Sub

    Sub DataReturnedEH(ByVal ReturnedDS As System.Data.DataSet)
        DataGrid1.DataSource = ReturnedDS
    End Sub

    Private Sub cmdBeep_Click(ByVal sender As System.Object, _
     ByVal e As System.EventArgs) Handles cmdBeep.Click
        Beep()
    End Sub
End Class
```

The first new thing that you might notice is the declaration for the `ServiceWrapper` object. Because you are declaring the `ServiceWrapper` object `WithEvents`, you must declare it at the module level. Next, inside the `cmdGetData_Click` method, you use the `AddHandler` function to define a procedure that will handle the `DataReturn` event from the `ServiceWrapper`. Then you kick the `ServiceWrapper`'s `GetData` method off on its own thread.

As you know, the `GetData` method in `ServiceWrapper` calls the Web service and then returns an ADO.NET `DataSet` using the `DataReturn` event. Your event handler, named `DataReturnEH`, handles the event and receives the dataset that is passed as a parameter. Inside the event handler, you set the `DataGrid`'s `DataSource` property to this returned dataset.

You might notice that the `DataGrid`'s `DataMember` property is not being set. Actually, Windows controls are not the best examples to use for multithreading because there are a number of issues with them, the main one of which is that many methods of controls are not thread-safe, which means you cannot call them from any thread except the thread on which they are running. For this example, leave things as they are and run the project. The grid will show a small plus sign in the upper-left corner when the dataset is back. If you expand the tree view by clicking the plus sign, you will see a list of the `DataTable` objects in the dataset. Only one table is listed, and if you click on that, you will see the data in the grid. You can see this in Figure 11.2.

FIGURE 11.2
The grid displaying a list of available DataTables in the DataSet.

Multithreading with Forms and Controls

Choosing the `DataTable` is probably not something you want to have to do. You might be tempted to modify the code to set not only the `DataSource` property, but also the `DataMember` property, as shown here:

```
Sub DataReturnedEH(ByVal ReturnedDS As System.Data.DataSet)
    DataGrid1.DataSource = ReturnedDS
    DataGrid1.DataMember = ReturnedDS.Tables.Item(0).ToString
End Sub
```

Because there is only one table in the `DataSet`, you can use `Tables.Item(0).ToString` to retrieve the name of the first table in the `DataTables` collection.

Having made this change, if you happen to run the application, the results are less than desirable. In fact, you get an error, part of which says

```
Controls created on one thread cannot be parented to a control on a different
thread.
```

The problem is probably not what you'd expect. The error arises from the fact that most controls are not thread-safe; in other words, they don't work well across multiple threads. You might think you're safe here because the base thread of execution—the form with all the controls— starts a new thread, which has an object that calls the Web service. The object then raises an event, which is handled in your form code. Now, for a quiz: Where does the event handler run? Is it on the thread of the main form or the thread for the `ServiceWrapper`?

If you answered the thread for the form, you'll be disappointed. The event handler code is actually running on the same thread as the `ServiceWrapper`. If you want proof, it's pretty easy to see. You can modify your `DataReturnedEH` to look like this:

```
Sub DataReturnedEH(ByVal ReturnedDS As System.Data.DataSet)
    MsgBox("I'm blocking execution of my thread")
End Sub
```

Now, if you run the application, the message box will appear when the `GetData` method raises the error. However, if you try to click back on the form, you'll find that you can. Click away on the Beep button and you'll see that the user interface is not blocked, even though the message box is still displayed. This lets you know that the message box and, therefore, the error handler, are not on the same thread as the user interface elements.

Microsoft warns you that multithreading actually is best for calling procedures and class methods, not for working with forms and controls. However, you might want to multithread parts of a user interface, as you have done here. If so, try to execute the methods of a control on the thread on which it was created. If you do call a method from another thread, use `Control.Invoke`.

Using `Control.Invoke` sounds simple enough, but there are a few things you have to know about it. First, it can only consume a delegate, which means you have to create a procedure that calls the control, and then create a delegate for the procedure. Then it is the control that is calling the procedure, so it runs on the same thread as the control.

Here is one possible implementation of this process. Your `ServiceWrapper` remains unchanged, but your form code now looks like this:

Creating Multithreaded Visual Basic .NET Applications

CHAPTER 11

251

11

CREATING
MULTITHREADED
APPLICATIONS

```vbnet
Public Class Form1
    Inherits System.Windows.Forms.Form

#Region " Windows Form Designer generated code "

    Dim WithEvents SW As New ServiceWrapper()
    Delegate Sub delFillGrid()
    Dim myDS As System.Data.DataSet

    Private Sub cmdGetData_Click(ByVal sender As System.Object, _
     ByVal e As System.EventArgs) Handles cmdGetData.Click
        Dim threadGetData As New System.Threading.Thread(AddressOf SW.GetData)
        threadGetData.Start()
    End Sub

    Sub DataReturnedEH(ByVal ReturnedDS As System.Data.DataSet) _
     Handles SW.DataReturn
        myDS = ReturnedDS
        Dim dFG As New delFillGrid(AddressOf FillGrid)
        DataGrid1.Invoke(dFG)
    End Sub

    Sub FillGrid()
        DataGrid1.DataSource = myDS
        DataGrid1.DataMember = myDS.Tables.Item(0).ToString
    End Sub

    Private Sub cmdBeep_Click(ByVal sender As System.Object, _
     ByVal e As System.EventArgs) Handles cmdBeep.Click
        Beep()
    End Sub
End Class
```

The creation of SW as an object of type ServiceWrapper is the same as before. Immediately after that, however, is a line that creates a Delegate called delFillGrid. Later, you'll create a new instance of the delFillGrid delegate. You also create myDS at the module level because of the difficulty in calling a sub and passing a parameter when using the Invoke method.

When you click the Get Data button, the code executed is the same as before. However, when the ServiceWrapper fires the DataReturn event (now being handled by a Handles clause instead of the AddHandler function), the DataReturnedEH first assigns the returned DataSet to the module-level myDS variable. Then a new instance of a delegate is created, and this delegate points to the FillGrid procedure. You then call the DataGrid's Invoke method, and pass in the delegate that points to FillGrid.

This is a long and somewhat complicated way to make the `DataGrid` call the `FillGrid` method. By using `Invoke`, you are assured that the `FillGrid` method runs on the same thread as the control itself, so there will not be any problems with calling the control's properties and methods.

If you run the application, you can verify that everything works just fine. You click the Get Data button, and you can happily click the Beep button, and it will respond well. After the data is back, the grid fills normally.

There is another caveat with working with forms and controls, but it will be discussed in the synchronization section later in this chapter.

Passing Parameters to Threads

It is very common to have methods or procedures that accept parameters. Recall from previous discussions, however, that the procedure that is passed to the thread when it is created cannot have a return value and cannot accept parameters. This complicates your work because you have to find some way to get data into the procedure without using the standard method of passing parameters on the procedure call.

Just as with returning a value, there are two ways to pass parameters to procedures running on other threads: You can use module or global variables, or you can use properties or fields. There are plusses and minuses with each approach, of course. You'll examine both methods now, but understand that your current example using the `Orders` Web service doesn't really lend itself to accepting parameters, because the `GetOrders` method does not accept any parameters. Rather than recoding the `Orders` Web service, you'll just create a new procedure and class to handle parameters.

Passing Parameters with Global Variables

To see how to pass parameters using global variables, you'll need to create a new procedure inside of your `Form1` class. This procedure will mimic the example you saw in Chapter 3, but you'll do more with it as far as passing parameters.

First, add two controls to your form. Add a button and name it `cmdPassParam`. Add a text box and name it `txtCounter`. Clear out the `Text` property of `txtCounter`, and change the `Text` property of `cmdPassParam` to Pass Params.

Now, add the following code to your form:

```
Dim mlCount As Long

Private Sub cmdPassParam_Click(ByVal sender As System.Object, _
 ByVal e As System.EventArgs) Handles cmdPassParam.Click
```

Creating Multithreaded Visual Basic .NET Applications

CHAPTER 11

253

11

CREATING
MULTITHREADED
APPLICATIONS

```
    mlCount = 100000
    Counter()
End Sub

Sub Counter()
    Dim lCount As Long
    For lCount = 1 To mlCount
        txtCounter.Text = lcount
    Next
End Sub
```

In this code, you create a module-level variable named mlCount, which is set to 100,000 in the cmdPassParam_Click sub. Feel free to adjust this number higher or lower depending on how long you want the thread to run.

In the Counter routine, you simply execute a loop the number of times set in the mlCount variable. The number is displayed in the txtCounter text box. If you run this project and click on the Pass Params button, you'll notice that if you then try to click on the Beep button, nothing happens because execution is blocked on the main thread as long as the loop in Counter is executing. You'll also notice that you don't see the number changing in the text box; that is because the control is not able to grab the necessary processor cycles to display the new value. This is what you saw in the example in Chapter 3.

In this example, you could have easily passed the value of mlCount into counter as a parameter. There's no need in this example for the module-level variable mlCount. However, you are about to multithread this example, and you won't be able to pass parameters after you run Counter on its own thread. Therefore, this example already has the value of the number of loop iterations set in a module-level variable.

Now, modify the code to use threads. Change the cmdPassParam_Click sub to look like this:

```
Private Sub cmdPassParam_Click(ByVal sender As System.Object, _
 ByVal e As System.EventArgs) Handles cmdPassParam.Click
    mlCount = 100000
    Dim threadCounter As New System.Threading.Thread(AddressOf Counter)
    threadCounter.Start()
End Sub
```

After making this change, you can run the code again. This time, the Beep button will respond to you while the Counter routine is running. In addition, you will see that the number in the txtCounter text box climbs as the loop executes. This means that you have successfully multithreaded your application, and from the Counter procedure, which is running on a new thread, you are able to pick up a value using the module-level variable approach.

What are the minuses with this approach? First, as discussed earlier in this chapter, some purists feel that global variables are inherently bad. Another, perhaps more important minus is that if you were to spawn multiple threads that all called Counter, they all would have to use the same value of mlCount. To get around this limitation, you will probably want to use the second approach, which is to use fields or properties of an object.

Passing Parameters with Fields or Properties

A more common approach to passing a parameter to another thread is to create a wrapper class, much like this chapter's earlier ServiceWrapper. You then create properties or fields (public variables) in the class and set those. You then call the method, but you place the method on its own thread before you execute it. This allows you to have multiple objects in memory, each with different values for the parameters, and you can run them all at the same time if you choose.

To see this, add a new class to your project and name it Counter.vb. Add the following code to the class:

```
Public Class Counter
    Public mlCount As Long

    Public Sub Count()
        Dim lCount As Long
        For lCount = 1 To mlCount
            'do nothing
        Next
        MsgBox("Thread done, mlCount was " & mlCount.ToString)
    End Sub
End Class
```

In the Counter class, you are creating a field named mlCount, and a method named Count. The Count method simply runs through a loop, but doesn't update a text box as you saw in the previous example. When it is done, it displays a message box saying that it is done, and how many times it ran through the loop.

Back in the form, modify the code for the cmdPassParam_Click sub to look like this:

```
Private Sub cmdPassParam_Click(ByVal sender As System.Object, _
 ByVal e As System.EventArgs) Handles cmdPassParam.Click
    Dim count1 As New Counter()
    Dim count2 As New Counter()
    count1.mlCount = 1000000000
    count2.mlCount = 99999999
    Dim threadCounter1 As New System.Threading.Thread(AddressOf count1.Count)
    Dim threadCounter2 As New System.Threading.Thread(AddressOf count2.Count)
    threadCounter1.Start()
    threadCounter2.Start()
End Sub
```

Now you are creating two instances of the Counter class, called count1 and count2. Each class gets a different value for the mlCount field, and you might want to modify these for your particular computer. You then spawn two threads, one for the Count method of each class. You then start both threads, so they are running simultaneously.

When the threads finish, they will display message boxes showing that they are done, and the number of times you executed the loop in that particular thread. This shows how you can pass parameters into an object before you start the thread, which gets you around the problem of not being able to pass parameters to procedures operating on a different thread.

If you look at Figure 11.3, you will see the two message boxes that appeared. These message boxes are from two instances of the same class, running on different threads, and having different values passed in, thanks to fields on the object.

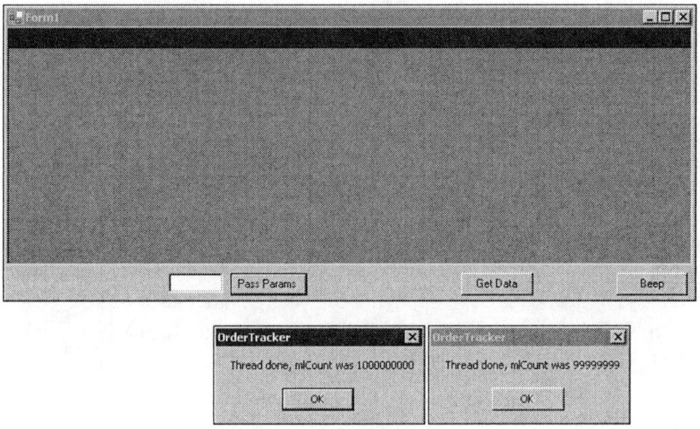

FIGURE 11.3
Two message boxes from two instances of the same class, running on two different threads and containing different field values.

Thread Maintenance and Synchronization

So far, you have started threads using the Start method, and they have died naturally. It is also possible to suspend, restart, and kill threads. You can check the states of threads at any time. Threads can also be assigned priorities, which control the size of the time slice they are given by the processor. In addition, threads can be foreground or background threads.

Foreground and Background Threads

Given the current state of your application, there is something interesting you can do with it. If you run the application and click the Pass Params button, the code will execute and two message boxes eventually will be displayed, one from each of the threads you created. When the message boxes are displayed, you can click back on the main form without clearing them because they are running on a different thread from the thread handling the user interface. Now, if you close the main form, the message boxes remain.

Your initial thought might have been that the message boxes would go away. After all, in classic Visual Basic, you could create a component and when you closed the program, all references to the component went away and the component would drop out of memory. Threads, however, are not components. The threads containing the message boxes are still alive, and your application is therefore still running.

The threads that you have created are *foreground threads*, which is the default for a new thread. Foreground threads run indefinitely, but background threads are killed when the last foreground thread has stopped.

You can see the behavior of foreground and background threads by adding one line to your cmdPassParam_Click sub. Make your code look like this:

```
Private Sub cmdPassParam_Click(ByVal sender As System.Object, _
  ByVal e As System.EventArgs) Handles cmdPassParam.Click
    Dim count1 As New Counter()
    Dim count2 As New Counter()
    count1.mlCount = 1000000000
    count2.mlCount = 99999999
    Dim threadCounter1 As New System.Threading.Thread(AddressOf count1.Count)
    Dim threadCounter2 As New System.Threading.Thread(AddressOf count2.Count)
    threadCounter1.IsBackground = True
    threadCounter1.Start()
    threadCounter2.Start()
End Sub
```

The only change here is that you have set the threadCounter1's IsBackground property to True. This means that the thread with the larger mlCount will close when all foreground threads close.

Run the application and click on the Pass Params button. After both threads have displayed the message box, click on the OK button for the message box from threadCounter2 (the one with the lower number of iterations). At this point, you still have the form open and one message box. Close the main form, and you'll notice that the message box closes immediately. This is because the message box was running on a background thread, and all foreground threads in the application have terminated.

Thread Priority

Not all threads are created equal; some threads have higher or lower priorities than other threads. All threads do get a turn at the processor, but some threads get a longer time slice than other threads.

There are five thread priorities:

- Highest
- AboveNormal
- Normal (the default)
- BelowNormal
- Lowest

These thread priorities are easy to set: just use the `Priority` property of the thread method. For example, if you add the following line to your code after you create `threadCounter1`, and then run the application, you'll see that `threadCounter1` now runs much faster.

```
threadCounter1.Priority = Threading.ThreadPriority.AboveNormal
```

In fact, on the test machine used for this code, `threadCounter1` finished before `threadCounter2` after the priority was changed, despite the fact that `threadCounter1` runs through the loop more times by a factor of ten.

Thread States

Threads have a variety of states in which they can exist. You can check the state of a thread at any point in time by examining the `ThreadState` property of a thread. Numerous states are possible for a thread, depending on what methods you have called. For example, when you call the `Start` method, the thread enters the `Running` thread state.

It is possible to suspend a thread at any point using either the `Sleep` or the `Suspend` method. The `Sleep` method puts the thread to sleep for a specified period of time, with the time being passed as either an `Integer` or `TimeSpan` data type. `Sleep` puts the thread in the `WaitSleepJoin` thread state. The `Suspend` method does not take any arguments, and suspends execution on the thread until the thread is `Resumed` or `Aborted`. `Suspend` puts the thread in the `Suspended` state. Threads in the `WaitSleepJoin` state are restarted with the `Interrupt` method.

The `Resume` method restarts a thread that has been suspended. After the thread has been resumed, it is back in the `Running` thread state.

You can check the fact that threads are being suspended and changing thread state by using the following code. Modify the code in your application by changing it to the following:

```
Dim threadCounter1 As System.Threading.Thread

Private Sub cmdBeep_Click(ByVal sender As System.Object, _
 ByVal e As System.EventArgs) Handles cmdBeep.Click
   Beep()
   MsgBox(threadCounter1.ThreadState.ToString)
   threadCounter1.Resume()
End Sub

Private Sub cmdPassParam_Click(ByVal sender As System.Object, _
 ByVal e As System.EventArgs) Handles cmdPassParam.Click
   Dim count1 As New Counter()
   Dim count2 As New Counter()
   count1.mlCount = 1000000000
   count2.mlCount = 99999999
   threadCounter1 = New System.Threading.Thread(AddressOf count1.Count)
   Dim threadCounter2 As New System.Threading.Thread(AddressOf count2.Count)
   threadCounter1.IsBackground = True
   threadCounter1.Start()
   threadCounter1.Suspend()
   threadCounter2.Start()
End Sub
```

The first change you have made is to move the definition of the threadCounter1 variable to the module level. Inside of cmdPassParam_Click, you instantiate threadCounter1, start it, and immediately suspend it. The thread will stay suspended indefinitely, so after it is suspended, you can click on the Beep button. The Beep button now first displays the thread state to you in a message box, and then resumes threadCounter1.

You can destroy a running thread, which is something you haven't done. Make the following changes to your code, which just involves removing the Suspend in cmdPassParam_Click and then modifying the cmdBeep_Click sub:

```
Private Sub cmdBeep_Click(ByVal sender As System.Object, _
 ByVal e As System.EventArgs) Handles cmdBeep.Click
   Beep()
   threadCounter1.Abort()
End Sub

Private Sub cmdPassParam_Click(ByVal sender As System.Object, _
 ByVal e As System.EventArgs) Handles cmdPassParam.Click
   Dim count1 As New Counter()
   Dim count2 As New Counter()
```

```
    count1.mlCount = 1000000000
    count2.mlCount = 99999999
    threadCounter1 = New System.Threading.Thread(AddressOf count1.Count)
    Dim threadCounter2 As New System.Threading.Thread(AddressOf count2.Count)
    threadCounter1.IsBackground = True
    threadCounter1.Start()
    threadCounter2.Start()
End Sub
```

You'll notice here that you are starting `threadCounter1`, but `cmdBeep_Click` now has a call to the `Abort` method on the `Thread` class. `Abort` kills a running thread. To test this, run the application and make sure that you press the Beep button before the `Count` method is done on `threadCounter1`. If you click the Beep button before `threadCounter1` finishes, it will be killed. You could verify this by waiting and noticing that the message box is never displayed. Or, you could watch the Output window in the VB .NET IDE and you will see when the thread has terminated.

Synchronization

The final topic for threading is that of thread synchronization. In some applications, you might want a thread that retrieves the information, another that sorts the data retrieved, and a third that loads the data into a grid. You might want these on three separate threads because it might be possible to re-sort later without having to fetch the data again. Therefore, you want these three actions to run on three separate threads, but at times they must run in sequence. It wouldn't make sense to run the data retrieval and data sorting threads at the same time. Therefore, you will need to have the sorting thread wait until the retrieval thread is finished.

Events are the common way to notify various parts of the program when certain threads are done. You saw this when you were looking for a way to return data from a thread; you passed that data back as the parameter of the event.

VB .NET provides you with a way of synchronizing shared data: the `SyncLock` statement. `SyncLock` allows you to control access to shared resources, much as locks in a database prevent multiple people from accessing the same item at the same time.

If you have a class with shared properties or methods, you can place a `SyncLock` block inside a shared member to make sure that only one thread accesses that shared member at a time. For example, create the following class in the same file as your `Form1` class:

```
Class SyncTest
    Public Shared Sub SyncMe()
        Dim lCount As Long
        For lCount = 1 To 1000000000
            'do nothing
        Next
```

```
        End Sub
End Class
```

So far, this is nothing special. Now, you'll stretch the purpose of the Beep button. Add the following code to `cmdBeep_Click`:

```
Private Sub cmdBeep_Click(ByVal sender As System.Object, _
 ByVal e As System.EventArgs) Handles cmdBeep.Click
    Dim oST1 As New SyncTest()
    Dim oST2 As New SyncTest()
    Dim threadX As New System.Threading.Thread(AddressOf oST1.SyncMe)
    Dim threadY As New System.Threading.Thread(AddressOf oST2.SyncMe)
    threadX.Name = "threadX"
    threadY.Name = "threadY"
    threadX.Start()
    threadY.Start()
End Sub
```

Here, you are instantiating two instances of the `SyncTest` object, and then calling the `SyncMe` method on two different threads. The way to watch this is to monitor the Output window in the IDE. As Figure 11.4 demonstrates, you can see when the threads finish executing, and they are easier to see because you set the `Name` properties for them. Time how long it takes for both to finish. On the test machine, it took twenty seconds, but both threads finish at almost exactly the same time.

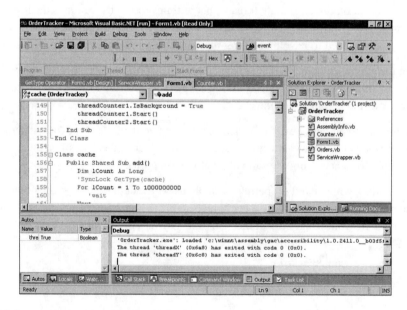

FIGURE 11.4

The two threads have finished, as noted in the Output window inside the Visual Studio .NET IDE.

Now, modify the code in the SyncTest class to look like this:

```
Class SyncTest
    Public Shared Sub SyncMe()
        Dim lCount As Long
        SyncLock GetType(SyncTest)
            For lCount = 1 To 1000000000
                'do nothing
            Next
        End SyncLock
    End Sub
End Class
```

The only difference here is that you have added the SyncLock statement to synchronize access to the shared SyncMe method. This means that you will allow only one thread to access the shared resource at a time, much like locking an update to a record in a relational database. Now, run the project again and time how long it takes the threads to end. The total time should be about the same, but the first thread, threadX, finishes at the halfway mark, and threadY finishes at the end of the time. This is because the threads are now running in sequence rather than parallel, thanks to the SyncLock command.

Summary

Much of what you have seen in this chapter presents some challenges for classic VB developers. After all, VB developers have had ten years of not worrying about multiple threads. Multithreading is important, however, to building robust and scalable applications.

If you question the scalable claim, remember that not all computers only have a single processor. On single-processor machines, the threads are getting time slices on the processor; so, in truth, only one thread can run at a time. On multiprocessor machines, however, multiple threads can run at the same time, which can make your application much more scalable. In addition, this just drives home the need for synchronization.

If you think that you could do all this with DoEvents, you need to understand something. Assume that you have a loop that had a DoEvents in it. If you click a button, DoEvents would yield to that processing. However, nothing in that Click event handler has to return control to the routine with the loop! In other words, the code inside the Click event handler could have its own loop—one without a DoEvents—and execution of the original loop would be blocked while the code in the Click event handler runs. With multithreading, such blocking would not take place.

Monitoring Performance with VB .NET

IN THIS CHAPTER

Performance tuning is usually one of the last things performed by developers. Unfortunately, given VB .NET's unfinished state, it's hard to perform any valid performance testing at this time. However, the .NET Framework does include new tools for monitoring performance that allow you to greatly increase your ability to monitor performance on your computer, or any computer on your network. In addition, you can create your own performance counters and monitor parts of your application with ease.

Monitoring Performance

For years, Windows NT included the Performance Monitor tool, commonly called Perfmon. This tool also exists in Windows 2000, and is handy for monitoring all manner of resources on the computer. Most common is the monitoring of the processor's busy time, but the Performance Monitor can include dozens of categories, such as Processor and FTP Server (if the FTP service was installed).

Windows includes a number of performance counters, which monitor these various aspects. The performance counters monitor what Microsoft calls *performance objects*, which fall into two categories. Performance objects can be physical objects, such as memory or processors; or they can be system objects, such as threads, processes, or compilations. It is these performance objects that are divided into various categories, and then you have the counters within those categories.

.NET includes a `PerformanceCounter` class in the `System.Diagnostics` namespace. This class allows you to connect to the performance counters on a computer and retrieve values in your code. The `PerformanceCounter` class also allows you to create your own custom counters, as you will see later in this chapter.

Accessing Performance Monitors

The `PerformanceCounter` class allows you to easily access performance counters on NT or Windows 2000 machines. You can use the `PerformanceCounter` easily by using the Server Explorer.

Create a new Windows application project and name it PerfTest. Open the Server Explorer window by hovering over the Server Explorer button next to the Toolbox button. You'll want to expand the Servers node, and then the server in which you are interested. In Figure 12.1, you can see that the server is named culaptop in this example. Next, expand the Performance Counter's node, and you'll see a list of the categories available for this server. The actual categories will vary depending on what you have installed on the server you are exploring.

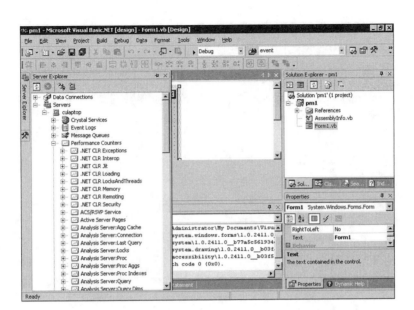

FIGURE 12.1
The Server Explorer allows you to easily add performance counters to your application.

Expand the Processor node to see what counters are available. You'll see such counters as % Interrupt Time, % User Time, and DPC Rate. If you try to add one of the counters to the form by dragging it over, however, you'll see that it doesn't work. Instead, you'll have to expand the counter in which you are interested, and you'll see more choices. These choices are called *instances*, and are available to allow you to access the counter for multiple objects. For example, a computer could have more than one processor, so you'd need a way to be able to access each processor separately. There's also a _Total instance that will give you a total for all the processors. You can see two instances in Figure 12.2 for the % Processor Time counter. The zero represents the one processor on the server, and the _Total represents all the processors. On single-processor systems, of course, these are the same.

Make sure that you have the instances showing for the % Processor Time counter, and click on _Total and drag it onto your form. When you do this, a new control is added to the component tray, with the name PerformanceCounter1. If you click on the control once and examine the properties, you'll see that the properties match what you'd expect given the terminology. The CategoryName is Processor, the CounterName is % Processor Time, and the Instance is _Total. The MachineName property lists the name of the server on which you are monitoring the counter.

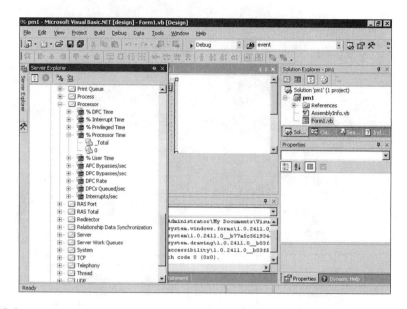

FIGURE 12.2

The instances of the % Processor Time counter.

Now, go to the Toolbox and open the Windows Form tab. Add a Label and a Timer to the form. Click once on the `Timer1` control, which will appear in the component tray. Change the `Interval` property to 1000 and make sure that `Enabled` is set to True.

Now, go into the code for the form and add the following code:

```
Private Sub Timer1_Tick(ByVal sender As System.Object, _
  ByVal e As System.EventArgs) Handles Timer1.Tick
    Label1.Text = PerformanceCounter1.NextValue.ToString
End Sub
```

This simple code takes the `NextValue` of the `PerformanceCounter1` object and places it in the label each second. This way, you can monitor the CPU utilization of your system. Go ahead and start the application and watch it run for a few moments. Perform some actions that will tax the processor, such as starting up large applications or performing a search for files on the computer.

Understanding the Performance Counters

Looking at the percentage utilization is fairly easy to understand. However, if you look at the categories and counters available, not all are intuitive. If there are counters on which you want more information, you can find descriptions for them by starting the Performance Monitor application. You can start it in Windows 2000 by selecting the Administrative Tools menu and then selecting Performance. Or, you can simply open a command prompt, and type **perfmon**, and press the Enter key.

After you start the Performance Monitor application, you click on the plus sign button to add counters. This opens the Add Counter dialog box, which has a drop-down list box labeled Performance object. This box shows the available categories. If you choose `System` as the performance object, the available counters will appear in the list box on the left. The list box on the right will show the available instances, although there are none in the case of the System category.

Select the Context switches/sec counter. If you aren't sure what this means, click the `Explain` button and a new window appears beneath the Performance Monitor, as shown in Figure 12.3. This window will stay open until you explicitly close it, and it will stay in sync as you switch categories or counters. This is a handy way to find out more information about some of the counters, if the names themselves are confusing.

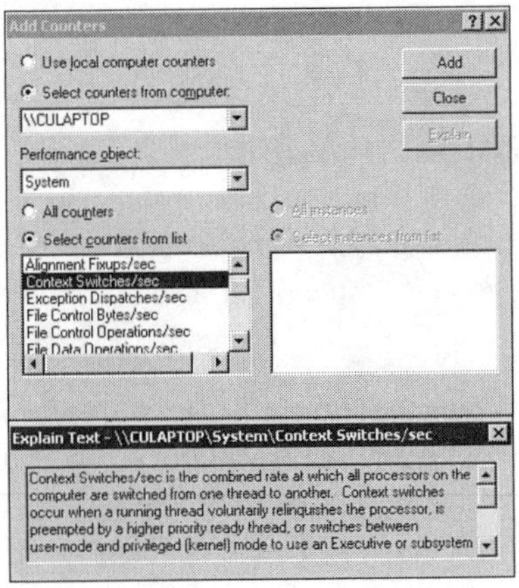

FIGURE 12.3

Clicking the Explain button in the Performance Monitor gives you a description of the various counters.

A better way to get a description of a particular performance counter is available in VS .NET, however. Choose the performance counter in which you are interested using the Server Explorer, right-click on the category of the counter, and choose View Category. This opens the Performance Counter Builder dialog box in read-only mode. This dialog box, shown in Figure 12.4, displays the category, the category description, all the counters, and the data type and description for each counter. This is the same dialog you will use in a few moments to create your own custom performance counters.

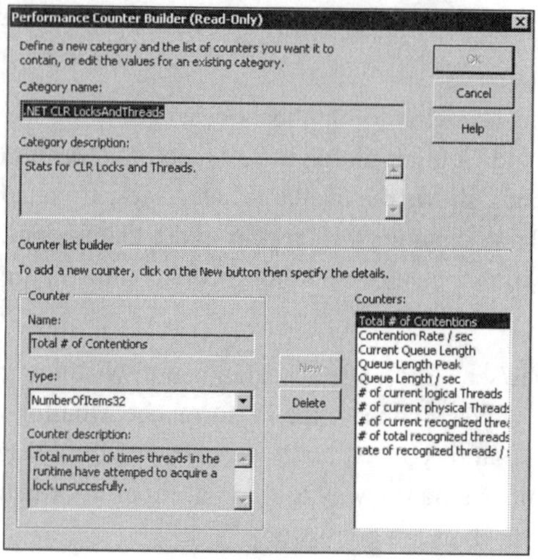

FIGURE 12.4

The Performance Counter Builder dialog box displaying the information for a particular category.

Instantaneous and Calculated Values

You can retrieve two types of values from counters: instantaneous and calculated. All values are samples taken from the actual object. However, instantaneous values are just that: They are a moment in time snapshot. A good example of an instantaneous value is a count; for example, the number of open file handles or the count of threads for a particular process.

Calculated values, on the other hand, require that at least two samples be present. The counter you are viewing for the processor utilization is actually a calculated value, based on the last two samples taken. This is why, when you first run the program, your very first value is zero. Most counters that include a time component are calculated, such as the Context Switches/sec you read about in the previous section.

When you use the PerformanceCounter class, two methods appear to be very similar: NextSample and NextValue. NextSample actually returns a CounterSample structure. This CounterSample contains the raw (uncalculated) value for the performance counter. This is no different from making a call to the RawValue property of the PerformanceCounter class the first time. On subsequent calls, however, you could also use the NextSample's Calculate method to calculate over the last two values, usually in a case in which you want an average to help smooth out wildly fluctuating values.

NextValue, on the other hand, returns a calculated value only. This is similar to using the NextSample.Calculate method, except that it is done for you. The return value of the NextValue method is a single-precision floating-point number, not a structure as with the NextSample method.

Adding Performance Counters Through Code

Adding performance counters to your application via the Server Explorer is fairly easy to do. However, you can also access the performance counters programmatically. The PerformanceCounter class is in System.Diagnostics, and using it allows you access to the counters just as you had with the Server Explorer.

To do the previous example using code, you can delete the PerformanceCounter1 control, and change your code to the following, making sure you change the MachineName property to the name of a machine to which you have access:

```
Dim pcProc As New PerformanceCounter()

Private Sub Form1_Load(ByVal sender As System.Object, _
 ByVal e As System.EventArgs) Handles MyBase.Load
   pcProc.CategoryName = "Processor"
   pcProc.CounterName = "% Processor Time"
   pcProc.InstanceName = "_Total"
   pcProc.MachineName = "culaptop"
End Sub

Private Sub Timer1_Tick(ByVal sender As System.Object, _
 ByVal e As System.EventArgs) Handles Timer1.Tick
   Label1.Text = pcProc.NextValue.ToString
End Sub
```

Here, you programmatically create a PerformanceCounter object called pcProc. This is created outside any procedure to make it module-level in scope.

In the Form_Load sub, you set all the necessary information: the category, counter, instance, and server names are all set in the Form_Load sub. Then, just as in previous examples, the value is displayed in the label when the timer fires.

Creating Your Own Performance Counters

The performance counters provided to you by the operating system are often useful for a variety of tasks. However, what if you want to provide counters from your application, such as the average orders per second entered into a database? In the past, you would have simply coded some variables into the application and tracked them yourself, perhaps writing them to a file or database. Now, however, the PerformanceCounter class allows you to create your own counters on the fly, and these counters can be exposed through the Performance Monitor application.

There are two ways to create custom counters and categories: You can use the Performance Counter Builder or you can create the categories and counters in code. Creating the categories and counters are not two steps of a process; instead, you must create the category and counters at the same time, which you will see in the examples. In addition, you cannot create categories and counters on remote machines.

Creating Counters with the Performance Counter Builder

If you want to add new categories and counters easily, you can do so by using the Performance Counter Builder, which is available via the Server Explorer. Open the Server Explorer and right-click on the Performance Counters node. In the pop-up menu, choose Create New Category, and the Performance Counter Builder will appear. Unlike what you saw in Figure 12.4, the dialog will be empty when you first create a new category.

In the Category Name text box, type **LearningVB**. In the Category Description text box, type **Example counters used for learning how to create counters in VB .NET**.

Notice that at this point, the OK button is still disabled. That is because you cannot create a category without counters. In the Counter List Builder section, click the New button. In the Name text box in the Counter section, type **ClickCount** and set the Type drop-down list box to NumberOfItems32. In the Counter Description text box, type **The number of clicks performed in the test application**. When you are done, verify that your dialog box looks like the one in Figure 12.5, and click the OK button.

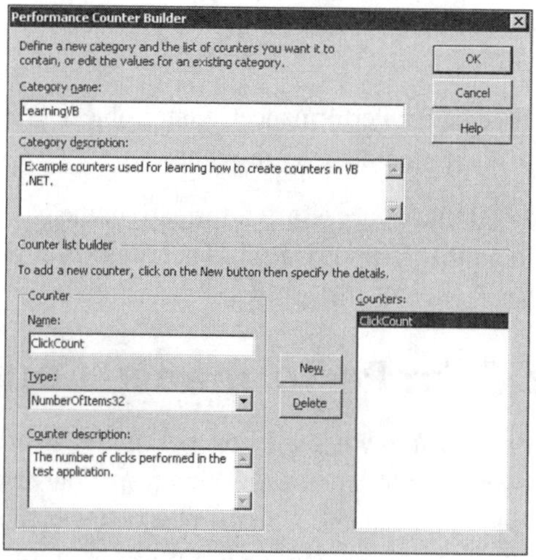

FIGURE 12.5

The Performance Counter Builder dialog box with your new custom counter.

If you look in the Server Explorer, you'll notice the category LearningVB has been added. If you expand that node, you'll see the counter ClickCount, as shown in Figure 12.6.

FIGURE 12.6

The new custom Performance Counter has been added to the Server Explorer list of available categories and counters.

Not only does the new counter appear in the Server Explorer, but it also appears in the Performance Monitor application. If you open Performance Monitor and click the plus sign button, the Performance Object drop-down list box will show you the new LearningVB category. Selecting this category will then show all the counters in the list box for counters. Figure 12.7 shows what you should see in the Performance Monitor application.

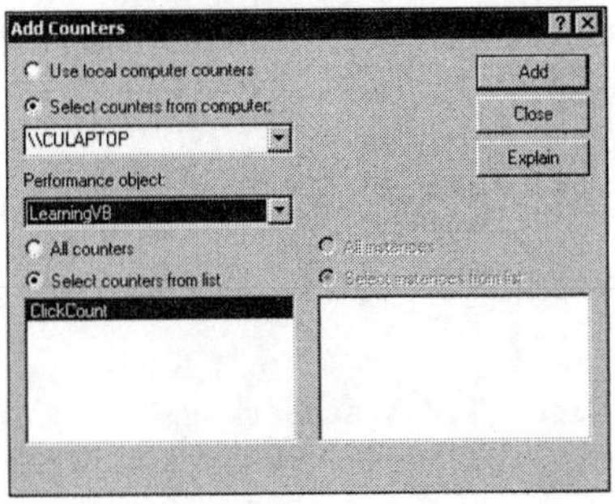

FIGURE 12.7

The new performance category and counter you added in VS .NET appear in the Performance Monitor application.

Go ahead and click the Add button in the Performance Monitor's Add Counter dialog box to add this counter to the Performance Monitor window, and then click the Close button. You should see Performance Monitor start to monitor that counter, which is currently at zero. Let the Performance Monitor run while you return to VS .NET.

Back in VS .NET, add a new form and accept the default name of Form2. Make this your startup form by setting it as the startup object using the project's properties dialog box. On Form2, add a text box and four buttons. Leave the text box named TextBox1, but set the following properties for the four buttons:

	Name	**Text**
Button1	cmdAdd1	Add 1
Button2	cmdAddX	Add X
Button3	cmdSubtract1	Subtract 1
Button4	cmdSubtractX	Subtract X

Now, open the Server Explorer and find the ClickCount counter under the LearningVB category that you added. Drag ClickCount onto your form. An object named `PerformanceCounter1` is added to the component tray of your form. Click once on `PerformanceCounter1` and look at the Properties window. Change the `ReadOnly` property to False, which will allow you to modify this counter in your application.

Now, add the following code to your application:

```
Private Sub cmdAdd1_Click(ByVal sender As System.Object, _
 ByVal e As System.EventArgs) Handles cmdAdd1.Click
    PerformanceCounter1.Increment()
End Sub

Private Sub cmdAddX_Click(ByVal sender As System.Object, _
 ByVal e As System.EventArgs) Handles cmdAddX.Click
    PerformanceCounter1.IncrementBy(TextBox1.Text)
End Sub

Private Sub cmdSubtract1_Click(ByVal sender As System.Object, _
 ByVal e As System.EventArgs) Handles cmdSubtract1.Click
    If PerformanceCounter1.RawValue > 0 Then
        PerformanceCounter1.Decrement()
    End If
End Sub

Private Sub cmdSubtractX_Click(ByVal sender As System.Object, _
 ByVal e As System.EventArgs) Handles cmdSubtractX.Click
    If PerformanceCounter1.RawValue >= TextBox1.Text Then
        PerformanceCounter1.IncrementBy(-1 * TextBox1.Text)
    Else
        PerformanceCounter1.RawValue = 0
    End If
End Sub
```

The `cmdAdd1_Click` sub is designed to simply increment by counter by one. The `Increment` method adds one to the current value of the counter, so a simple call to `Increment` is all that is required.

The `cmdAddX_Click` sub uses the `IncrementBy` method to add a number other than one to the counter. In this case, you read the value in the text box and increment the counter by that amount.

> **NOTE**
>
> If you had `Option Strict` turned on, you'd have to explicitly convert the value in `TextBox1` to a `Long` data type. Your code would end up looking like this:
>
> ```
> PerformanceCounter1.IncrementBy(CLng(TextBox1.Text))
> ```

The `cmdSubtract1_Click` sub is designed to reduce the counter by one, so you call the `Decrement` method to decrease the counter by one. You do perform a check here to make sure that the counter is still above zero. Failure to perform this check causes the counter to roll back from zero to its maximum value of 4,294,967,295. Therefore, you'll normally want to ensure that you do not go below zero.

Finally, `cmdSubtractX_Click` reduces the counter by the value typed into the text box. However, there is no `DecrementBy` method, so you employ the trick of using `IncrementBy` with a negative number. This allows you to add in a negative number, thus decreasing the counter. Notice that if you are trying to decrement the counter by more than is in the counter, you simply set the `RawValue` to zero. This works well because the counter is an instantaneous value, not a calculated value.

Go ahead and run the application. Make sure that you can see both your form and the Performance Monitor application, which should be tracking the ClickCount counter. Now, click once on the Add 1 button. You'll notice that the counter rises to one. Click the Add 1 button twice more, and notice the counter climb to three. Now, type a 5 into the text box and click the Add X button, and you'll see the counter climb to eight. Now, click the Subtract 1 button once and the counter will drop to seven. With the five still in the text box, click the Subtract X button to drop the counter to two. Click the Subtract X button again, and the counter will drop to zero.

Figure 12.8 shows you what you will see in the Performance Monitor if you perform these steps fairly quickly. Take your time, and make sure that you understand what is happening as you increment and decrement the counter.

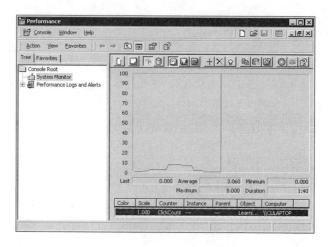

FIGURE 12.8
The Performance Monitor displaying the value of the new counter you created, as you manipulate it through code.

Adding Custom Counters to Other Computers

You created a new performance counter called ClickCount in a LearningVB category, but you created it only on the local computer. What if you need to install this application on another computer? You could manually create the same counter on that machine, but that is not the best way to do it. You could also add code to your application to create the counter, which you will see in a moment.

However, VS .NET gives you an easier way to add these counters to other computers. Return to the designer for Form2, and click once on the PerformanceCounter1 control in the component tray. If you look in the Properties window, you'll see an `Add Installer` link, just as you saw when you created a Windows service. You can see this link in Figure 12.9.

If you click on the Add Installer link, a ProjectInstaller.vb file is added to your project. The designer of this file has a `PerformanceCounterInstaller` control on it, and this will handle adding the ClickCount counter in the LearningVB category to any machine that runs this application.

Creating Counters Programmatically

In the previous section, you created a new category and counter with the Performance Counter Builder. You could also create new counters using code. With code, you can create a new category and a single counter by calling the Create method of the `PerformanceCounterCategory` class. This creates the category and counter at the same time.

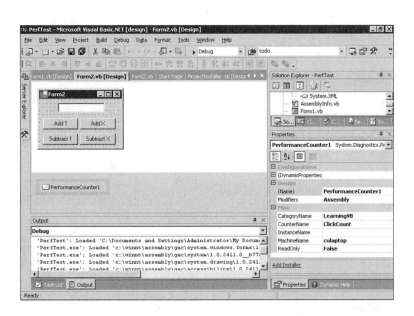

FIGURE 12.9

The Property window for your PerformanceCounter control will include a link to add installers for the counter to your project.

If your needs are more complex and you need to create more than one counter, you have to use the CounterCreationData class to create new counters and add them to a CounterCreationDataCollection collection. This collection is then passed to the Create method, which creates the category and all of the counters at once.

Suppose that, as an example, you want to record the number of transactions you were able to process per second. In addition, you want to track the average time it takes to process a certain part of your application. You want to create these two counters via code, and access them programmatically.

To create the counters programmatically, create a new form named Form3, and set it as your startup object. Add a button, and then add the following code:

```
Private Sub Button1_Click(ByVal sender As System.Object, _
 ByVal e As System.EventArgs) Handles Button1.Click
    Dim CountColl As New CounterCreationDataCollection()
    Dim counterTxPerSec As New CounterCreationData()
    Dim counterAvgTime As New CounterCreationData()
    Dim counterAvgBase As New CounterCreationData()
```

```
    With counterTxPerSec
        .CounterName = "Transactions"
        .CounterHelp = "Number of transactions per second"
        .CounterType = PerformanceCounterType.RateOfCountsPerSecond32
    End With
    With counterAvgTime
        .CounterName = "Time to Process"
        .CounterHelp = "Average time to process the request"
        .CounterType = PerformanceCounterType.AverageTimer32
    End With
    With counterAvgBase
        .CounterName = "Base Time to Process"
        .CounterHelp = "Average time to process the request"
        .CounterType = PerformanceCounterType.AverageBase
    End With

    CountColl.Add(counterTxPerSec)
    CountColl.Add(counterAvgTime)
    CountColl.Add(counterAvgBase)
    PerformanceCounterCategory.Create("VbNetCounters", _
      "Counters created while learning VB .NET", CountColl)
End Sub
```

This code looks complicated, but it is fairly straightforward. First, you create a new
CounterCreationDataCollection because you will be creating multiple counters, and they must be
in a collection. Then, you create three individual counters: counterTxPerSec, counterAvgTime,
and counterAvgBase. Even though you just wanted a counter to record the average time for a
task, you'll need to create two counters to perform the calculation.

Next, you set the names, descriptions, and types for the counters. You then add all three to the
collection, create the category, and pass in the collection as a parameter.

This creates a new category named VbNetCounters. Close the Performance Monitor (it does
not refresh the list automatically). Now, run the application, and click on Button1. Reopen the
Performance Monitor, and drop down the Performance Object list to verify that VbNetCounters
exists. Choose to add the counter named Transactions.

Close your VB .NET application, and add two more buttons to the form, and a text box. Add
the following code to your application:

```
Private Sub Button2_Click(ByVal sender As System.Object, _
  ByVal e As System.EventArgs) Handles Button2.Click
    Dim TxPerSec As New PerformanceCounter()
    TxPerSec.CategoryName = "VbNetCounters"
    TxPerSec.CounterName = "Transactions"
    TxPerSec.ReadOnly = False
```

```
    TxPerSec.IncrementBy(textbox1.text)
End Sub

Private Sub Button3_Click(ByVal sender As System.Object, _
  ByVal e As System.EventArgs) Handles Button3.Click
    PerformanceCounterCategory.Delete("VbNetCounters")
End Sub
```

`Button2_Click` creates a new instance of the `PerformanceCounter` object, something you accomplished earlier by dragging the counter from the Server Explorer and dropping it on your form. You bind to a particular category and counter, and then set the `ReadOnly` property to False. When you run the application, you'll increment the counter by the value in the text box. However, this is not a constantly incrementing counter. Instead, its data type is `RateOfCounts PerSecond32`, which means it will check the number that occurred in a second, display that number, and then reset to zero.

`Button3_Click` simply removes the new category you created.

Start the project and make sure that you can see your form and the Performance Monitor. Type **10** into the text box and click on `Button2`. You'll see the Transactions counter rise to 10 and then fall back to zero. Change the text box to 50 and click `Button2`. Again, you'll see the counter rise to 50 and fall back. Change the text box back to 10, but this time, click `Button2` as many times as you can in five seconds.

Because you are able to click the button more than one time per second, you can get the transactions per second up to 20, 30, 40, or even higher. As soon as you stop clicking, of course, the counter falls back to zero.

This would be an ideal counter for situations in which you are trying to determine the number of records per second you are serving up through a Web service, the number of transactions per second your component is handling, or any other similar measure. The Performance Monitor lets you set alerts on any counter, so you could be notified if certain events occurred.

Summary

Monitoring performance counters from within VB .NET is a useful function because it allows you to monitor almost any aspect of your current computer, or any other machine on your network, provided you have the appropriate access rights.

The fact that .NET makes it easy to create your own performance counters and programmatically access them brings a new level of functionality to VB developers. Your applications can now create their own categories within the Performance Monitor tool, familiar to most administrators and many power users. You can supply performance counters for a variety of functions within your application, allow easy monitoring through a standard Microsoft tool.

More importantly, you have an easy way to monitor how well your application is running. If you want to know how well it performs on one server versus another, place some performance counters in your application and watch the application performance on each server. There's no need to compile in debug information or other hooks that will later have to be removed.

Deployment and Configuration

IN THIS CHAPTER

Some of the last steps you'll take when developing your applications are configuration and deployment. These steps are necessary so that your application will function properly on any computer on which it runs.

With VB .NET and the .NET Framework, deployment and configuration are easy tasks, and quite different than with VB6 applications.

Deploying .NET Apps

Before you dig into the mechanics of deploying your VB .NET applications, it's important to first cover some of the concepts and advantages that .NET offers you over classic environments.

First, remember that all .NET applications emit metadata, which makes them self-describing. All the settings and deployment parameters are contained with the application itself, and there is no need to enter them in the registry or rely on other dependencies. This also means that each application is a completely standalone entity, and won't interfere at all with other applications. In fact, you can even have multiple versions of the same application deployed on one computer, and they won't interfere with each other!

Another benefit of self-describing applications is that they are very easy to deploy. You simply need to copy your files from one computer to the other. No complex installer routines are necessary.

Not only is getting your application to another computer easier, but there are now more options to do so as well. The quick and dirty way to deploy is to just use XCOPY, but you can also deploy over the Internet or by using the Microsoft Installer. Updating applications is also flexible, allowing you to update single components at a time via XCOPY or Internet.

In this chapter, you examine three ways to deploy your applications: via the Windows Installer, via CAB files, or via the Internet and Internet Explorer 5.5.

Windows Installer

The Windows Installer is an installation and configuration application that provides a standard method for deploying your applications. It allows you (or your users) to selectively install parts of your application and leave others out, or choose to install them at a later time. These installation files typically end in the `.msi` extension, and you've probably seen this standard interface in quite a few places. Figure 13.1 shows the Windows Installer in use when installing Microsoft Office.

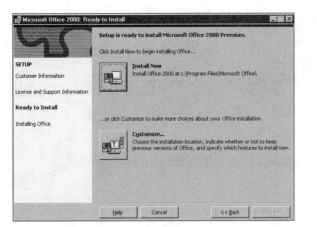

FIGURE 13.1

The Windows Installer in action.

If you've used the Windows Installer before, you'll know it offers you quite a few features for configuring your installation, thus reducing the time spent on deployment for the developers and end users. This is the Installer's *raison d'etre* (that's "reason for being" for those non-French speaking readers).

Visual Studio .NET provides a wizard allowing you to customize the way you deploy your application via the Windows Installer. Using VS .NET, you can very easily and quickly build a deployment solution without having to do anything other than clicking a few buttons.

Open a new or existing VB .NET project in VS .NET. Figure 13.2 shows an empty project created just for this exercise.

In the Solution Explorer, right-click on the solution and choose Add, New Project. In the Add New Project dialog box, choose Setup and Deployment Projects in the Project Types and Setup Wizard in the Templates, and give it an appropriate name. After you click the OK button, VS .NET will add another project to your solution, and display the File System window, shown in Figure 13.3.

The left pane shows what the file system on the installation machine will look like when deployed. Recall that because deployment involves only copying files, there are no options here for editing registry values or including dependencies. The right pane shows the items that will be installed in each folder (by default, it simply lists the same things as the left pane).

13

DEPLOYMENT AND
CONFIGURATION

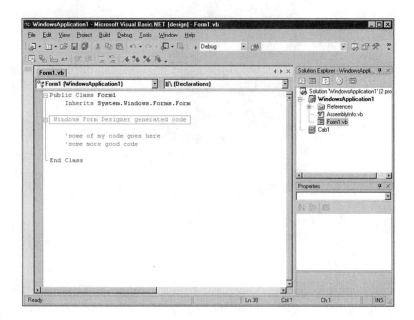

FIGURE 13.2

A typical application ready for deployment.

FIGURE 13.3

The File System window allows you to customize your installation.

The Application Folder is where your main application files will be installed. This typically includes your .exe or .dll files, .resource files, and so on. In the properties window (lower right in Figure 13.2), you can configure where exactly this folder will be located on the user's machine. By default, it is c:\Program Files*your company name**your app name*. This is specified with the syntax [ProgramFilesFolder][Manufacturer]\[ProductName]. Typically, you'll want to leave this as is, to make it easier for your users. You can create subdirectories under this folder by right-clicking on the Application Folder and selecting Add, Folder.

The properties window has a few additional elements you can set. The first, AlwaysCreate, specifies that this folder should be created even if the folder is empty. The Condition property allows you to specify rules that will be enforced during installation. For example, specifying VersionNT>=500 means that the installation will occur only if the target machine is Windows 2000 or later. For more information on conditional phrasing, see the VS .NET documentation with the topic Deployment Conditions.

DefaultLocation, Description, DisplayName, and Name are all self-explanatory. Property provides users a way to override the paths of custom folders for your application. If you leave this property blank, users cannot change or rename the target folders during installation.

Finally, Transitive specifies whether the Condition property should be evaluated only upon first installation, or every time the installer is called. For example, you could use it to enable reconfiguring the application after it has been installed. Typically, you'll leave this property at False.

Next, the Global Assembly Cache Folder (GAC) specifies any custom assemblies that should be copied to the target computer's Global Assembly Cache. These assemblies would be loaded every time the CLR is started on the target machine, and thus would be available to many different applications. This folder has the same property options as the Application Folder.

User's Desktop contains, obviously, the items that will be installed to the target machine's desktop. These will normally include shortcuts to your application. User's Programs Menu likewise contains shortcuts to your application that will be placed in the Start Menu, Programs folder.

Additionally, if these four folders are not enough, you can right-click on File System on Target Machine, select Add Special Folder, and add any number of additional special folders to which you can deploy files. These include the Windows System folder, the Start menu, Fonts folder, and so on.

After you've configured your application properly, select Build from the Build menu, and your deployment package will be created with an .msi file extension. Browse to your application solution folder (c:\Documents and Settings*user*\My Documents\Visual Studio Projects*appname* by default), and you'll see a new folder with the same name as your

Deployment solution (Setup3, in this case). Inside this folder, you'll see Debug and Release folders, which contain debug and release versions of your installer. By default, your installer will have been placed in the Debug folder. Inside, you'll see the installer file (again, Setup3.msi in this case). Double-click on this, and you'll be greeted with the familiar Windows Installer application, shown in Figure 13.4.

FIGURE 13.4

The Installer application.

All you need to do is distribute this file and you're done! An end user can now execute this file again for further options such as repairing installation or removing the application. A user can also go to the Add/Remove Programs Control panel to manipulate the program.

> **NOTE**
>
> Your users must have the .NET Framework installed for this installation package to work.

CAB Files

A CAB file is basically a compressed version of your application files. This allows you to distribute your application more easily, especially over the Internet.

Creating a CAB file for your application is an easy process. Just as you did to create a Windows Installer project, go to the File menu and select Add Project, New Project, and select Cab Project from the Add New Project window. The CAB project will appear in your Solution Explorer. Add the necessary files by right-clicking on the CAB solution, selecting Add, File. Anything you put in this solution will be compressed.

These CAB files can be distributed with your Windows Installer application, or via the Internet, as you'll see in the next section.

┌─────────────┐
│ **Note** │
└─────────────┘

The Beta 2 version of the .NET Framework has a few limitations on CAB files. Specifically, you can place only one assembly in a single CAB file, and the CAB file must have the same name as the assembly inside it. It is unclear if this will be the case in the released version.

Internet Explorer

There are numerous ways to take advantage of the Internet for your applications. As you learned in Chapter 8, "Building Web Applications with VB .NET and ASP.NET," one method is to use ASP.NET to build a fully functional application. Users can simply visit your Web site and execute your Web application. Chapter 9, "Building Web Services with VB .NET," showed you how to build Web services, another way to distribute your application components via the Internet. Both of these methods often use assemblies to provide supporting resources to your application. The users never need to execute anything on their side other than Internet Explorer.

The CLR also allows your executable applications to be accessed over the Web with Internet Explorer 5.5 or later simply by typing the name of your application in the address bar—something that was not possible prior to .NET. For example, by typing `http://www.yourserver.com/MyApp/MyApp.exe` into your browser, the application will be instantiated and run on the client's machine. Figure 13.5 shows such a situation using the simple application we built earlier in this chapter.

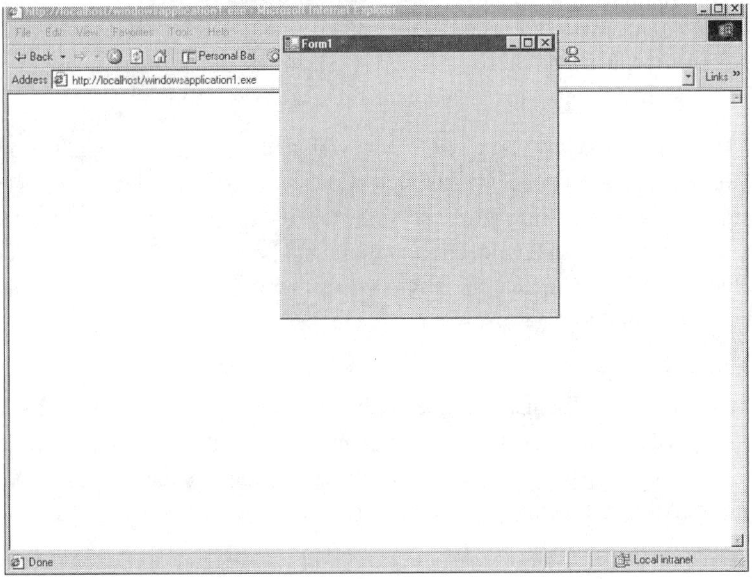

13

DEPLOYMENT AND CONFIGURATION

Figure 13.5

Executing an application through Internet Explorer 6.

Supporting files for your application (such as configuration or CAB files) must be located in the same directory as your `.exe` file for this method to work. These files will be downloaded by the client as necessary.

Configuring .NET Applications

Once upon a time, configuration for applications was quite a pain. With desktop-based applications, you were often required to manipulate registry values or deal with external `.ini` files. These were both good places to store configuration information, but were lacking in flexibility.

The registry was a repository of application information, and a logical place to store your custom information. However, the registry was hardly portable, so settings on one machine were not transferable to another without a registry dump. Also, if anything occurred that caused your application to become out of sync with the registry (such as the application path changing), you were out of luck. For settings to be restored, you often had to simply reinstall the entire application.

`.ini` files were a bit more flexible, allowing you to move your settings with your applications. The problem with these files, however, was that the information contained within was very specific. It applied to only one application, and could not affect the operating system or other apps.

With ASP applications, configuration was an entirely different, and more unpleasant, issue. Settings had to be registered in IIS, and thus were not transferable. Configuring an application often required being physically located at the server. Many ASP developers will recall spending quite a bit of time at client sites setting up applications and servers. If anything ever needed to change, that meant another trip to the client site—a costly chore.

With VB .NET, developers have an entirely new way to configure their applications. The .NET Framework introduces the `.config` file, which allows you to customize all the settings you could ever want, from controlling where session state data is saved to custom database connection strings. This file is an XML file, and therefore can be easily transferred and deployed along with the rest of your application. No more writing registry values or manually configuring IIS—just make your changes using a simple text editor such as Notepad, save, and your settings take effect.

VB .NET applications use the name of the application for this file. For example, if your application is called `Calculator`, the corresponding configuration file will be called `Calculator.config`. It is stored in the same directory as the application, along with other application files. ASP.NET configuration files are always named `web.config`.

These files can contain all sorts of configuration information, and in the next few sections, you'll see how to use them in VB .NET and ASP.NET applications.

> **NOTE**
>
> .NET maintains a system-level config file that maintains default settings for all your applications and the CLR. This file is called `machine.config`, and is typically located in the `c:\winnt\Microsoft.NET\Framework\version\Config` folder.

VB .NET Configuration

The `.config` file for a VB .NET application can have nearly any structure you want (as long as it's XML), but the base element must always be `<configuration>`. Let's look at an example in Listing 13.1.

LISTING 13.1 A Sample `.config` File

```
<configuration>
   <configSections>
      <!-- handlers here-->
   </configSections>
   <myruntime>
      <!-- runtime configuration settings here -->
   </myruntime>
   <appSettings>
      <!--application specific settings -->
    </appSettings>
</configuration>
```

The `.config` files are created for you in an ASP.NET application, and they are always called Web.config. With any other type of project, you have to manually create the `.config` files, and they are the name of the application. For example, an application named App1 would need a configuration file named App1.config. Or, you could give the configuration file a generic name, app.config, which would then work for the current application.

Whether or not you're familiar with XML, this listing is easy to comprehend. On line 1 is the root configuration element, `<configuration>`. This element is required. Next, on line 2, the `<configSections>` element defines handlers (in other words, .NET classes) that will be used to process the settings further down in the `.config` file. The following code snippet is a more detailed example:

```
<configSections>
   <sectionGroup name="system.web">
      <section name="browserCaps" type="System.Web.
➥Configuration.HttpCapabilitiesSectionHandler,System.Web "/>
   </sectionGroup>
</configSections>
```

The second line (sectionGroup) defines a group of settings that will be used later in .config, and the third line (section) defines the class that will be instantiated to handle the browserCaps setting. The type attribute specifies the class, followed by the assembly that it belongs to.

.NET already provides almost all the handlers you'll ever need in the machine.config file's configSections element (refer to the previous note). So, you'll most likely not have to modify this element at all (remember that you can inherit or override these values).

However, if you want to add your own custom sections that do not have declared handlers in the base machine.config file, you'll need to add a <configSection> element to your file. A typical handler for most sections is System.Configuration.NameValueFileSectionHandler, which returns a name/value collection of settings.

Line 5 specifies a section named myruntime. Because this is a custom section with no handler declared in the machine.config file, you must add one to your configSection element. The handler you use will depend on the type of data you want to store in this section. You'll see in a moment how to retrieve these values from your application.

Finally, the appSettings section is a special element for .NET applications. This is where you'll most likely store any custom information for your application because the CLR provides a very easy mechanism for accessing these values, which you'll examine in the next section.

Retrieving Configuration Settings from Your Application

What good are configuration settings if your application can't read them? After you've set up your .config file, .NET provides easy access to the settings contained within. Listing 13.2 shows a simple .config file that you'll use to retrieve settings from.

LISTING 13.2   MyApp.config

```
<configuration>
   <appSettings>
      <add key="appName" value="MyApp" />
      <add key="DSN" value="MyDBConnection" />
   </appSettings>
</configuration>
```

This file contains only two settings, appName and DSN, stored in the appSettings element. Note that you must use the add keyword to add elements to this section, followed by a key name and value. To retrieve either of the two settings, simply use the syntax:

```
ConfigurationSettings.AppSettings("appName")
```

Or:

```
ConfigurationSettings.AppSettings("DSN")
```

That's all there is to it! When your application loads, it populates the AppSettings collection of the System.Configuration.ConfigurationSettings class with all the values in the .config file. Thus, you can easily access these values just as you would those in a dictionary created programmatically. Let's look at a very simple VB .NET application that uses this method, shown in Listing 13.3.

LISTING 13.3 Reading Configuration Values from an Application

```vb
Imports System
Imports System.Configuration

Public Class MyConfigurationReader
    Public Sub ReadSettings()
        Dim strAppName as String

        StrAppName = ConfigurationSettings.AppSettings("appName")

        Console.Writeline("This application is named:")
        Console.Writeline(strAppName)
    End Sub
End Class
```

Put this code in Notepad and save it as MyConfigurationReader.vb, and compile it from the command line with the command:

```
vbc /t:exe /r:System.dll MyConfigurationReader.vb
```

This will generate an executable file named MyConfigurationReader.exe. Next, save the .config file from Listing 13.2 as MyConfigurationReader.exe.config (don't forget to include the .exe!), and execute the application by typing MyConfigurationReader at the command line. You should see the following output:

```
This application is named:
MyApp
```

> **NOTE**
>
> In this case, you are creating the configuration file using Notepad. Inside of the VS .NET IDE, however, you could choose to add a new item, and one of the options is to add an application configuration file. This allows you to edit the file inside the IDE.

13

DEPLOYMENT AND
CONFIGURATION

You can retrieve any setting from the appSettings section in your .config file with this simple method call, and because the .config files are loaded along with your application by the CLR, there is no overhead involved.

There is another, more general method to retrieve configuration values, without relying on the appSettings section: GetConfig. Just like the .AppSettings collection, the GetConfig collection is populated at run-time, and you can access any property with the command:

```
ConfigurationSettings.GetConfig("setting_name")
```

The difference between the AppSettings method and GetConfig is that the latter returns an Object data type, which means you'll need to cast it to the appropriate type. GetConfig also retrieves a section of values, rather than a single value. For example, modifying Listing 13.3, you end up with Listing 13.4.

LISTING 13.4   Using GetConfig to Retrieve Configuration Values

```
Imports System
Imports System.Collections.Specialized
Imports System.Configuration

Public Class MyConfigurationReader
    Shared Sub Main()
        Dim colAppSettings as NameValueCollection
        Dim strAppName as String

        colAppSettings = CType(ConfigurationSettings.
        ➥GetConfig("appSettings"), NameValueCollection)
        strAppName = CType(colAppSettings("appName"), String)

        Console.Writeline("This application is named:")
        Console.Writeline(strAppName)
    End Sub
End Class
```

Because you know the handler for the appSettings section returns a NameValueCollection object, you have to import the appropriate namespace, System.Collections.Specialized. Inside the Sub Main, you instantiate a NameValueCollection object named colAppSettings to hold the results returned from GetConfig. You then retrieve the appSettings section using GetConfig, casting it to a NameValueCollection type using the CType function. The colApp Settings object now contains the settings stored in MyConfigurationReader.exe.config.

You then retrieve the appName property from the colAppSettings collection and store it in strAppName. The value is then written to the console using Console.Writeline. Compile this source using the same command as before, and you'll end up with the same output:

```
This application is named:
MyApp
```

It is a bit more complex to use `GetConfig`, but it provides you the added flexibility of retrieving any section in the `.config` file, rather than just `appSettings`.

ASP.NET Configuration

As mentioned earlier this chapter, ASP.NET applications use the `web.config` file as their configuration setting repository.

The `web.config` file uses a hierarchical configuration. This means that your application can inherit settings from another application, and vice versa. In an ASP.NET application, which typically consists of a directory structure several levels deep, a subfolder will inherit the parent's `web.config` settings, unless overridden by another `web.config` file.

For example, imagine the directory structure shown in Figure 13.6.

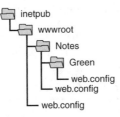

FIGURE 13.6
A typical ASP.NET directory structure.

The entire Web application would automatically use the settings contained in the `web.config` file in the wwwroot directory. The Notes directory contains its own `web.config` file, so it and its subdirectories would have access to those values. If any settings in the `web.config` files in the Notes and wwwroot directory differ, the Notes directory will use its own. Likewise, the `web.config` file in the Green directory would use the settings inherited from both parent folders, overriding those specified by its own `web.config`.

It might be a bit confusing at first, but the methodology is a blessing. Take a look at the sample `web.config` shown in Listing 13.5.

LISTING 13.5 A Sample `web.config` File

```
<configuration>
   <configSections>
      <!-- handlers here-->
   </configSections>
```

LISTING 13.5 Continued

```
<system.net>
   <!-- .NET runtime configuration settings here -->
</system.net>
<system.web>
   <!-- ASP.NET Configuration settings here -->
</system.web>
</configuration>
```

The base element, again, is `<configuration>`, which contains the settings for all other pieces of the .NET Framework. This element is required in every web.config file.

Next, the `<configSections>` element performs the same function as in the VB .NET application .config file; it defines handlers that will be used to process the settings further down in the web.config file.

The next element, `<system.net>`, contains settings that control the .NET runtime itself. You typically won't want to mess with these settings, so don't worry about that section.

The final element, `<system.web>`, controls ASP.NET application settings, such as security and session state. Table 13.1 lists the subelements available in this section.

TABLE 13.1 The ASP.NET Configuration Sections

Section	Description
`<authentication>`	Settings for authentication in ASP.NET. Can be used only by site-, machine-, and application-level config files (disallowed by subdirectories).
`<authorization>`	Authorization settings.
`<browserCaps>`	Configures the browser capabilities component.
`<compilation>`	Compilation settings used by ASP.NET.
`<customErrors>`	Custom error messages displayed by ASP.NET applications.
`<globalization>`	Contains settings for the define region and culture-specific information.
`<httpHandlers>`	The IHttpHandler classes that handle incoming requests.
`<httpModules>`	HTTP modules in the application.
`<httpRuntime>`	ASP.NET HTTP runtime settings. Can be used only by site-, machine-, and application-level config files (disallowed by subdirectories).

TABLE 13.1 Continued

Section	Description
`<identity>`	The identity used by the ASP.NET application.
`<machineKey>`	Configures keys to use for encryption of forms authentication data. Can be used only by site-, machine-, and application-level config files (disallowed by subdirectories).
`<pages>`	Page-specific configuration settings.
`<processModel>`	The process model used by IIS.
`<securityPolicy>`	Defines named security levels to policy files. Can be used only by site-, machine-, and application-level config files (disallowed by subdirectories).
`<sessionState>`	Configures the session state information.
`<trace>`	Settings for the ASP.NET trace service.
`<trust>`	The code access security permission for a particular application. Can be used only by site-, machine-, and application-level config files (disallowed by subdirectories).
`<webServices>`	Configures Web services.

In addition to these ASP.NET specific settings, you can also use the `appSettings` section and `ConfigurationSettings.AppSettings` method just as you did for VB .NET applications. Each of these sections provides a bevy of options to play with, so I won't cover them all here. Refer to the .NET Framework documentation for more information.

One of the most common uses for the `web.config` file is to secure your ASP.NET applications, so let's take a deeper look at the security features in the next section.

Security

Security is a very important topic to any program, especially ASP.NET applications, because you are essentially allowing any one in the world to access your server's file system. Even with desktop-based applications, you are often exposed to unknown and potentially threatening code (as demonstrated by the prolificacy of computer viruses in today's world).

The CLR takes a number of precautions to prevent unauthorized access by applications or users. In addition, the security framework is consolidated and integrated into .NET, so any application can use the same concepts and objects to prevent misuse. Now you'll take a deeper look into how security works with .NET.

Basic Concepts

Everything in .NET security is based on permissions. Code must have permission to access certain resources, users must have certain permissions to access certain code, and so on. Everything you do in the .NET Framework, whether you realize it or not, requires permissions. The .NET Framework even provides a number of objects that represent permissions.

Permissions are determined from a number of sources. User permissions can be determined by the credentials supplied when identification occurs, or by the role that the user fulfills. Code can be granted permissions based on who executes it, and security policies written by administrators.

There are three different types of permissions: code access, identity, and role-based. Each of these fulfills a specific function in the .NET Framework. Code access is used to determine the code's access to file system resources, such as files or environment variables. Identity permissions apply to assemblies, and determine what resources they have access to. This is done by examining features of the assembly (called *evidence*), such as where the assembly originated from, digital signatures, and so on. Finally, role-based permissions determine user-related access. You'll examine code access and role-based permissions later in the chapter.

Finally, after permissions are established, .NET can proceed with authentication and authorization. The former is the process of verifying the requesters are who they say they are. The latter is the process of allowing or denying authenticated users access to resources. These two concepts apply heavily to ASP.NET applications, and you'll examine them in more detail later in the chapter.

Code Access Security

Code access security is a new concept introduced by .NET. This system determines what resources a particular application or piece of code has access to. This might not seem revolutionary, but first you need to see how security was implemented prior to .NET.

Security used to be based on user identities. In other words, a user tries to access resources by supplying valid credentials (such as a username and password) and then is given varying permissions based on those credentials. A major flaw with this system is that even trusted users can execute malicious code, whether intentionally or not, that causes havoc to an operating system. This explains why so many users have been infected by computer viruses.

For example, just because you log in using the administrative account on your computer doesn't mean that you won't accidentally open an attachment in an e-mail message that is actually a virus. Even worse, hackers might gain access to such administrative accounts and execute all sorts of unruly things.

Code access security solves these issues by not relying on user identities and permissions. Rather, the code that is executed is granted permissions based on its credentials, which tend to be harder to fake than user credentials. These include the code's source and digital signatures.

In this situation, if an administrative user attempts to open an unauthenticated e-mail attachment, the request fails, even though the user is an administrator. The user must specifically override the settings to allow this action to be performed. Although code access doesn't stop this occurrence, it does prevent code from being executed unknowingly or unintentionally.

You can write code without targeting the .NET code access system; in fact, you've been doing so for the past 12 chapters. However, you won't be able to provide information about your code to the runtime, leaving interpretation to the CLR, and therefore it might be denied security access. Thus, you can use special attributes in your code to specifically request permissions, as you'll see in the next two sections.

Requesting Permissions from the Runtime

Ideally, it should not be left to the CLR to determine what permissions your code should have access to. Thus, you can specify upfront the permissions your application will need. Note that this doesn't necessarily mean that your application will get those permissions—all the rules of code access security still apply—but it helps to ensure that your code cannot be used maliciously and will operate properly in tight security situations.

There are three ways you can request permissions: request the minimum allowed by the CLR, request optional permissions that are not crucial to the functionality of your application, and explicitly deny permissions, even if the CLR will grant them. All of these methods are performed with nearly the same syntax:

```
<assembly: PermissionObject(SecurityAction.method, Flags := flags)>
```

This code must be placed at the assembly level. Listing 13.6 shows an example that requests the `FileIOPermission`, which allows the application to read and write to the file system.

LISTING 13.6 Requesting Permissions Explicitly

```
Imports System
Imports System.Security
Imports System.Security.Permissions
<assembly: FileIOPermission(SecurityAction.RequestMinimum,
➥Unrestricted := True)>

Namespace MyNamespace
    Public Class MyHappySecureClass
```

LISTING 13.6 Continued

```
    Public Shared Sub Main()
        'do file system access here
    End Sub
  End Class
End Namespace
```

This listing looks just like any other code you've seen, except for the `assembly` attribute after the `Imports` statements. This code requests the minimum security file I/O permissions allowable by the CLR, specifying that the access is unrestricted. If you wanted to optionally request the file I/O permission, change the fourth line to read:

```
<assembly: FileIOPermission(SecurityAction.RequestOptional,
➥Unrestricted := True)>
```

And if you want to disallow your own code to access the file system, use the following:

```
<assembly: FileIOPermission(SecurityAction.RequestRefuse,
➥Unrestricted := True)>
```

When your application is compiled, it places this `assembly` attribute information into the assembly manifest (that is, the metadata), which is then examined by the CLR during load.

Additionally, rather than requesting individual permissions, you can request permission sets. These sets are built-in groups of permissions that fit different requirements. The syntax is

```
<assembly: PermissionSetAttribute(SecurityAction.method, Name := "set_name")>
```

Table 13.2 lists the built-in permission sets.

TABLE 13.2 Built-in Permission Sets

Name	Description
Execution	Permission to execute, but not to access protected resources
FullTrust	Full access to all resources
Internet	The permission to use for content from an unknown source
LocalInternet	The permission set to use content from an unknown source, but from within an enterprise
Nothing	No permissions (do not execute)
SkipVerification	Try to skip permission verification

Requiring Permissions of Your Users

In addition to informing the CLR of the permissions your application needs at runtime, you can also require that users of your application have certain permissions during execution. Just because your application was granted the unrestricted `FileIOPermission` permission doesn't necessarily mean that you want to enable the user of your code to delete any and all files. Thus, anywhere in your code, you can require users to have permissions before execution will occur.

This method of declaring security is very useful when you don't really know beforehand what resources the user will be accessing. For example, in the case of Microsoft Word, you initially want to obtain permissions to access the file system, and allow the users to open and write files. However, you do not want them to overwrite certain crucial files, such as system files. Because you have no way of knowing what files the users will try to access, you should implement security procedures in your application in the places where unauthorized access could occur.

There are two methods to do this: declarative and imperative. The first, declarative security, can be used only at the assembly, class, or member level. This means that certain permissions must be met before *any* of the code is executed. Imperative security methods can be placed anywhere in your code, and are very useful when you want your code to conditionally execute based on information obtained during execution. You'll look at the declarative security syntax first.

The syntax for this method is very similar to requesting permissions from the CLR. Place the following code before any member that you want to protect:

```
<MyPermission(SecurityAction.Demand, flag = flags)>
```

Replace *MyPermission* with the appropriate permission object, and use `SecurityAction.Demand` to indicate that this particular permission must be met before any of the code will be executed. Again using the `FileIOPermission` as an example, Listing 13.7 shows a code snippet from a typical class.

LISTING 13.7 Using Declarative Security Permissions

```
<FileIOPermission(SecurityAction.Demand, Unrestricted = True)>
Public Class MyClass
   Public Sub New()
      'The constructor is protected by the security call.
   End Sub

   Public Sub MyMethod()
      'This method is protected by the security call.
   End Sub

   Public Sub MyMethod2()
      'This method is protected by the security call.
   End Sub
End Class
```

Because the declarative attribute is placed at the class level, all methods within also require the specified permission. Similarly, you could place the attribute at the assembly or method level to affect an entire assembly or a single method, respectively.

Imperative security works a bit differently. It can be used only inside a method call, and you work with the permission objects directly. Listing 13.8 shows an example.

Listing 13.8   Using Imperative Security Permissions

```
Public Class MyClass
   Public Sub MyMethod()
      'This method is protected by the security call.
      Dim objPerm as New FileIOPermission(Unrestricted)

      objPerm.Demand()
      'code
End Sub

   Public Sub MyMethod2()
      'This method is not protected by the security call.
   End Sub
End Class
```

In this code, you create a new `FileIOPermission` object, passing it the `Unrestricted` permission state variable. Then you simply call the `Demand` method to demand the user have security permission from that point forward. If the user does not have permission, an access denied message will be raised.

Role-Based Security

Role-based security is based on granting permissions to users based on the roles they fulfill. For example, you might perform the administrative role on your own computer, but are only a power user on your computer at work. The role you perform is granted certain permissions, and therefore, multiple people can be in each administrative or power user role without having to assign individual permissions.

Role-based security in .NET is based on two key concepts: identities and principals. They are very similar, but it is important to see the distinctions. An identity represents a user; it contains information about the user's name, password, validation type, and so on. A principal, on the other hand, represents the application or code and its permissions. Thus, there are two security checks for role-based security—one based on the user, and one based on the code being executed. Both are necessary to ensure security of your operating system.

.NET provides two built-in versions of each of these objects: generic (the `GenericIdentity` and `GenericPrincipal` objects) and Windows (the `WindowsIdentity` and `WindowsPrincipal` objects). The generic objects are provided so that you can implement your own custom security checks after obtaining the user's and code's credentials. The Windows-based objects are used when you want to rely on Windows authentication to dole out permissions. No matter the objects you use, the syntax is still the same. Listing 13.9 shows a very simple application that performs role-based security checks.

LISTING 13.9   Role-Based Security Application

```
Imports System
Imports System.Security.Permissions
Imports System.Security.Principal
Imports System.Threading

Public Class RoleCheck
    Public Shared Sub Main()
        Dim strUserName, strPassword as String

        Console.Write("Enter your user name: ")
        strUserName = Console.Readline()

        Console.Write("Enter your password: ")
        strPassword = Console.Readline()

        if strUserName = "JoeSmith" AND strPassword = "password" Then
            Console.Writeline("Permission granted")
            Dim arrUserInfo As String() = {"Administrator", "User"}
            Dim objIdentity as New GenericIdentity("JoeSmith")
            Dim objPrincipal as New GenericPrincipal(objIdentity, arrUserInfo)
            Thread.CurrentPrincipal = objPrincipal
        end if
    end sub
end class
```

Performing role-based security involves only a few steps in addition to what you already know. First, you import the `System.Security.Permissions` and `System.Security.Principal` namespaces.

The first part of the code should look familiar. You're simply displaying output to the user, and reading in values from the command line. Next, you have a simple `If...Then...Else` statement that checks whether the supplied credentials match the strings `JoeSmith` and `password`. You then use `Console.Writeline` to write a response to the user. After the `Console.Writeline`, however, is where it starts to get interesting.

Using the `GenericIdentity` object, you instantiate a new identity named `JoeSmith`. Next, you use this identity object to create a new `GenericPrincipal` object, supplying an array of role information (this array holds the names of the roles this identity fulfills).

Finally, after you've created your principal and identity objects, you need to make sure that the rest of the application executes under the specified permissions. You do this by setting the `CurrentPrincipal` property of the `Thread` object to the principal you just created. Now, anything that executes in this application after you set the thread's `CurrentPrincipal` property will execute using the identity and principal declared here. (See Chapter 11, "Creating Multithreaded Visual Basic .NET Applications," for more information on threads.)

For example, the following code snippet could be placed anywhere else in the listing, and security checks would be performed:

```
Sub MyProtectedMethod()
    Dim objPermission as New PrincipalPermission("JoeSmith", "Administrator")
    objPermission.Demand()

    'perform secure functionality
End Sub
```

This method creates a new permission object based on the identity `JoeSmith`, with the role `Administrator`. Then you call the `Demand` method just as you did with imperative security. If you had not granted the `Administrator` role to the identity `JoeSmith` in Listing 13.9, this code snippet would not execute. (The `PrincipalPermission` object on the second line is just another permission object, much like `FileIOPermission`.)

You can also perform role-based declarative security checks with the syntax:

```
<PrincipalPermissionAttribute(SecurityAction.Demand, Name:="JoeSmith",
➥Role:="Administrator")>
```

Using the identity and principal objects, you can ensure the utmost security for your application no matter who accesses it.

ASP.NET Security

Security concepts in ASP.NET are very similar to VB .NET desktop-based applications; a user assumes an identity and supplies credentials, and is given certain permissions based upon them. This should now be old hat to you. The methods of securing your applications, however, are very different in ASP.NET.

ASP.NET relies on three steps to secure its applications. The first step, authentication, is the process of making sure that a user is who she says she is. This is the same concept as in VB .NET security. The second step, authorization, is determining the resources authenticated users have access to—again, the same concept from VB .NET. The third step, impersonation, however, is a new concept. All these methods can be implemented through the `web.config` file.

Impersonation allows the ASP.NET engine to impersonate the user that accesses an application, thereby restricting its own power. For example, in a typical Web site, anonymous visitors are allowed access. When such an anonymous visitor starts executing ASP.NET pages, the pages are executed with the visitor's permission set, rather than ASP.NET's permission set, which has many more permissions than an anonymous user. This prevents visitors from attempting to access resources that they shouldn't be able to by hacking ASP.NET, much as code access security protects users from inadvertently executing malicious code.

Next, we'll examine the three steps to ASP.NET security, and how each is implemented.

Authentication

You can implement authentication with just one additional line to your `web.config` file. The syntax for implementing authentication is as follows:

```
<configuration>
   <system.web>
      <authentication mode="mode" />
   </system.web>
</configuration>
```

There are three modes ASP.NET can use to implement authentication. The first, `Windows`, relies on IIS and Windows authentication. This methodology is the same as used to secure any ASP.NET application, so we won't cover it here. See *Sams Teach Yourself ASP.NET in 21 Days* for more information.

Passport authentication is the second method. This relies on Microsoft's Passport technology—a central location of user information used for validation—to function. This allows a user to log in to one Passport-enabled site, and automatically be logged in to *every* Passport site. It works similarly to `Forms` authentication, which will be discussed in a moment. To use Passport authentication, you must first register with the Passport service (this requires paying a fee, which explains why it won't be covered in this book). Then when users visit your site, they will first be redirected to Microsoft's Passport login form and, if valid credentials are supplied, will be redirected back to your secure pages. Visit `www.passport.com` for more information.

The third method, `Forms` authentication, is very common. You've probably seen Web sites that present you with a form for username and password information—this is `Forms`-based authentication. You enable this method with the following `web.config` file:

```
<configuration>
   <system.web>
      <authentication mode="Forms">
```

```
        <forms name="name" loginUrl="url"/>
      </authentication>
    </system.web>
</configuration>
```

When a user now attempts to access your Web site, he will first be redirected to the URL specified by the `loginUrl` property. This page should contain a login form for the user to enter credentials. Using the `FormsAuthentication` object, you can then verify a user's identity. Listing 13.10 shows an ASP.NET page that provides a login form and validates a user upon submission.

LISTING 13.10 A Forms Authentication ASP.NET Page

```
<%@ Page Language="VB"%>

<script runat="server">
    sub Login(obj as Object, e as EventArgs)
        if tbUserName.Text = "JoeSmith" and tbPassword.Text = "password" then
            FormsAuthentication.SetAuthCookie(tbUsername.Text, false)
            Response.Redirect("securepage.aspx")
        else
            lblMessage.Text = "<font color=red>Sorry, invalid username or " & _
                "password!</font><p>"
        end if
    end sub
</script>

<html><body>
    Please enter your username and password.<p>
    <form runat="server">
        <asp:Label id="lblMessage" runat="server"/>
        Username:
        <asp:Textbox id="tbUserName" runat="server" /><br>
        Password:
        <asp:Textbox id="tbPassword" TextMode="password" runat="server" /><p>
        <asp:Button id="Submit" runat="server" OnClick="Login" Text="Submit"/>
    </form>
</body></html>
```

The lines inside the `<form>...</form>` tags simply present a form to the user to enter a username and password. When the user presses the submit button created as an ASP.NET server control, the form posts back to itself and executes the `Login` method.

The code in the `Login` procedure is a simple check of the supplied credentials. Here, the username and password must be "JoeSmith" and "password," respectively. The next line contains the only new code in this listing: You call the `SetAuthCookie` method of the `Forms Authentication` object to set a cookie on the visitor's computer to indicate that he is a valid user and is allowed access to the site. The first parameter of this method is the username the visitor will be identified by in your application, and the second indicates whether this authentication cookie should persist after the visitor leaves your site. `False` means that the user will have to log in every time he visits, whereas `True` means that he has to log in only the first time; all subsequent visits will use the same authentication cookie to validate the user. Then, you simply redirect the user to the secure part of your site.

If the validation fails, you display an error message if the credentials are invalid. Figure 13.7 shows the output of this page when the credentials don't match the hard-coded values.

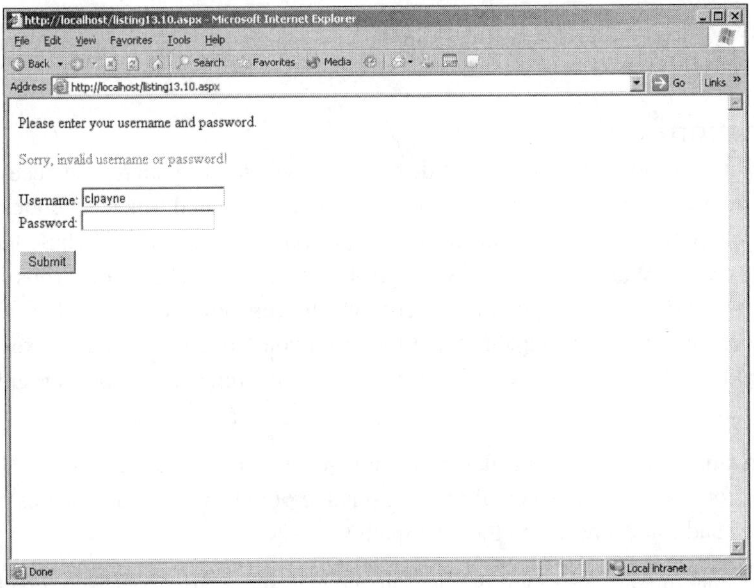

FIGURE 13.7
Access is denied with the page fails the hard-coded security values.

You can also supply valid username and passwords in your `web.config` file with the following syntax:

```
<configuration>
   <system.web>
      <authentication mode="Forms">
         <forms name=AuthCookie" loginUrl="login.aspx">
            <credentials passwordFormat="format">
               <user name="clpayne" password="helloworld" />
```

```
            </credentials>
          </forms>
        </authentication>
      </system.web>
    </configuration>
```

The password format indicates whether the password should be encrypted before being sent. The `Clear` format indicates no encryption, and `MD5` and `SHA1`, indicate well-known encryption schemes.

If you specify user credentials in your `web.config` file, you'll have to modify your login page slightly. Change the Authenticate call to the following line:

```
if FormsAuthentication.Authenticate(tbUserName.Text, tbPassword.Text) then
```

The `Authenticate` method compares the supplied username and password to the `web.config` file.

Authorization

Recall that authorization is the process of determining whether users have the necessary permissions to access resources, *after* they have been authenticated. Like authentication, authorization can be implemented in a number of different ways. You can use file-based authorization, which relies on Windows NT Access Control Lists (ACLs). These are permission lists maintained by the operating system that specify which users have access to which files. An ACL can be created for every single file and folder on your computer, which makes it a very powerful and flexible security system. See the Windows documentation for more information on using ACLs.

URL authorization, on the other hand, can be implemented through your `web.config` file. This method relies on the hierarchical configuration scheme of `web.config`, and denies or allows access to files and folders based on the URL path.

For example, enabling authorization in your `web.config` file at your root Web directory will enable authorization for *all* files in your Web directory, including subdirectories. These values can be overridden by other `web.config` files in those subdirectories, just as the rest of the settings in `web.config`.

To enable authorization, place the following XML elements in your <system.web> web.config element:

```
<authorization>
    <allow users="comma-separated list of users"
           roles="comma-separated list of roles" />
    <deny users="comma-separated list of users"
           roles="comma-separated list of roles" />
</authorization>
```

Simply place the users and roles you want to allow or deny in the appropriate `allow` or `deny` element. That's all there is to it!

You can also use special wildcards to allow or deny groups of users at once. The `?` operator means allow or deny all anonymous users, and `*` means allow or deny all users. The default behavior when authorization is not otherwise specified is to allow all users:

```
<authorization>
    <allow users="*" />
</authorization>
```

Impersonation

Impersonation can be a difficult concept to comprehend. As discussed earlier, it allows ASP.NET to execute code under a specified user's identity.

By default, impersonation is disabled. As the user moves from IIS authentication to the ASP.NET application, ASP.NET itself takes on the identity that IIS is configured to use (by default, this is the local System identity). Typically, this identity has permissions to access all files and folders. Other security measures must be used to handle access, such as URL authorization.

When impersonation is enabled, ASP.NET takes on the role of the identity that IIS passes to it. If the user is unauthenticated, ASP.NET will impersonate the anonymous user, and if the user is authenticated, ASP.NET will take on that identity. Now that ASP.NET is impersonating another user, Windows can restrict access to the application as a whole by using ACLs.

An ASP.NET application is a user of the system's resources. It accesses files and folders, memory, and so on. By default, the ASP.NET application has fairly liberal permissions, and generally can access everything the system has to offer. This is necessary because ASP.NET must use these resources to operate correctly. However, you might want to restrict access to certain resources, depending on who's using the ASP.NET application. For example, an anonymous user shouldn't be able to take advantage of the application's permissions and access all the system's resources. Thus, an ASP.NET application can impersonate its users in order to restrict access.

To enable impersonation, you need to add only one line to your `web.config` file, under the `<system.web>` element:

```
<identity impersonate="true" username="user" password="pw" />
```

The `username` and `password` attributes are optional, and can be used if you want ASP.NET to impersonate a specific identity, other than the one that IIS passes to it.

For more information on any of these ASP.NET security concepts, check out *Sams Teach Yourself ASP.NET in 21 Days*.

Summary

You have covered a lot of territory in this chapter. You learned all about deployment and configuration, and took a crash course on security topics as well.

Deployment is as easy as using XCOPY or FTP to transfer files from your development computer to the target computer. There are, however, additional tools that help you deploy easier and faster, such as the Windows Installer and CAB files. Each of these can be used to package the components in your application and deliver them quickly to the target computer, taking the guesswork away from the user. You can also execute applications and distribute CAB files via Internet Explorer.

Configuration settings in .NET are stored in .config files. These are simple XML-formatted text files that store any sort of configuration information you want. The special appSettings element provides a central location and easy access for settings. You can use the ConfigurationSettings.AppSettings or GetConfig methods to read in configuration values from your application.

ASP.NET configuration is done with the web.config file. This is also an XML file. All ASP.NET settings go into the <system.web> subelement. Table 13.1 lists the various settings available to you.

Security is an important concept in .NET; it is integrated throughout every part of the framework through various mechanisms. Code access security is used to verify that questionable code should be executed. This prevents otherwise trusted users from executing malicious code, intentionally or not. Role-based security is like code access security, but applies to users instead of code. This scheme prevents unauthorized users from accessing protected resources.

Both code access and role-based security can be implemented via declarative or imperative methods. The first is used to request or prevent access to an entire portion of your application—such as an assembly or class. Imperative methods are used when you aren't sure prior to execution whether a user will attempt to access protected resources, but will need to access non-protected ones.

Finally, ASP.NET security is implemented in three stages: authentication, authorization, and impersonation. All these settings are configured easily through the web.config file with the <authentication>, <authorization>, and <identity> elements.

.NET Interoperability with COM

IN THIS CHAPTER

Most companies that have been developing with Microsoft development tools have a large investment in their existing systems, especially the business logic they have coded into COM components. Those components are being used by Windows applications and Web applications, and are often used as the workhorse of applications for enforcing business rules and allowing for reusability of those rules across multiple applications.

The .NET Framework provides many benefits, but it is impractical to think that all companies will immediately update all their business logic components to .NET. To address this issue, and the opposite issue of needing to call a new .NET assembly in a COM-based application, Microsoft provides you with an interoperability library that allows .NET to use COM, and COM to use .NET.

Thanks to Microsoft's implementation of interoperability, COM does not know when it is calling .NET, and .NET can easily call COM components. .NET can also make calls out to the Windows API.

As you have read, .NET code that is executing is handled by the .NET Framework and is called *managed* code. Code not running inside the .NET Framework is called *unmanaged* code. VB .NET and C# were designed to write managed code because they were built to use the .NET Framework. C++ can write either managed or unmanaged code. Previous versions of VB technically create unmanaged code because VB applications do not use the .NET Framework.

Using COM Components from .NET

Perhaps the most common use of interoperability will be the calling of COM components within a .NET application. This makes sense because many companies have invested a significant amount of time and money getting their business logic coded into reusable COM components.

COM components did offer a few of the same benefits seen by the .NET Framework. Specifically, COM looked the same at the binary level, so a client written in VB or an ASP client using VBScript could call a COM component written in C++. COM components written in VB could be called by C++ applications. In fact, non-Microsoft products, such as Delphi and PowerBuilder, could create and consume COM components with ease.

COM looked the same at the binary level because all COM components had to expose a standard set of interfaces, including IUnknown and IDispatch. Because all COM components exposed these interfaces, you were assured that any COM client could call any COM component, regardless of the languages used.

.NET, on the other hand, uses an assembly's manifest to gather the necessary information for calling and using an assembly. COM components do not have a manifest, of course, so .NET gives you the means to create a manifest from the type library of a COM component.

Creating .NET Metadata from a COM Component

.NET gives you three primary ways of generating .NET metadata from a COM component. Those methods are

- Automatic conversion inside of Visual Studio .NET
- The Type Library Importer tool (`tlbimp.exe`)
- The `TypeLibConverter` class for generating the metadata in memory at runtime

There is actually a fourth way to create the metadata, which is to create them from scratch. This option will not be explored in this chapter.

Creating the Sample COM Component

Before seeing how the .NET metadata is created from a COM component, you need to create a COM component. This component will be kept rather simple because the focus here is not on learning how to create VB COM components. Instead, the component will have a field, a property, and a method.

Open up Visual Basic 6.0 (yes, the unmanaged version of Visual Basic). Start a new ActiveX DLL project. Name the project `Interop`, and name the class module `Employee`. In the `Employee` class module, enter the following code:

```
Public Name As String
Dim mdDOB As Date

Public Property Get DateOfBirth() As Date
    DateOfBirth = mdDOB
End Property

Public Property Let DateOfBirth(pdDOB As Date)
    mdDOB = pdDOB
End Property

Public Function GetEmployee(piEmpID As Integer) As String
    Dim sEmpInfo As String

    'pretend this is a database lookup
    sEmpInfo = "Employee Name: " & Name & _
        "; Employee Date of Birth: " & mdDOB
    GetEmployee = sEmpInfo
End Function
```

This code creates a component with two properties, although one is called a field because it is implemented with only a public variable, not a `Public Property Get`/`Let` pair. The field is simply called `Name` and accepts or returns a string. The property is called `DateOfBirth` and is of type `Date`. The single method accepts a parameter that simulates an employee ID. If this were a real example, that employee ID would be used to query a database and the employee's information would be returned. To keep this example simple, `GetEmployee` simply returns a string with the employee's name and date of birth in it.

Now, choose File, Make Interop.dll from the menu. Place the DLL in some location that you will remember as you work through the examples.

You now have a COM component that you will call from .NET. The next challenge is getting .NET to see the component.

Automatic Metadata Creation in Visual Studio .NET

In the first example, you will let VS .NET handle the metadata creation for you. Open Visual Studio .NET, and create a new VB .NET Windows application. Name this project `ComInterop`. After the project is open, right-click on the References node in the Solution Explorer, and choose Add Reference. This will open the Add Reference dialog box.

The second tab of the Add Reference dialog box is COM, so click on this tab. Just as in VB6, VS .NET now scans the registry, looking for all the registered COM components. When the list box is filled in, scroll down and locate the `Interop` component you just compiled. Highlight `Interop` and click the Select button in order to add `Interop` to your project. Your dialog box should look like the one in Figure 14.1.

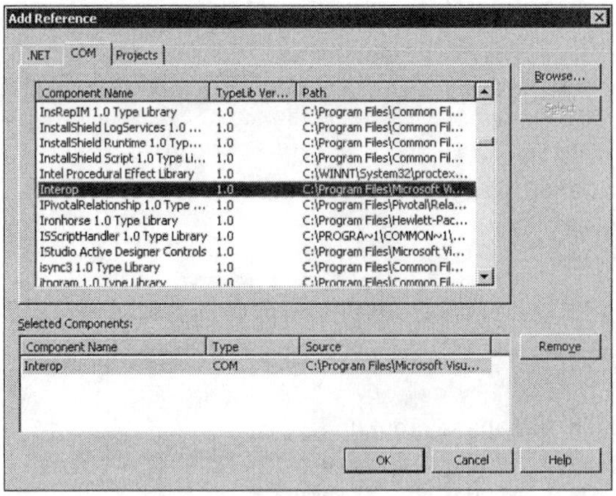

FIGURE 14.1
The Add Reference dialog box can show you all the COM components on your machine, and allow you to use them in your .NET project.

You are likely thinking you are nearly done, based on prior experience. Click the OK button, and something new happens: You are presented with the message box shown in Figure 14.2.

This box informs you that a primary assembly for the `Interop` COM component doesn't exist, and asks if you would like to have a wrapper generated for you. Click Yes to generate the wrapper.

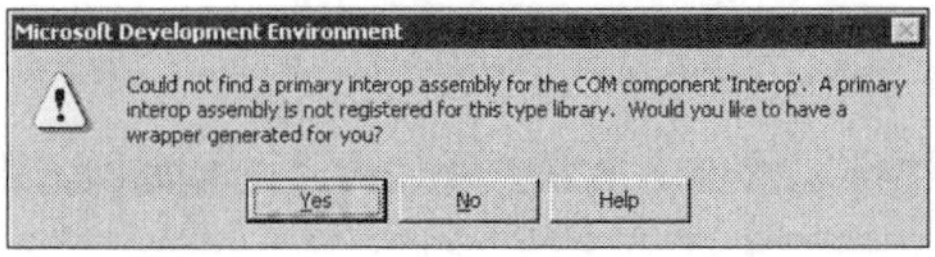

FIGURE 14.2
This message box informs you that an assembly does not exist for this COM component and allows you to create a wrapper for it.

The term *wrapper* is probably new to you. .NET exposes COM components to .NET clients using a proxy called a *runtime callable wrapper*, or RCW. Recall from your out-of-process COM work (often called *DCOM*) that a proxy is something that looks like an object to the client, but its actual job is to marshal calls from the client process and communicate with the real object, running in some other process. Similarly, the RCW looks like a standard .NET object to the client, but the RCW handles the task of taking the calls from the .NET client and marshaling them to the COM component.

The good news is that, just as with COM proxies, the nasty details of the RCW are hidden from you.

Now, look in the Solution Explorer. If the References node is not already expanded, expand it now. You'll notice that `Interop` appears in the References tree view, along with all the other System namespaces. If you click on the `Interop` node and look at properties, you'll see that it references something called Interop.Interop_1_0.dll.

This DLL is what your .NET application is actually calling. To your application, it appears to be a standard .NET assembly, because it *is* a standard .NET assembly. The fact that it acts as a runtime callable wrapper, and sends all calls on to a COM component, is immaterial to your client.

If you want to verify that the DLL is a standard .NET assembly, you can use the ILDasm.exe program to view it. ILDasm stands for IL Disassembler, and it allows you to view the metadata for an assembly that has been compiled to Intermediate Language. In Beta 2, ILDasm is not included in any of the program groups on the Start menu, so you'll have to locate it yourself. When you have found the executable, launch it and then use the File, Open command to navigate to your `ComInterop\bin` directory, which now holds the Interop.Interop_1_0.dll file. Open the DLL in ILDasm, and expand the Employee node.

14

.NET
INTEROPERABILITY
WITH COM

As shown in Figure 14.3, you can see the properties and one method that you created. However, there are also three calls to `System.Runtime.InteropServices`. This namespace has classes designed for accessing COM components and native APIs. This shows you that Interop.Interop_ 1_0.dll is a .NET assembly in the real sense, but it acts as a proxy to the actual COM component behind the scenes.

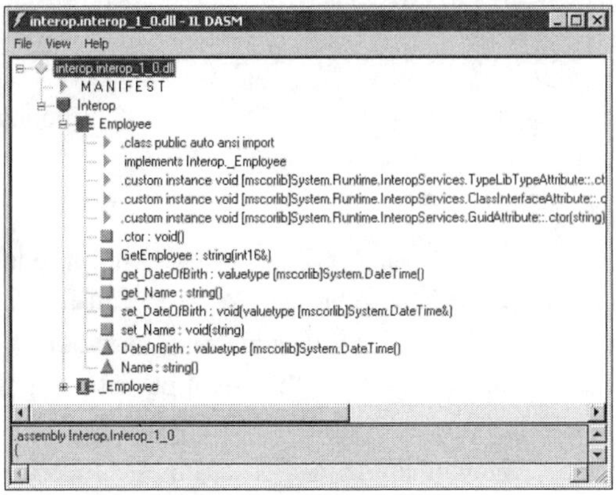

FIGURE 14.3

ILDasm showing you the assembly that was built to enable your .NET application to call a COM component.

Now that you have created a wrapper capable of calling the COM component and returning values, you'll want to test your application. Add a button to your WinForm, and enter the following code:

```
Private Sub Button1_Click(ByVal sender As System.Object, _
 ByVal e As System.EventArgs) Handles Button1.Click
    Dim Emp As New Interop.Employee()
    Emp.Name = "Torrey Spinoza"
    Emp.DateOfBirth = "12/10/91"
    MsgBox(Emp.GetEmployee(1))
End Sub
```

This code merely creates an instance of the object, passes in a name and date of birth, and then calls the `GetEmployee` method. `GetEmployee` is simulating a database lookup, so you have to pass in an integer as an employee ID, but the actual value is ignored. The return from the `GetEmployee` method is displayed in a message box.

Run the project and verify that everything works as you would expect. Congratulations! You have just called a COM component from within a .NET application.

Creating the Metadata with the Type Library Importer

Another way to create the .NET assembly's metadata is to use the Type Library Importer, or Tlbimp.exe. This console application takes a type library and generates the appropriate wrapper assembly that you can then call in your .NET application.

In VB6, the default is to have the type library built into the component instead of as a separate file. The type library is like a table of contents for the component: It contains a list of all the classes, along with the properties methods, and events of each. It also has information about the parameters and data types of those parameters. While each class in a component has at least one interface, there is just one type library for the entire component, regardless of how many classes are in it.

With the type library being built into the COM component, you'll use the actual COM DLL as the input to Tlbimp.exe. If you had compiled the type library out into a separate .tlb file, that would be your input to the Tlbimp.exe utility.

> **NOTE**
>
> In VB6, you can compile a type library into a separate .tlb file by throwing a single switch. Choose Project, *<project name>* Properties, and on the Component tab, check the Remote Server Files check box.

Locate the Tlbimp.exe file, which should be in the \Program Files\Microsoft.NET\ FrameworkSDK\Bin directory. Make sure that it is in the path or be prepared to type the entire path when you call it.

Open a command prompt and move to the directory containing your COM component, which means the VB6 project you compiled earlier. Once there, type the following line:

```
Tlbimp Interop.dll /out:InteropNet.dll
```

This single line of code takes the COM DLL as an input, which is the first argument. You then specify that the new file that should be generated will be named InteropNet.dll, which is controlled by the /out switch. If you did not specify the name for the .NET assembly, it would attempt to create it with the same name as the COM DLL. Because you don't want to overwrite the COM DLL (you'll be calling it, remember), you need to create a new name.

After Tlbimp.exe is finished, you have a new DLL named InteropNet.dll. If you desire, you can browse this with ILDasm.exe to verify that it looks like the Interop.Interop_1_0.dll that you examined earlier.

Now, return to Visual Studio .NET. Create a new Windows application named ComInterop2. Right-click on the References node, but this time, stay on the .NET tab. If you scroll down, you don't see the `InteropNet` assembly that you just added. This shouldn't come as a surprise; recall that assemblies are not placed into the registry, so .NET doesn't know anything about them automatically. Instead, click on the Browse button and navigate to the directory where you just created InteropNet.dll. Select InteropNet.dll and click the Open button. InteropNet.dll is added to the Add Reference dialog box, so you can click the OK button.

Once again, you see the assembly added to the References node in the Solution Explorer. Return to the form, add a button, and add the following code:

```
Private Sub Button1_Click(ByVal sender As System.Object, _
  ByVal e As System.EventArgs) Handles Button1.Click
    Dim Emp As New InteropNet.Employee()
    Emp.Name = "Hailey Spinoza"
    Emp.DateOfBirth = "4/8/1995"
    MsgBox(Emp.GetEmployee(1))
End Sub
```

Run the application, and verify that things work as they did before.

Before moving on, answer one question: What is the location of the InteropNet.dll file you just executed? It's not where you just created it. Instead, it's in the `ComInterop2\bin` directory. You can verify this by examining the Output window, where you will see this line (or something similar):

```
'ComInterop2.exe': Loaded 'c:\documents and settings\administrator\
my documents\visual studio projects\cominterop2\bin\interopnet.dll',
No symbols loaded.
```

Notice here that the DLL is in the `ComInterop2\bin` directory. If you return to the Solution Explorer, click once on the InteropNet node under References, and look at the Properties window, you'll notice that the `Copy Local` property is set to `True`. This copies the DLL into the local application's directory structure when the application is built.

The `TypeLibConverter` Class

A third way to create an assembly from the type library of a COM component is to use the `TypeLibConverter` class. This class allows you to create a dynamic assembly, which is an assembly that is stored only in memory but can be saved to disk, if you choose to do so.

The `TypeLibConverter` class is found in the `System.Runtime.InteropServices` namespace, and contains a method named `ConvertTypeLibToAssembly`, which allows you to pass in a type library and have it converted to an assembly on the fly. You can then reference the new assembly and call it just as you have the two previous assemblies.

Using .NET Components in COM Applications

As you saw, using COM components in a .NET application was an easy task. Now, it's time to look at the reverse situation, in which you will call a .NET component from a COM application. This situation is not quite as clean as using COM components in .NET because you have to perform some tricks to get it to work.

Preparing the .NET Component for COM Clients

The first thing you want to do to have a .NET component that can be called by a COM client is to create your .NET component as you normally do. Start a new Class Library named NetInterop. Inside Class1.vb, you'll change the class name to EmpNet and enter the code that gives you the same functionality as the COM component from earlier. Your final code should look like this:

```
Public Class EmpNet
    Public Name As String
    Dim mdDOB As Date

    Public Property DateOfBirth() As Date
        Get
            DateOfBirth = mdDOB
        End Get
        Set(ByVal Value As Date)
            mdDOB = Value
        End Set
    End Property

    Public Function GetEmployee(ByVal piID) As String
        Dim sEmpInfo As String
        sEmpInfo = "Employee Name: " & Name & _
            "; Employee Date of Birth: " & mdDOB
        GetEmployee = sEmpInfo
    End Function
End Class
```

This code will work the same as the previous example that was written in COM: You have a field called Name, a property called DateOfBirth, and a method called GetEmployee that accepts a single parameter as an argument. The GetEmployee method returns a string to your client.

At this point, you need to build your assembly, so choose Build from the Build menu. Now, things are about to change.

14

.NET
INTEROPERABILITY
WITH COM

You have compiled a .NET component, or assembly, and it is located in the bin directory of the project. You could leave it where it is, but you'll want to move or copy it for reasons that will be obvious in a moment.

You have several choices for your next step, but it is easiest if you create a new directory on your hard drive. For this example, I'll use C:\Interop as the directory. Copy (or move) the NetInterop.dll to the C:\Interop directory. What you now have is a .NET assembly in a directory all by itself.

To use this .NET assembly in a COM client application, you need to register the component in the registry. You might be tempted to reverse the process from before: Tlbimp.exe read the type library and created a .NET assembly. Conversely, there is a Tlbexp.exe that takes a .NET assembly and creates a type library.

Unfortunately, the type library that is created with Tlbexp.exe is not registered, so VB6 won't be able to automatically locate it. Further, the .tlb that is generated cannot be registered directly with Regsvr32.exe, the registration tool familiar to many VB developers.

Using Regasm.exe

The answer, therefore, is to use the Regasm.exe utility. This utility is designed to read an assembly and place the necessary type information into the registry so that COM clients can call the assembly.

First, if Regasm.exe is not in the path, you'll need to locate the Regasm.exe utility on your machine and either move it to a directory that is in the path, or type the entire directory name in front of the utility.

Next, open a command prompt and move to the directory where you placed the .NET component, which for this book's example is C:\Interop. Type the following command at the prompt:

```
regasm /tlb:NetInterop.tlb NetInterop.dll
```

You should receive the following messages:

```
Types registered successfully
Assembly exported to 'C:\Interop\NetInterop.tlb', and the type
library was registered successfully
```

What you are actually doing in the command is two steps that could be done separately. The Tlbemp.exe mentioned in the previous section would generate a type library but not register it; the Regasm.exe with the /tlb switch creates a type library *and* registers it. The Regasm.exe also registers the assembly's types in the registry. You could run this as two separate commands, but this line allows you to register the type library and the types at the same time.

Creating the COM Client Application

The next step is to create a COM client that can use the component. Open VB6 and create a new Standard EXE application. When the project is open, select Project, References and look at the References dialog box. Scroll down until you find the `NetInterop` type library being displayed, and check the box next to it. As you can see in Figure 14.4, the reference is pointing to the type library file you created in the `C:\Interop` directory. When done, click the OK button.

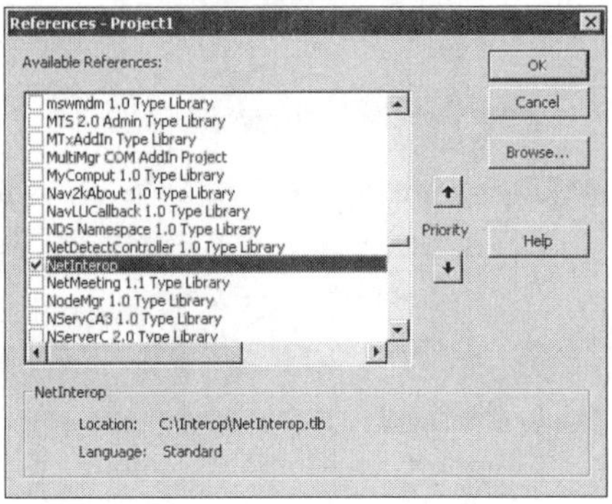

FIGURE 14.4

The .NET assembly shows up in the References dialog box, thanks to being registered by the Regasm.exe utility.

Now, add a button to your form, and add the following code to the project, and do not be alarmed if things don't appear to be working properly:

```
Private Sub Command1_Click()
    Dim Employee As EmpNet
    Set Employee = New EmpNet
    Employee.Name = "Jane Doe"
    Employee.DateOfBirth = "4/1/91"
    MsgBox Employee.GetEmployee(1)
End Sub
```

The first thing you might have noticed when you started typing was the complete lack of Intellisense. When you typed the period after typing `Employee`, you did not get a list of the available properties and methods. This is an artifact of the way .NET works in COM clients. You'll just have to code without Intellisense and trust that the application will work.

After you have typed in the code, you'll probably be tempted to click the Start button in the VB6 IDE to test the application. If you do this, however, you'll get the error shown in Figure 14.5.

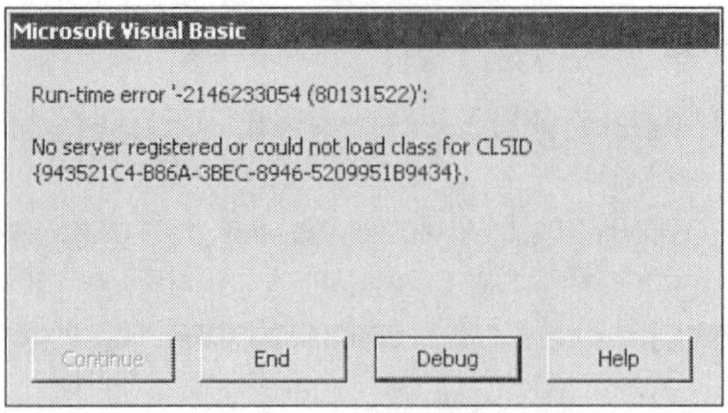

FIGURE 14.5

The result of trying to run your COM client in the IDE, where it is unable to locate the .NET assembly it is calling.

You might be wondering what in the world is going on. After all, you've already lost Intellisense, and now you can't run the client application in the IDE. Actually, there's a good reason for the client application not running at the moment.

.NET works differently from COM. .NET typically assumes that either the assembly will be in the local directory, or it will be loaded in the global assembly cache. You read about the global assembly cache in Chapter 4, "Building Classes and Assemblies with VB .NET," and you even placed an assembly in the GAC. If you had placed this assembly in the GAC, you would be able to run the client within the IDE.

Because your assembly is not in the GAC, however, .NET tries to serve it up from the local directory. The local directory to the VB6 IDE is the directory containing VB6.exe, which is C:\Program Files\Microsoft Visual Studio\VB98 by default. Because this is obviously not the directory containing the assembly, the call fails.

You could have placed the assembly in the same directory as VB6.exe and run Regasm in that directory. However, in this example, you can fix the problem by compiling the COM application into the same directory holding the assembly—in this case, C:\Interop. Choose File, Make Project1.exe, but make sure that you navigate to the same directory holding the .NET assembly you want to call. Once there, compile the program.

Now, from the C:\Interop directory, run Project1.exe. The project will run normally, and display the results in the message box, as shown in Figure 14.6. Congratulations! You have just called a .NET component from within a COM application.

A Note on Registering

One thing you should realize is the difference between registering COM components and .NET assemblies. .NET allows you to store copies of an assembly in multiple locations on the hard drive. By default, .NET applications use assemblies in their local directories. This means that the local copy of the assembly will be used.

FIGURE 14.6
The COM application is able to call the .NET component when they are both in the same directory.

This is basically the opposite of how COM works. With COM, you can have multiple copies of a component on the hard drive, but applications will use only the copy that has been registered. By default, COM applications go to the registry to find the physical locations of components. COM handles instantiating the component either in the same process space as the application, or by creating the component in another process and returning a pointer to that component.

So, when you create a COM client calling a .NET component, it is .NET that is finding the component. Therefore, the client and component have to exist in the same directory, or the component has to be placed in the GAC for it to be located. This is why you cannot run your client applications in the VB6 IDE unless you move the component into the same directory as VB6.exe and register it there.

Calling Windows API Functions

One of the major features of .NET is that it is platform independent. However, there are many powerful functions available in the Windows API, so there is little doubt that some developers will want to a call Windows API function from time to time. Fortunately, VB .NET includes the `Declare` statement, which allows you to call Windows API functions.

The `Declare` statement in VB .NET is very similar to the one from VB6, with some minor modifications. You might recall from your VB6 work that functions have both an ANSI and a Unicode implementation in the API: an A suffix means the ANSI version, whereas a W suffix indicates Unicode. Examine the following sample `Declare` statement:

```
Declare Function GetComputerName Lib "kernel32.dll" _
   Alias "GetComputerNameA" (ByVal lpBuffer As String, _
   ByRef nSize As Long) As Long
```

You see here that you are using a `Declare` to create a function that points to the ANSI implementation of `GetComputerName`. By default, the `Declare` statement assumes the ANSI version is what you will be calling; no modifier is needed. If you choose to call the Unicode version, you add a modifier to the `Declare` statement to force strings to be passed as Unicode.

```
Declare Unicode Function GetComputerName Lib "kernel32.dll" _
   Alias "GetComputerNameW" (ByVal lpBuffer As String, _
   ByRef nSize As Long) As Long
```

Whether you choose ANSI or Unicode is immaterial in most VB .NET applications.

Calling a Windows API Function

You can call a Windows API function using the `Declare` function and then calling the function as you would any other function. Create a new Windows application named `ApiTest`. Add a button to the application, and make your code look like this (with the Windows Form Designer generated code hidden, of course):

```
Public Class Form1
    Inherits System.Windows.Forms.Form
    Declare Function GetComputerName Lib "kernel32.dll" _
      Alias "GetComputerNameA" (ByVal lpBuffer As String, _
      ByRef nSize As Long) As Long

#Region " Windows Form Designer generated code "

    Private Sub Button1_Click(ByVal sender As System.Object, _
      ByVal e As System.EventArgs) Handles Button1.Click
        Dim sMachineName As String = Space(50)
        Dim lLength As Long = 50
        Dim lRetVal As Long

        lRetVal = GetComputerName(sMachineName, lLength)

        MsgBox("Current Machine: " & sMachineName)
    End Sub
End Class
```

In this code, you are using the Windows API to get the name of the current computer. You declare a function called `GetComputerName` that references the `GetComputerNameA` in the kernel32.dll.

Inside the click event sub, you create a string variable and fill it to a size of 50. You then create a long that you also initialize to 50. If you have done much with API calls, you know that you often have to pass in a string that has already been initialized to a large enough size to hold the value that will be returned. What is strange is that even though the `lpBuffer` parameter is defined with the `ByVal` keyword, the return value is actually passed back to the string. The `nSize` parameter is `ByRef`, and the size of the return is passed back through this parameter.

If you run this code, the message box will display the name of the computer on which the code is running. Congratulations! You have just called a Windows API function from within a .NET application.

Summary

Some people like to say that COM is dead. Microsoft might be moving away from COM, but given that some companies still have Windows 95 as their standard desktop operating system, COM will no doubt be around for a very long time. Therefore, Microsoft made .NET capable of integrating with COM in several ways.

First, .NET can call COM components. Accomplishing this is very easy for the .NET developer. VS .NET will create an assembly for you that acts as a wrapper to the COM component, or the developer can create the wrapper using the Tlbimp.exe utility.

Second, .NET can expose assemblies to COM components. Using the Regasm.exe utility, you can create a type library from an assembly's manifest, and have the type library registered in the registry. As long as the COM application and the .NET component are in the same directory, or the .NET component is placed into the GAC, your COM application can use the .NET component.

Finally, VB .NET allows you to continue to call API functions in the operating system using the Declare statement. This means you can take advantage of the power of the underlying operating system.

Writing Code for Cross-Language Interoperability

IN THIS APPENDIX

With .NET, you have the ability to create components in one language that can then be consumed by applications written in another language. This is nothing particularly new, because COM enabled you to write COM components in VB and call them from C++ applications, and vice versa. However, .NET gives you the ability to perform such actions as inheriting a VB .NET component in a C# application, or having your VB .NET application inherit a COBOL .NET component that is inheriting from a J#.NET component.

This level of interoperability is far beyond what COM gave you, but it doesn't come without its own set of rules. The rules can be broken within individual languages, but breaking the rules prevents you from being assured that the code you write can interoperate properly with other .NET languages.

The .NET Framework Class Library

The .NET Framework class library contains a number of base data types for use in your application. However, the .NET Framework class actually supports many base types that are not compliant with the Common Language Specification, or CLS. It is important to know what types are and are not available to the CLS, but first it is useful to understand the CLS.

What Is the Common Language Specification?

The *Common Language Specification* (CLS) is a subset of the language features directly supported by the Common Language Runtime. The runtime lays out a set of rules to guarantee cross-language interoperability. By defining types and rules that all CLS-compliant code must use, you are guaranteed that a class written in C# can be inherited by any other .NET language. You can rest assured that the data types of properties and parameters are compatible across languages.

By using only types that are included in the CLS, your component will be accessible to clients written in any other language that supports the CLS. Basically, the CLS specifies a set of rules to which all languages must adhere in order to have full cross-language interoperability under the .NET Framework. Realize that only what is exposed by your component needs to be CLS-compliant. Inside a method, for example, you can use private variables that are not CLS-compliant, but the method can still be CLS-compliant because all the exposed items are part of the CLS.

The CLS specifies not just data types, but also a number of rules. Right now, there are 41 rules that specify the CLS. For example, one rule specifies that the type of an enum must be one of the four CLS integer data types. Most of these rules are transparent to you as a developer because the Visual Studio .NET environment handles them for you.

Data Types and the CLS

Rather than focus on the actual rules of the CLS, it is more useful to examine the underlying data types in the CLR, how they map to VB .NET data types, and whether they are CLS-compliant. The good news is that all built-in VB .NET data types are CLS-compliant. However, it is possible to use data types in VB .NET that are provided by the .NET Framework that are not CLS-compliant. The following tables break the .NET Framework base types down into broad categories and then examine the .NET base data type, the built-in VB .NET data type, and whether it is CLS-compliant. If there is no built-in VB .NET data type, the data type is the same as the .NET base type. If a data type is not CLS-compliant, you would not want to expose a property with that data type, nor would you want a public method to have parameters or a return value of one of those data types.

Table A.1 lists the integer data types of various sizes. Table A.2 covers the floating-point numbers, of which there are only two. Table A.3 covers other data types, such as `Boolean` and `Object`.

TABLE A.1 Integer Data Types

VB .NET Type	CLS-Compliant?	.NET Base Type	Range	Size
Byte	Yes	System.Byte	0 to 255 unsigned	1 byte
System.SByte	No	System.SByte	-128 to 127	1 byte
Short	Yes	System.Int16	-32,768 to 32,767	2 bytes
Integer	Yes	System.Int32	-2,147,438,648 to 2,147,438,647	4 bytes
Long	Yes	System.Int64	-9,223,372,036,854,775,808 to 9,223,372,036,854,775,807	8 bytes
System.UInt16	No	System.UInt16	0 to 65535	2 bytes
System.UInt32	No	System.UInt32	0 to 4,294,967,295	4 bytes
System.UInt64	No	System.UInt64	0 to 184,467,440,737,095,551,615	8 bytes

TABLE A.2   Floating-Point Data Types

VB .NET Type	CLS-Compliant?	.NET Base Type	Range	Size
Single	Yes	System.Single	-3.402823e38 to 3.402823e38	4 bytes
Double	Yes	System.Double	1.79769313486232e308 to -1.79769313486232e308	8 bytes

TABLE A.3   Other Data Types

VB .NET Type	CLS-Compliant?	.NET Base Type	Range	Size
Boolean	Yes	System.Boolean	True or False	2 bytes
Object	Yes	System.Object	Any object	
Char	Yes	System.Char	A Unicode character	2 bytes
String	Yes	System.String	Fixed-length string of Unicode characters	
Decimal	Yes	System.Decimal	-79,228,162,514,264,337, 593,543,950,335 to 79,228,162,514,264,337, 593,543,950,335	12 bytes
IntPtr	Yes	System.IntPtr	Same as Int32 or Int64, depending on platform	Varies
UIntPtr	No	System.UIntPtr	Same as UInt32 or UInt64, depending on platform	Varies

As you create applications, you'll want to make sure that you stick to CLS-compliant types if you want to ensure interoperability with other .NET languages. Remember that this only applies to items that are exposed; private variables inside a Function or Sub can use System.UInt16 or any other non-CLS-compliant type, and you can still have full interoperability.

INDEX

SYMBOLS

A

Hey, you've got enough worries.

Don't let IT training be one of them.

Get on the fast track to IT training at InformIT,
your total Information Technology training network.

InformIT | **www.informit.com** | **SAMS**

■ Hundreds of timely articles on dozens of topics ■ Discounts on IT books from all our publishing partners, including Sams Publishing ■ Free, unabridged books from the InformIT Free Library ■ "Expert Q&A"—our live, online chat with IT experts ■ Faster, easier certification and training from our Web- or classroom-based training programs ■ Current IT news ■ Software downloads ■ Career-enhancing resources

InformIT is a registered trademark of Pearson. Copyright ©2001 by Pearson.
Copyright ©2001 by Sams Publishing.